I0540736

GUNBOAT JUSTICE

British and American Courts in China and Japan
(1842 to 1943)

Volume III

Revolution, Resistance and Resurrection (1927-1943)

Douglas Clark

Gunboat Justice

By Douglas Clark

Volume 1 - ISBN-13: 978-988-82730-8-9
Volume 2 - ISBN-13: 978-988-82730-9-6
Volume 3 - ISBN-13: 978-988-82731-9-5

This book has been reset in 10pt Book Antiqua. Spellings and punctuations are left as in the original edition.

HISTORY / Asia / General

EB056

Published by Earnshaw Books Ltd (Hong Kong)

In memory of my maternal grandfather

The Honourable Mr Justice Russell Skerman

Supreme Court of Queensland

Foreign Office Map Of The Main

Treaty Ports In East Asia, 1925

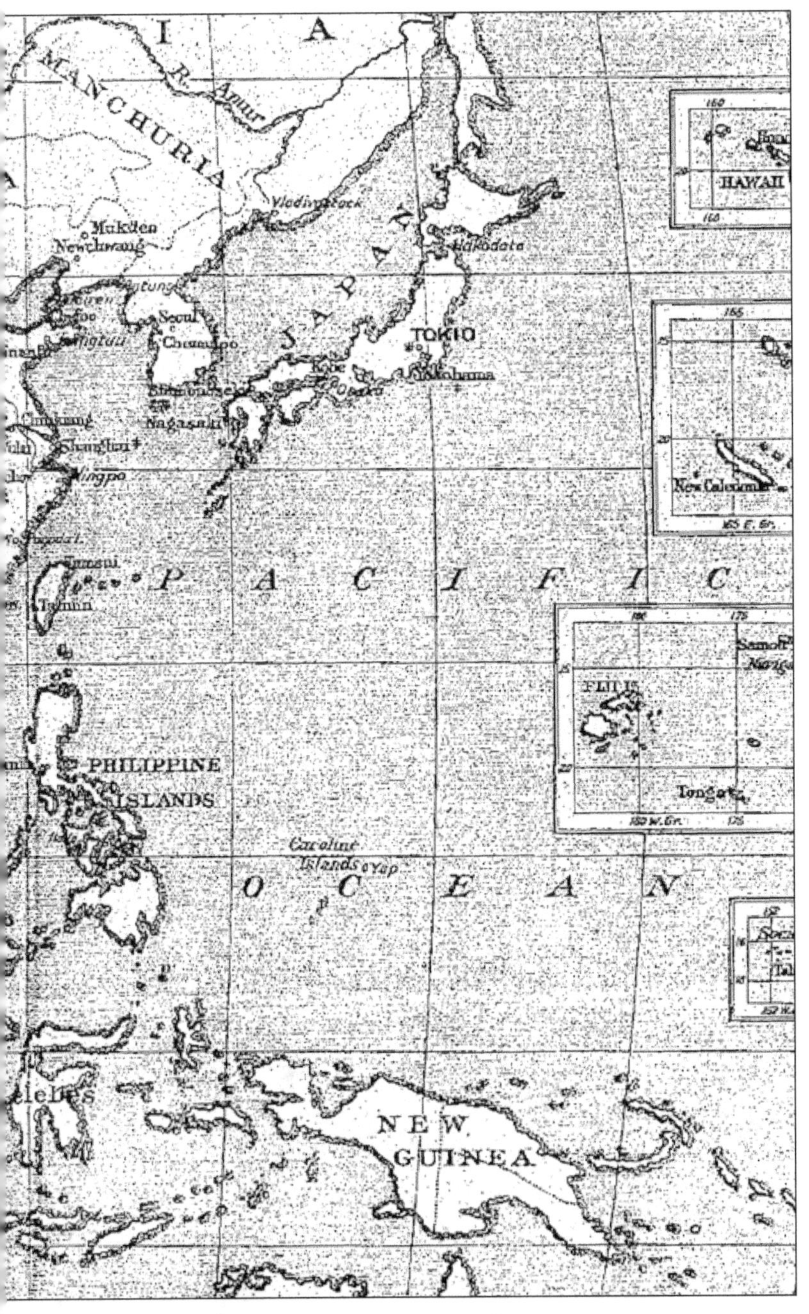

Contents

Volume I White Man, White Law, White Gun (1842-1900)

AUTHOR'S NOTES 1
Foreword 3

Introduction – Extraterritoriality: An Extraordinary System 7

Part One: The Beginning (1842 to 1865) 19
Chapter 1 – White Man, White Law, White Gun 21
Chapter 2 – Courting the Law: Consuls as Judges 39

Part Two: Establishing British Justice (1865 to 1878) 49
Chapter 3 – The Founder: Sir Edmund Hornby 51
Chapter 4 – Establishing the Court 59
Chapter 5 – Opening the Court: The First Cases 73
Chapter 6 – The Younger Generation: Learning the Ropes 83
Chapter 7 – Order Out of Legal Chaos 99
Chapter 8 – Bricks and Mortar: A Home for the Court 111
Chapter 9 – Reforming the British Courts in Japan 129
Chapter 10 – Building the New Japanese Legal System 147
Chapter 11 – Mixed Justice in China 159
Chapter 12 – The End of an Era: Hornby retires – Goodwin dies 177

Part Three: Reorganisation (1878 to 1881) 187
Chapter 13 – Reorganising the Courts 189
Chapter 14 – The Bullion Dollar Question: The Ross Case 219
Chapter 15 – The Chinese Challenge 229
Chapter 16 – Some Corner of a Foreign Field: The Death of George French 249

Part Four: Consolidation (1881 to 1891) 253
Chapter 17 – Jockeying for Promotion 255
Chapter 18 – Chinese Demand Justice 263
Chapter 19 – Enlarging Jurisdiction 277
Chapter 20 – Japan Demands Change 283
Chapter 21 – A New Arrival And A Fond Farewell 291

Part Five: Japan Rises – China Falls (1891 to 1900) 301
Chapter 22 – The Amalgamation 303
Chapter 23 – Japan Asserts Itself 319
Chapter 24 – Infidelity and Murder in Yokohama 337
Chapter 25 – Endings and New Beginnings 367
Chapter 26 – A Time for Rejoicing not Revenge 391
Chapter 27 – The Full Stop in the Wrong Place: Vale Sir Nicholas 401

Conclusion to Volume I 412

Index 414

Volume II Destruction, Disorder and Defiance (1900-1927)

Introduction to Volume II 3

Part Six: China Boxed In (1900 to 1905) 7
Chapter 28 – The Boxer Rebellion 9
Chapter 29 – The High Court of Weihaiwei 23
Chapter 30 – Ambition Achieved: Wilkinson CJ 31
Chapter 31 – 1905: A Year of Change 53

Part Seven: The United States Court for China 71
Chapter 32 – Taming the Wild East 73
Chapter 33 – The Wild East Fights Back 97

Part Eight: Dying Dynasties (1906 to 1911) 119
Chapter 34 – Korea's Hero: Ernest Bethell 121
Chapter 35 – The Ricshaw Coolie and the Sampan Man 135
Chapter 36 – For Better or Worse 145
Chapter 37 – The Law of the Land 157

Part Nine: Revolution and War (1911 to 1920) 169
Chapter 38 – The Republican Revolution 171
Chapter 39 – New Roles and New Faces 179
Chapter 40 – World War I 195
Chapter 41 – Farewells and Promotions 213

Part Ten: The Roaring Twenties (1920 to 1927) 223
Chapter 42 – Bad Behaviour at the Bar 225
Chapter 43 – Gun Runners 249
Chapter 44 – A Sad Farewell: Lobingier Retires 263
Chapter 45 – Rebel with a Cause: Lawrence Kentwell 273
Chapter 46 – The Rise of Nationalism 305
Chapter 47 – Intermingled Jurisdictions 327
Chapter 48 – Recognition, Retirements and Advances 337
Chapter 49 – The Dirty DA 349

Conclusion to Volume II 363

Appendix: Introduction to Vol I 366

Index 378

Volume III Revolution, Resistance and Resurrection (1927-1943)

Introduction to Volume III 3

Part Eleven: A New Hope (1927 to 1931) 7
Chapter 50 – The Rise of China 9

Chapter 51 – The Work of Two Men 35
Chapter 52 – Extraterritoriality to End 43

Part Twelve: The Japanese Empire Strikes Back (1932 to 1941) 55
Chapter 53 – Major Battles 57
Chapter 54 – The Last Judges 73
Chapter 55 – Predators 87
Chapter 56 – In the Shadow of the Gallows 105
Chapter 57 – The Badlands of North China 123
Chapter 58 – Dark Days 131
Chapter 59 – Live by the Gunboat... 159

Part Thirteen: The End (1937 to 1943) 183
Chapter 60 – The End of Extraterritoriality 185
Chapter 61 – Summing Up 195

Postscript - Life After Death 199

A note on the writing of this book 209

Acknowledgements 215

Further Reading and Places of Interest 221

Table of Appointments (British courts) 227

Judges and District Attorneys of the US Court for China 232

Appendix: Introduction to Vol I 233

Index 245

Table of Cases 280

Table of Jury Members 291

Tables of Illustrations 296

Photographs 302

Romanisation and place names

I have used transliterations of Chinese personal and place names in accordance with the transliterations used during the period covered by this book. Where someone is now much better known by a different transliteration, I have used this.

For place names in China, for any reference prior to the Communist Revolution in 1949, I have generally used the contemporaneous English names, such as Canton and Amoy. Beijing is referred to as Peking for the most part but also as Peiping for the period that was its official name. This is the way the names appear in the documents of the time and would have been spoken in English.

For street names in Shanghai, I have used the pre-World War II street names. Where appropriate I give the current street name in parentheses.

For references to places and personal names in China after the Communist Revolution, I have used Hanyu Pinyin, except where a person is much better known by a different transliteration.

For Japanese names, I have used modern romanisations. For Korean names I have used contemporaneous transliterations.

For all quotations or names of publications I have kept the original spelling.

Currencies in Shanghai

There were four major currencies in use in Shanghai during the period covered by this book. For almost the entire period, the Pound Sterling to United States Dollar exchange rate was £1 = US$5. For a time, the US dollar was also referred to as the Gold Dollar (G$). The other two currencies in use were Mexican silver dollars and the Chinese Tael (based on the price of silver). The value of these currencies fluctuated wildly. In 1930, US$1 was equal to about 3 taels and $3.5 Mex. However, at other times the Mexican dollar was equivalent to or worth more than the US$.

I have not attempted to give any conversions of currency in the book.

File References

Unless indicated otherwise, all files references are to the UK National Archive file reference for a document. PRONI files refers to the Wilkinson Papers kept at the Public Records Office of Northern Ireland. Where possible full file references have been given for the PRONI papers. However, these were not always available.

Cartoons and Illustrations

All cartoons and illustrations accompanying the text, with two exceptions, are contemporaneous drawings published at the time. The exceptions are the sketches of the Supreme Court and George French's grave which have been made from photographs.

Introduction to Vol III

Revolution, Resistance And Resurrection

Below is a short introduction for Volume III. For readers who do not have or have not read the earlier volumes, the Introduction to Volume I is reproduced as an appendix. This should be read first before reading the following.

Volumes I and II described the development of extraterritoriality in China, Japan and Korea from its early beginnings in the 1840s and 1850s to its abolition in Japan in 1899 following successful adoption of a Western legal system. Japan, now a major economic and military power, in 1910, annexed Korea bringing extraterritoriality to an end there. By the 1910s, China was the only country in North East Asia where foreigners still had extraterritorial rights.

China had started reforming its laws and legal system at the end of the Qing Dynasty and continued to do so after the Republican Revolution in 1911. However, the civil wars that followed Yuan Shikai's attempt to install himself as emperor and World War I held back the development of China and its new legal system. The chaos and disorder of warlord-controlled China allowed foreign powers a free hand to maintain their treaty rights and privileges.

The 1920s saw change with growing Chinese nationalism, marked most notably by the May 30 Movement following the killing of protesters by the Shanghai Municipal Police in 1925. The Nationalist Party in Canton was also growing military stronger. By the mid-1920s the Nationalists had been able to match (but not yet outgun) foreign military power in Canton. In 1926, they launched a Northern Expedition to recapture north China and the government of China.

Their revolution succeeded. This brought new challenges to the foreign powers - extraterritoriality only worked effectively when the host power was weak and foreign powers were strong. This was not the case in the late 1920s when Britain and America were hit hard by the Great Depression. The Chinese asserted themselves militarily taking over a number of minor foreign concessions. During the course of the fighting, the British and American courts were both forced to decide if the Nationalists were rebels or a new government. Once the Nationalists had taken firm control of China, Britain and America both reached agreements in principle with the Nationalists to bring an end to extraterritoriality. This drive stalled with Japan's invasion of Manchuria and attack on Shanghai in 1932. Japan's continued assertion of its "special rights" and invasion of China in 1937 brought an entirely different complexion to British and American extraterritoriality. Power came out the barrels of Japanese guns and the officials and courts of other foreign powers had to bend to this reality to avoid being broken.

Extraterritoriality, paradoxically, became useful to China by keeping foreign powers engaged with the country. It was a thorn in the side to the Japanese but they were not yet ready to spark a confrontation by abolishing it. The British and American courts in China found themselves challenged in ways they never had been before when dealing with a strong China and subsequently with a strong Japan. Many of the cases before the courts in the last 16 years of their existence involved dealing with this new reality. Chinese resistance to Japanese occupation also found its way in the courts – the most high profile case involving an application to free from the British Consular Gaol in Tientsin four Chinese suspected of assassinating another Chinese working for the Japanese puppet government in Tientsin.

Not all cases involved war or high politics. The courts still continued to handle other cases including a number of murders and the collapse of one of Shanghai's largest financial house. A major battle was fought over the right to inherit the many millions of dollars amassed by Silas Hardoon, an Iraqi Jew. In one case a Sikh Defendant was almost literally resurrected when he came as close to death as it is possible but surived!

World War II brought an end to British and American extraterritoriality in Japanese-occupied China. The British Supreme Court and the United States Court for China continued to exist in Free China but with very little work to do. Early 1943 saw the formal abolition of British and American extraterritoriality - and the last case in the United States Court for China with a special judge flown in from India.

It had been a very long journey of over 100 years for China to achieve the end to the unequal treaties. The formal abolition of extraterritoriality was greeted by the Chinese with joy. The abolition, however, occurred while China was fighting for its very life against Japan and the celebrations were tempered. At the beginning of 1927, there had been much stronger hope amongst the Chinese - and equal fear amongst foreigners – that this historic event would occur much more quickly. The Nationalists were on the march and it appeared they were unstoppable.

Part Eleven

A New Hope
(1927 to 1931)

Chapter 50

The Rise of China

1927 WAS A WATERSHED year for China.

Sun Yat-sen had died in 1925 and Chiang Kai-shek, the commander of the Whampoa Military Academy, had taken over as the leader of the Kuomingtang (Nationalist Party) in Canton. The Whampoa Military Academy had been set up by Chiang in 1924 to train, with Soviet assistance, an officer corps for the Nationalists. It had been a great success. In July 1926, Chiang launched a Northern Expedition from the Nationalists' base in Canton to take over the country. The warlord armies in the south of China were no match for the Nationalist Party's modern and well-trained army. By September 1926, the Nationalists' troops had captured Hankow on the Yangtze River and were poised to drive north onto Peking. In Hankow, the Nationalists took over the Hankow foreign concession. Other smaller concessions throughout the country were also occupied. The Nationalists captured Nanking in March 1927 and attacked the concessions there, causing outrage amongst the treaty powers.

Soon after, the Kuomingtang forces reached Shanghai where at one stage, given what had happened in Hankow and Nanking, there were serious concerns they would try to take over the foreign concessions. The British Cabinet in London met on numerous occasions to discuss the crisis. Unlike in the past, there was no clear consensus on what could be done to stop a Chinese advance. Gunboats were still an option. Two proposals were made to seek to force the Nation-

Sapajou does a round of the boundaries

alists to agree to leave foreign concessions alone. First, was a blockade of the Bogue at Humen sealing off the Pearl River and Canton's access to the sea. The second was to use the British naval power on the Yangtze to prevent the Nationalist armies crossing the river in their advance northwards.[1]

One thing that was agreed was that Shanghai had to be defended at all costs. The treaty powers including Britain, America, Japan and France all sent substantial numbers of troops to defend the concessions.[2] Britain alone sent 20,000, mainly Sikh, troops to Shanghai. Shanghai newspapers were full of pictures of the defences that had been built, including barbed wired fences surrounding the concessions entirely and maps showing the sectors controlled by the different troops of each nation. The *North China Herald* showed numerous pictures of Sikh troops and carried a Sapajou cartoons of: "Our Punjabi Visitors"[3] and Tamil and other

Our Punjabi Visitors

1 CAB/24/186. The Situation in China, March 29, 1927, Draft Report of the Joint-Chiefs of Staff Sub-Committee, presented to Cabinet.

2 W. Eberhard, *A History of China*, pp315 to 327.

3 Pictures of Sikh and French Vietnamese troops: *North China Herald*, January 29, 1927, p137; Sapajou's cartoon: *North China Herald*, February 5, 1927, p179. Photos of the armies and fighting in Shanghai: *North China Herald*, February 19, 1927, p271; March 26, 1927, pp490-491; April 9, 1927, p59.

troops.

The political branch of the Shanghai Municipal Police was particularly concerned that the Nationalist Party's North Expedition forces contained "subversive foreign agents" who would seek to propagate communism and nationalism amongst the Indian population in Shanghai.[4] This was not just paranoia. Numerous Sikhs were arrested and tried in the British Police court for sedition for trying to convince Sikh soldiers not to fight.[5]

Even more alarmingly, political assassination came to British Shanghai. In early April 1927 in broad daylight, Harbant Singh, walked up to the most senior Indian policeman in Shanghai, Senior Inspector Sirdar Sahib Budda Singh, at the gates of the Central Police Station on Foochow Road (Fuzhou Road) and shot him twice in the back and once in the chest, killing him almost instantly. Budda Singh lying on the ground was able to call out to another Sikh policeman, Bhan Singh, "Call for help, I am dying." Bhan Singh grabbed Harbant Singh from behind and sub-inspector Phillips, who had rushed from the police station, gun in hand, disarmed Harbant Singh.[6] The SMP raided the Sikh Gurdwara soon after this and arrested 10 other Sikhs for being part of the conspiracy to kill Budda Singh.

Sirdar Sahib Budda Singh: Assassinated

4 F. Wakeman, *Policing Shanghai*, 1927-1937, p145.

5 See, for example: *R v Sangat Singh* and *R v Amar & Dalup Singh*, *North China Herald*, March 26, 1927, p514.

6 "The tragic death of Sirdar Sahib Singh", *North China Herald*, April 9, 1927, p74; *R v Harbant Singh* (committal) *NCH*, April 16, 1927, p127; *R v Harbant Singh* (trial), *NCH*, May 21, 1927, p343. For the trial of the 10 conspirators see: *SMP v Harnam Singh et al*, *NCH*, May 14, 1927, p302; *North China Daily News*, April 9, 1927 (funeral); Shanghai Muncipal Council Annual Report, 1927, p35 (tribute to Budda Singh and date of Harbant's execution).

Harbant Singh was put on trial for murder before Peter Grain and a jury of 12.[7] Allan Mossop, the Crown Advocate, prosecuted. Mr A.E. Seddon defended Singh. Seddon had agreed to act for free in the public interest so that a man facing the death penalty would not be tried without a defence. Singh made Seddon's job very hard. He refused to cooperate with him and did not give him any instructions. When asked to plea, Singh responded coolly: "I did murder Sirdar Sahib Budda Singh, so I must plead guilty." Seddon asked, in accordance with the custom that a defendant could not plead guilty to murder, that a plea of "Not Guilty" be entered. Grain agreed to this. After the prosecution evidence was called, Harbant Singh made a statement from the dock admitting the crime and saying that he killed Budda Singh because "I wish he die and no make more trouble." After closing submissions and being instructed by Grain, the jury took only five minutes to find him guilty. Before sentencing Singh, Grain asked if he had anything to say. Singh replied: "I kill him because he was a bad man." Grain, without putting on the traditional black cap, then sentenced Singh to death. Grain, who was "visibly affected," then told the court:

> "Mr Crown Advocate, this case being concluded, I desire to pay a tribute to memory of the murdered man. Sirdar Sahib Budda Singh was a gentleman. He was brave, loyal, generous, courteous and kind hearted. He served his sovereign bravely and loyally. He carried out his duties in Shanghai conscientiously, courteously and with kind-heartedness. I knew him personally and it was with great sorrow that I heard of his death."

Harbant Singh became the martyr he obviously wanted to be. He was executed by hanging at Ward Road Gaol on June

7 The jury members were J.R. Moody, C. Reeves, W.J. Dexter, F.S. Ward, R. Bachrach, J. Acheson, D.W. Leach, J.R. Milligan, W.H. Ferris, J.Huxley, F.L. Barker and G.H. Ackerman.

18, 1927.

Budda Singh was given a grand funeral procession headed by Sikh police followed by the Municipal Band. His coffin was shrouded with the Shanghai municipal flag and his sword, Indian decoration and long service medal were placed on top of it. All senior members of the SMP joined the procession, including Captain Barrett, who was now Commissioner of Police. All off-duty Sikh policemen and foreign, special, Japanese and Chinese police joined the parade. Members of the fire brigade and French police also marched. Singh was cremated in accordance with Sikh custom. The *North China Daily News* made a point of farewelling Singh as a "very loyal Sikh officer and a gentleman."

The Municipal Council in its Annual Report for 1927 made specific mention of Singh's murder stating that he "was a most loyal officer and his death was directly attributable to his unceasing efforts against disaffected Indians in Shanghai."

The Shanghai Municipal Police believed that the assassination was part of the Nationalist-inspired move to instigate a strike amongst Sikh policemen supported by Russian agents.[8]

While this may have been true, Chiang Kai-shek had by this time decided to rid the Nationalist Party of leftists and to break with the Russians. Rather than agitating inside the concessions or seeking to occupy them, instead, in the same month that Budda Singh was killed, April 1927, Chiang launched a purge of the Nationalist Party to remove Communist Party members. This was tacitly supported by the foreign powers. In Shanghai, with the consent of Stirling Fessenden, now the Chairman of the Municipal Council, armed Chinese troops moved through the International Settlement to be in a position to attack communists who were on strike in Shanghai. A bloody purge followed in which many communists were killed. Eight months later, in December 1927 the Nationalists severed relations with

8 F. Wakeman, *Policing Shanghai*, 1927-1937, p145.

Soviet Russia and sent away its Soviet advisers.[9]

By 1928, the Nationalist Party had relatively firm control over the country from Canton up to Peking and was formally recognized as the government of China. A system of District and High Courts headed by a Supreme Court was introduced to handle legal cases. Additionally, military and naval courts, an administrative court, magistrate's courts and police tribunals were all established. In areas where there were foreigners without treaty rights, special courts were introduced with foreign advisers, interpreters and special prisons. The first place such courts were introduced was in Harbin in Manchuria where a large number of Russians, who had lost extraterrito-

Sapajou on the rendition of the Mixed Court

9 F. Hawks Pott, *A Short History of Shanghai*, 1928, pp298-302.

rial rights in 1922, lived.[10]

A provisional farewell to the Mixed Court

In Shanghai, as well, new Chinese courts were established. As a result of the Shanghai riot in 1925, the treaty powers agreed with the local government of Chekiang to abolish the Mixed Court in the International Settlement at the end of 1926. It was replaced with effect from January 1, 1927 by a Provisional Court with a Chinese Judge sitting alone for most cases. A deputy foreign consul was allowed to sit with the judge to watch proceedings where the case involved municipal regulations or the accused was an employee of a foreigner enjoying extraterritorial rights.

The judges of the Provisional Court were more than willing to exercise their newly returned sovereignty and power. One judge in particularly, Judge Ziar, refused to follow the old way of doing things. Y.S.Ziar had been a practicing lawyer in Shanghai for many years, had been educated in London and had qualified as a barrister in England. He had at times appeared in the British Supreme Court, in particular, it will be recalled, in the private prosecution of Superintendent Gabbutt for torturing Loh Tse Wah. In one case before Ziar, a destitute Russian, Mr Leontieff, was brought before the court on vagrancy charges. The prosecutor, Mr Maitland on behalf of the Municipal Council, sought a fine and expulsion order. Ziar responded, over protests from Maitland, that he did not have

JUDGE ZIAR
Of the Shanghai Provisional Court

Judge Ziar, British barrister, now a Chinese Judge of the Provisional Court

10 G. Keeton, *The Development of Extraterritoriality in China*, pp36 to 44.

E.T. Maitland prosecuting and Oscar Fischer defending in the Provisional Court before Judge Chiu

the power to make the order. He said to Leontieff:

"That you are poor does not necessarily mean to say we can deprive you of your liberty as this Court will make no distinction between the rich and the poor. You may go."[11]

In another case, when a British barrister, Mr Covey, appeared in a suit, Ziar told him he could not hear him unless he wore Chinese robes. Covey said he could not because British Bar Association rules prohibited him from "appearing in other courts than our own in the dress a foreign court may have laid down as to be worn by its nationals," nor was he allowed to wear his wig and gown in a foreign court. Covey pointed out that all recognised practitioners of other nationalities did not appear robed in the British courts. Ziar responded that he could not do anything about that. After consultation with the clerk of the Provisional Court, Covey returned to say he would need to withdraw from this and all other cases.[12] After negotiations, British barristers were allowed to appear in a normal business attire.

Interestingly, the British did not always assert their rights in the Provisional Court. In February 1927, a Charles Maitland was prosecuted by the Municipal Police in the Provi-

11 *SMC v Leontieff*, *North China Herald*, January 15, 1927, p75.

12 *North China Herald*, February 19, 1927, p292.

Sapajou on Judge Ziar's ruling that barristers appear in Chinese robes. R.N. MacLeod is in the centre. Reader Harris is to his right

sional Court for obtaining money by false pretences. He said in excellent Chinese that he was British but as he had not registered at the Consulate so was being prosecuted in the Provisional Court. The case proceeded without, it appears, there being any protest by the British authorities.[13]

Recognizing a rebel government

The Nationalists' rise to power created a new problem for both the American and British courts. In the US Court, the question was whether the Nationalists had the right to sue as the Government of China and when did they acquire it? In

13 *SMC v C Maitland, North China Herald,* February 12, 1927, p248.

the British Court the question was: should edicts of the revolutionary army be binding?

Since 1924, the United States had not recognized any government of China. In that year, it gave *de facto* recognition to Marshal Tuan Chi-jui who controlled Peking, but once his government had collapsed in 1926, it had not recognized any new government.

In February 1926, a fire had destroyed the Chinese Government Telephone Administration Exchange buildings in Wuchang next to Hankow (both cities are now part of Wuhan). Merchants Fire Assurance Corporation of New York and the Great American Fire Assurance Corporation of New York had insured the building and equipment. The Nationalists captured Wuchang in 1926 and took over the property.

By early 1928, the Nationalists had occupied most of China, but had not yet captured the capital, Peking. They wished to bring an action under an insurance policy against the insurance companies claiming $135,000 Mex. They instructed H.D. Rodger and Nick Char to bring proceedings in the US Court for China. In April 1928, Rodger first asked the US Consulate for a certificate "stating when the United States Government ceased to recognize the Chinese Government - either the present so-called Peking Government or the Nationalist Government at Nanking." This was passed on to the State Department. The legation was instructed to reply that since Tuan's administration had collapsed, the American government had not dealt with any regime as the Government of China but had dealt with "certain authorities on the basis of regional jurisdiction." The US authorities declined to give Rodger a certificate.[14]

Two months later, after the Nationalists had captured Peking, Rodger wrote again asking if the Nationalist govern-

14 *Republic of China v Merchants Fire Assurance Corporation of New York*, 30 F.2d 278 (1929), Gilbert, Rudkin and Dietrich, District Judges (also published in *North China Herald*, March 23, 1929, p501.) Foreign Relations of the United States, Correspondence, 1928, pp179 and 189.

ment could now sue as the *de facto* government of China. He got a pass-the-buck reply that while the US government now dealt with the Nationalists as the *de facto* government, the question of whether they could sue in the US Court was a question for the US Court for China. Rodger, therefore, then filed suit in the US Court. Judge Purdy declined jurisdiction on the basis that the Nationalist Party was not the recognized government.

Rodger with his partner, Nick Char, appealed to the Ninth Circuit in San Francisco, who had an easy decision to make. By the time the appeal was heard in early 1929, the US had recognized the Nationalist Party as the government for China and entered into a Treaty of Commerce, although it had not yet been ratified by the Senate. On this basis, the Ninth Circuit ruled that the US Court for China now had jurisdiction. It did add that Purdy's original decision was correct but the change in recognition now meant the Nationalists had taken over the rights of the Chinese government.

Norwood Allman acted for the Merchant Fire Insurance Company. In his memoirs he wrote that:

> "Our client was perfectly willing to pay. There was no question about that. The sole problem was to pay whom."[15]

Not true. Allman was suffering from selective memory.

The case came back to the US Court for China, where both insurance companies first sought to have the case dismissed because the fire had happened before the Nationalists had captured Wuchang. When they had taken Wuchang, the "incoming forces got only the partially burned buildings, and acquired no capital in the insurance policy." Purdy dismissed these arguments without giving detailed reasons.[16]

15 N. Allman, *Shanghai Lawyer*, pp137-138.

16 *North China Herald*, April 27, 1929, p158.

The cases were then tried in June 1929. The insurance companies made some of the usual arguments about there being no proper evidence of loss and that the claim had not been made in time. Purdy rejected these and gave judgment against the Great American Insurance Company.[17]

The Merchants Fire Assurance Company, Allman's client, however, had an interesting defence which caused Purdy considerable difficulties. This was that the former Chinese Government had reached an agreement on March, 27 1928 to settle the claim. A judgment had been granted by consent in the US Court for China on April, 23 1928 recognizing this agreement. (Consent judgments are judgments agreed between the parties and while officially made by the court are usually not reviewed by the court in detail.) Rodger attacked the agreement as having been made by a government with no legal capacity to sue in the court, for the same reasons that the Nationalist government had not been able to sue at the time. Purdy agreed. He said that the agreement and the judgment had clearly been entered into by collusion between the parties. If the judgment had been an act of the purported Chinese government he would have been able to treat it as having no effect.

He faced a difficulty, however. The judgment was not an act of the Chinese government; it was an act of the United States Court for China. He had to give it effect until it was formally set aside. Purdy said that he was satisfied the Nationalist Government should recover on the policy, but very reluctantly concluded that until the previous judgment was set aside, he would have to give effect to it. He was forced to dismiss the claim, but did so without prejudice to the Plaintiff bringing a new claim once the previous judgment had been set aside.

If this was a case of a client being "perfectly willing to pay," imagine what a case would have looked like if the client

17 Trial report: *North China Herald*, June 15, 1929, p448; Judgments: *North China Herald*, August 17, 1929, p257.

was not willing to pay.

The devalued tael

The Nationalists capture of Hankow in 1927 produced another insurance case, this time in the British Supreme Court for China. The issue in the case was a very important one that produced a rare occasion where the Full Court overturned a decision of the Judge of the Court.[18]

The issue was relatively simple. Wo Ho Tong Co in Hankow bought insurance from the Commercial Assurance Co Ltd in March 1927. The policy provided that any payments under the policy would be paid in Hankow Taels. Hankow Taels did not, in fact, exist as a unit of currency but were used as an accounting unit. When payment was to be made, Hankow Taels were converted into silver dollars at the daily rate of exchange.

Soon after the contract was signed, the Nationalists captured Hankow and on April 18, 1927, Mr T.V. Soong the Nationalist Finance Minster issued regulations fixing the exchange rate of Hankow Taels at 71 taels to $100. On June 30 there was a fire at Wo Ho Tong's premises. The damage was assessed and agreed at 4,006.16 taels. The new Nationalist regulations provided that only the notes of three banks at Hankow, the Central Bank, Bank of China and Bank of Communications were allowed to be in circulation. The effect of these regulations was to depreciate the value of the Hankow Tael by 80%. That is, it was only worth 20% of its previous value. The insurance company paid the claims with the notes of one of the approved banks. Wo Ho Tong rejected the payment on the basis that the payment should have been in silver dollars, the currency of China. Wo Ho Tong argued that the Nationalist Government was not the legitimate government

18 *Commercial Union Assurance Co Ltd v Wo Ho Tong Co*, (Full Court), *North China Herald*, January 19, 1929, p115. Leave to appeal application: *North China Herald*, February 2, 1930, p206.

THE FULL COURT IN SESSION
Judge Sir Peter Grain, Judge Sir Henry Gollan (presiding) and Judge G. W. King

of China or Hankow at the time of the fire and payment. The British Supreme Court should not give effect to the regulations, which were those of a rebel government. At the trial, Peter Grain agreed with this argument and ordered that the money should be paid in the legal silver currency of China.

The insurance company appealed to the Full Court, made up of Sir Henry Gollan, the Chief Justice of Hong Kong, presiding, Grain, and Gilbert King. Reader Harris appeared for the insurance company and Ranald McDonald for Wo Ho Tong. The decision of the Full Court was given in January 1929. Because Gollan had returned to Hong Kong, Grain read out Golan's judgment. This must have been hard for him, because Gollan disagreed with Grain entirely. Gollan considered that the Nationalist Government was at the time in *de facto* control of Hankow and therefore entitled to issue the regulations. Payment in the notes of the Hankow banks was acceptable. King agreed with him. Both Gollan and King did express the hope that the insurance company, having established the principle, "will realize that there may be another view of the facts of this case besides one which only regards strict legal rights as between the parties."

Grain wrote a powerful dissenting judgment. For him, the question was not whether the Nationalist Party was in *de facto* control of Hankow, the question was "were they the government of the country with the power to alter the currency of the Nation?" He said that at the time the Government of the Republic of China was still in existence and functioning. The Nationalists had occupied Hankow by force, but their power "did not run beyond the places they were holding by force."

> "They were in fact at that moment rebels, as a rebel is an individual who rises against and rebels against constituted authority of the nation. No doubt rebels do often in due course become the constituted authority if successful in defeating the authority in being."

Grain wanted to make it clear he was not picking on the Nationalists and added an example from English history:

> "As for instance, Oliver Cromwell was a rebel and in rebellion against the King, the lawful authority of England at that date, until he entirely defeated the King's forces and established himself as Lord Protector of England in place of a king."

He concluded that the Nationalist Party was at the time not the lawful government of China and had no power to alter the national currency. He added that "as it happened the Nationalist Party have become successful" and become the lawful government. But, it may have been that they had not become successful and been "turned out of Hankow shortly after the regulations in question were promulgated." He then asked what would have happened should the court have then been asked to decide if the bank notes were legal tender.

Leave to appeal to the Privy Council was granted, but it appears the appeal did not go ahead. The insurance company is then likely to have taken another view of the facts of the case, including the fact they would have to spend a lot of money to fight in the Privy Council and possibly lose and made an offer to settle.

Chinese Americans

By 1928, the Nationalist Chinese authorities around Shanghai started taking a stricter interpretation of extraterritorial rights, especially in relation to Chinese Americans, whom in many cases they considered to be Chinese. In some cases, Chinese Americans brought problems upon themselves by trying to have the best of both worlds and be Chinese or American when it suited them. In other cases, Chinese authorities asserted jurisdiction over Chinese Americans solely because they had failed to take appropriate steps to renounce their Chinese nationality.

This new reality was brought home to Chinese American lawyer Nick Char who had with H.D. Rodger represented the Chinese government in the Wuchang Insurance cases in the US Court. He was not able to attend court when Purdy gave his judgment because he was sitting in a Chinese jail serving a three months sentence for assault.

Char had been born in Hawaii to Chinese parents. At a baseball game at Pioneer Field in the southeast corner of the French Concession in June 1927, he assaulted a Chinese, Jui Hsoh-hsien. The attack had been quite vicious and two years later, Jui was still confined to his bed. Jui filed a complaint against Char in the Provisional Court. Char originally did not object to this and appeared to defend the charge. Char and his partner, H.D. Rodger, thought, correctly, that the Provisional Court would treat Char lightly. Char also wished to represent Chinese clients before the Provisional Court. Under the new rules applying in there, foreigners were not allowed to represent Chinese. He therefore chose not to assert his American citizenship.[19]

Even though they could clearly see that Char was seeking to take advantage of his dual nationality, the US Consulate in Shanghai took steps to assist him. A consular official told the Provisional Court before the trial that Char was American and that he could easily be prosecuted in the US Court for China because he lived in the International Settlement. However, the judge said that in his application to the Chinese authorities for the right to appear in the Provisional Court, Char had described his origin as "Canton Province." The court considered this sufficient evidence to hold he was Chinese. In October 1928, Char was fined $300.

Jui was not satisfied with the light penalty and appealed the decision to the Chinese Court of Appeal. In early February 1929, Char was arrested in the International Settlement on the orders of the Chinese Court of Appeal and was detained by the Shanghai Municipal Police. The US Consulate suggested to the President of the Court of Appeal that Char be granted bail so that an agreement could be reached on his citizenship status. This was rejected.

Rodger then appeared in the Provisional Court seeking Char's release. Rodger said that Char was an American citizen not subject to the jurisdiction of the court. He produced a US army discharge certificate showing Char had fought in the US Army in World War I. Judge Shen said that the matter was before the Court of Appeals and he could not deal with it. Mr H.E. Stevens, the US Vice-Consul and the Senior Consul's deputy at the Provisional Court, made a formal statement that Char was a United States Citizen and could not be prosecuted in the Chinese courts. The Chinese authorities could arrest him but he must be handed over to the American authorities if a request was made. Mr Bryan, the prosecuting solicitor appearing on behalf of the Police said that the Police would hold

19 Foreign Relations of the United States, 1929, Vol II, pp513 to 518; *North China Herald*, February 9, 1929, p252 and February 16, 1929, p287.

Char until they received information from the United States Consul-General that Char was American.

The United States Consul-General, Edwin Cunningham, felt strongly that if action was not taken in this case, the Chinese government would seek to assume jurisdiction over all Chinese Americans. First, the consulate sought to achieve a diplomatic resolution. Cunningham wrote to the Commissioner of Foreign Affairs, Mr Wunsz King, seeking Char's release. Mr Stevens and Mr C.D. Meinhart, American Vice-Consuls, went on appointment to see Mr King. King snubbed them. When they arrived they were informed he was not in. The US Consulate then felt that it had "no alternative" but to ask the SMP to release Char on the grounds he was an American. Cunningham reported to the Secretary of State that: "This request the police complied with as is the usual custom in Shanghai when a Consul of an extraterritorial power makes a request." On his release, Char was advised not to leave the International Settlement.

Char's appeal hearing was scheduled the following day, on February 8. Char had already been released and did not appear. The Court of Appeal waited one hour for Char to appear and then handed down a judgment in his absence. The court said that "to a poor man" a fine of $300, "would be a heavy punishment, but as the accused is a rich man this fine is no punishment so he is sentenced to imprisonment." The court then imposed a sentence of three months imprisonment.

Thomas Sellett, the US District Attorney, was asked for his opinion on the case. He advised that because Char was a dual national, he could be tried in the Chinese courts or the US Court. Consul-General Cunningham disagreed with this. He held to the view that Char could not be prosecuted in a Chinese court as long as he lived in a treaty port and had not "expatriated" himself; that, is done things inconsistent with his status as a US citizen. Cunningham reported the case to the US Secretary of State, Henry Stimson, asking for guidance as to how to handle cases of this type in the future.

Sellett, despite thinking Char had been properly tried in the Chinese courts agreed to try Char in the US Court. A letter was sent to the Commissioner for Foreign Affairs requesting this to be done. The Commissioner for Foreign Affairs, or more likely his superiors, had other ideas. Char had been friends with the Commissioner for many years. Char had been discussing some matters concerning his clients with the Commissioner on the telephone. The Commissioner invited Char to come to his office in the Chinese part of Shanghai outside the International Settlement. Once there, he was promptly arrested. He was allowed to telephone the US Consulate General but was subsequently placed in a Chinese jail outside the Settlement. The US Minister in China, John MacMurray, on July 15, 1929 immediately cabled Washington for instructions on what to do, adding that the case was "attracting considerable attention locally." He said that the imprisonment of Char outside the Settlement was a breach of the Mixed Court rendition agreement that required imprisonment in the Settlement.

The next day before he received a reply, he sent another cable requesting "early action," and that there was "an important principle involved which will affect large numbers of Sino-American citizens if the Chinese authorities are permitted without prejudice to arrest and arbitrarily detain Char without judicial authority." Secretary of State Stimson was in no mood for "early action" or to save Char. He cabled back one month later, essentially agreeing with Sellett's earlier opinion that Char had brought the issue on himself and instructed the US officials in China to take "no action looking for Char's release from the custody of the Chinese authorities." Cunningham, on being informed of this, still wanted to make the best of a bad lot and obtained MacMurray's approval to tell the Chinese authorities that they were not requesting Char's release because of his past actions and so to avoid "silence on our part [being] interpreted to mean that we acquiesce in the Chinese view on the question of jurisdiction over persons of dual Chinese and American nationality."

Cunningham was right to be concerned. Two months after this, in October 1929, two more cases arose involving Chinese Americans who both lived in the International Settlement and registered as US citizens every year. In the first case, Dr T.C. Lieu was served with a criminal summons in the Provisional Court charging negligence causing death. Sellett had already investigated the case and decided not to prosecute. Lieu could not be arrested if he remained in the International Settlement, but if he left the Settlement to see patients, he ran the risk of being picked up by Chinese police. In the second case, Fong Koon Look was sued in a civil action in the Provisional Court and a judgment was given against him. MacMurray cabled the Secretary of State to ask for instructions as to what could be done to protect them. He received the simple answer to "afford them such protection as is possible and proper" under the treaties granting extraterritoriality. Lieu's case appears to have been resolved, but in the case of Fong, the Commissioner of Foreign Affairs upped the ante saying that he was a Chinese citizen because he had not obtained a certificate of denaturalization. The Provisional Court also ruled that Fong was subject to its jurisdiction for the same reason.[20]

Fong remained safe if he stayed in the International Settlement or French Concession, but like Char could be arrested if he left. He was also stuck in the difficult situation that he was now unable to obtain a certificate of denaturalization because he had a civil judgment outstanding against him. Cunningham recommended that negotiations be entered into with the Chinese regarding the status of dual nationals and that they be advised when registering with the US Consulate to obtain

20 Details of these cases and the advice to the consul in Canton are *in Foreign Relations of the United States*, 1929, pp519-523.

certificates for denaturalization.

In 1928, the Department of State had advised the Consul-General in Canton to recommend dual nationals apply for denaturalization. However, having considered the matter further, the Department of State wrote to the Charge d'Affaires specifically ordering US consular officials not to advise Chinese Americans to denaturalize. Their concern was Article 14 of the Chinese Nationality Law. This provided that if a Chinese denaturalized, they would lose any property that a non-Chinese could not hold unless it was transferred to a Chinese citizen within a year. The US Government did not want to be responsible for Chinese Americans losing property and therefore advised its consuls to merely tell Chinese nationals of the possibility of obtaining denaturalization certificates.

The British also continued to face similar problems with Hong Kong Chinese. A few years later, the Shanghai Consul-General, J.F. Brenan, wrote to the British Minister about a case of a Hong Kong Chinese widow, Tseng Wu Cho, which brought "home forcibly the disadvantages attaching to dual nationality in the absence of any agreement with the Chinese Government on the subject." Tseng's husband had been a registered British subject in Hankow and Shanghai. Following his death, the British Supreme Court for China granted probate to his widow, also a Hong Kong Chinese. Mr Tseng's Chinese relatives brought an action in the Chinese courts against the widow. Brenan wrote a letter claiming jurisdiction but the Chinese court issued a preliminary ruling that it had jurisdiction. Brenan noted that in "view of the Chinese Nationality Law, the Court could not have ruled otherwise and it would be useless for me to protest against the judgment." Under Chinese law Mrs Tseng would only be entitled to part of the estate. Brenan said it was unjust for her to be subject to two jurisdictions but he was unable to do anything about it.[21]

21 FO 656/219 Letter from J.F. Brenan to British Minister dated February 22, 1933.

A New Special District Court

The agreement to establish the Provisional Court in place of the Mixed Court only had a term of three years. In 1929, negotiations began with the Chinese government over the establishment of new courts in Shanghai, leading to an agreement in February 1930 signed by Britain, the United States, Brazil, Norway and Holland establishing a District Court and a branch High Court in Shanghai. Appeals from the High Court lay to the Supreme Court of China.[22]

Any Chinese arrested in the International Settlement were, at least, to face a preliminary hearing in the District Court to determine if they should be transferred to another court. Foreign lawyers were allowed to practice before the court when a foreigner was a party, but only to act for the foreign party. The Municipal Council was allowed to nominate policemen to serve as judicial police and "as far as practicable" they should be Chinese. The court took over all cases pending before the Provisional Court and all judgments of the Mixed Court and Provisional Court were agreed to remain binding.

The agreement provided that the practice of consular assessors sitting on the bench be abolished in all cases. However, a declaration annexed to the agreement provided that the foreign parties did not give up any rights under existing treaties, meaning that under the Chefoo Convention, a consular official could still attend cases as an observer when a national of their country was a party.

The Shanghai Special District Court was opened in the old Provisional Court Building (which was itself the old Mixed Court building) on April 1, 1930 in a very impressive ceremony.[23] A total of 26 judges were sworn in beneath a portrait of

22 Agreement relating to the Chinese Courts in the International Settlement at Shanghai, made at Nanking February 17, 1930. For further details of the Mixed Court, Provisional Court, Special District Courts and High Court, see, Tseng Yu-Yao, *the Termination of Unequal Treaties*, pp455-516.

23 "Special Shanghai District Court", *North China Herald*, April 8, 1930, p52. Hsu's name

Dr Sun Yat-sen. Dr Sun's will was read, followed by three minutes silence. Dr Showin Wetzen Hsu the new Judge of the 2nd Branch Kiangsu Provincial Higher Court said that "he would ensure impartial administration of justice by those under his control." He then added a very serious note that it was clear "that the reputation of China and her diplomatic future, was in the hands" of the judges who had all been sworn in this morning.

Dr Showin Wetzen Hsu, former President of the Provisional Court, new Judge of the Kiangsu Higher Court

There was no immediate purge of foreigners involved with the court. Mr R.T. Bryan, who had served as "Police Advocate", remained on as "Municipal Advocate" and the Judicial Police remained a foreign domain with Chief Inspector W. Whiting appointed as head, assisted by Inspector N. White and two foreign sergeants.

Handover of Weihaiwei

The Chinese takeover of British and foreign interests continued further north. In 1930, Belgium returned its concession in Tientsin. Of greater importance, on April 18, 1930, Britain and China entered into a Convention for the Rendition of Weihaiwei to China. The Convention came into force on October 1, 1930. Under the agreement, Weihaiwei was returned in its entirety to China. Britain agreed to remove its garrison within one month. All decisions of the British Courts in Weihaiwei were to remain in full effect as if made by a Chinese court. The Supreme Court

was variously spelt Wei-chung, Wei-Chin and Wei-tsen.

for China and the United States Court for China resumed extraterritorial jurisdiction over British and American subjects in Weihaiwei with effect from October 1, 1930.[24]

Up until the rendition of Weihaiwei, Peter Grain had continued to preside as Judge in Weihaiwei. Two years before the return, Grain, the Crown Advocate Allan Mossop and Mossop's assistant, Victor Priestwood, travelled to Weihaiwei to try a very sad murder case against a Chinese. Chiang Liang-shi, a concubine of the late Chiang Yu-ho, was accused of murdering the first wife, Chiang Miao-Shih. The trial was heard by Grain with a jury including one Chinese juror, H.W. Sun. Mossop represented the Crown and Priestwood defended.

The concubine had poisoned the first wife because she ill-treated her. The only real defence offered, which at the time was not a defence, was "battered second wife syndrome." The defendant gave evidence as to how she had been beaten by the husband and first wife. Then, after the death of the husband, she said the first wife had tried to sell her as a wife to other men. The jury returned a verdict of guilty but with a recommendation for mercy. Grain, as required by law, sentenced her to death, but also supported the recommendation for mercy. Her sentence was commuted to 10 years imprisonment.[25]

Just before the return of Weihaiwei, Grain heard two more sad cases in early 1930 where life had been taken.[26] In the first case, Liu Chang-te was accused of killing his mother. The evidence from the family was that he was an "undutiful son" and lazy. The mother had been found beaten to death in a cellar under the house. Blood was found on a splintered piece of wood in the kitchen and on Liu's clothing and shoes. Liu had fled when villagers had tried to catch him and later when the police had tried to arrest him. The jury took a very short time

24 S.3 Weihaiwei Order in Council, 1930 dated November 27, 1930.

25 *R v Chiang Lian-shi*, *North China Herald*, December 3, 1927, p419. "Battered wife syndrome" is occasionally accepted as a defence to murder charges in British courts.

26 *R v Liu Chang-te* and *R v Chang Yung-fu*, *North China Herald*, January 23, 1930, p137.

to find Liu guilty. Grain sentenced Liu to death and told him he could appeal to the Commissioner.

The last case was much sadder for all concerned. Chang Yung-fu, a chauffeur, had been driving through a small village. Motorcars were still new to China and particularly to Weihaiwei. Traffic rules required that cars drive through villages at five miles per hour (8 km/h), close to walking pace. This was necessary because people were not used to the speed of cars and could be easily hit. Chang by his own confession was driving at 15 m/h (24 km/h). A little girl of five years old ran out onto the road. Chang braked hard and swerved to the right, but his rear wheel struck the little girl killing her.

Chang was charged with manslaughter. Grain told the jury that the only question was whether Chang was driving too fast so as to deserve to be convicted. The jury returned a verdict of "not guilty", which Grain said he agreed with. But he encouraged Chang to compensate the family. Chang said he had offered money but it had been refused; the owner of the car had refused to help and even with the help of others he had not been able to get the child's family to compromise. In what must have been a very sad moment for all concerned, the girl's father remained in court for a long time to argue the decision was unfair. The *North China Herald* commented that the villager may not have understood that "British justice endeavours to fit the punishment to the crime and that British law is not founded on the old world notion, 'an eye for an eye; and a tooth for a tooth.'"

Weihaiwei was returned to China on October 1, 1930. The Chinese and British flags flew side by side throughout the day and the British flag was lowered at sunset. Chinese courts thereupon took jurisdiction over Chinese while the British Supreme Court for China, the United States Court for China and other consular courts resumed jurisdiction over their own nationals.

There were some reports that locals regretted the departure of the British, but perhaps the father of the little five-year-old girl would have thought that the Chinese justice system was preferable.

Chapter 51

The Work of Two Men

Gilbert King worked for the British Court for almost exactly the same period of time Weihaiwei was a British colony. In April 1931, King returned home on leave, the *North China Herald* reporting that he was in "indifferent health." He had remarried, to Muriel Waugh, in 1928 and his new wife was encouraging him to retire. A photo taken the year before, in 1930, showed him looking decidedly unwell. By November, he decided to retire after only four years as Assistant Judge. King died six years later in 1937 at his home at Reigate, England at the age of 66.[1]

On news of his death reaching Shanghai, Allan Mossop said that "he was certain the members of the Bar would share with the judges and staff of the Court the great sense of loss which was felt at Mr King's passing." The *North China Daily News* described him as a "brilliant man" who gave "loyal and faithful service." "As a magistrate his work on the Bench was marked with great understanding and humanity … while as an Assistant Judge he brought to his work an erudition and application of the highest quality."[2]

The *Times,* in what for someone who had only served as an Assistant Judge was a long obituary was glowing its praise:

1 *North China Herald,* April 28, 1931, p123; *Times* Obituary, 24 December 1937 ; *North China Daily News* Obituary, December 30, 1937.

2 *Shanghai Times,* December 29, 1937; *North China Daily News* December 30, 1937 (Mossop Law Reports).

> "He was an extremely learned Judge, and some of his decisions form an important part of the archives of the British Court in Shanghai. More than all else, perhaps, he will be remembered for his quiet, friendly, unassuming nature and the dry wit of his conversation. No man of his time was more genuinely liked in the Far East by all who knew him. These certainly included those who appeared before him as Registrar and Judge, in which capacity he well knew how to temper justice with humanity."

King had for almost the entire three years prior to his retirement been carrying out the work of two men. When he was promoted to Assistant Judge a new Registrar was not appointed. The Chief Clerk of the Court, Idwal Morris, a solicitor, had for most of the time acted as Registrar. When Morris was unavailable, A.J. Martin took over his responsibilities. Between April and August 1930, Charles Graham Overbeck Anderson, a mixed-race barrister who worked for the consulate, acted as Registrar. However, King would have been supervising their work.

Two men were appointed in 1930 and 1931 to take over from him as Registrar and Assistant Judge.

New Registrar

In 1930, Cyril Henry Haines was appointed Registrar. Haines was born on March 2, 1895 and was 35 at the time. He was the son of Walter John Haines OBE, former Deputy Chief Inspector of Customs and Excise in the United Kingdom. Haines joined the Scottish Education Department in 1914, but almost immediately joined the army and was on active service during World War I. He joined the Foreign Office in 1920 and was admitted as a barrister of the Middle Temple in 1926. He was Assistant to the Anglo-Mexican Revolutionary Claims Commission in 1928. Haines served as Registrar for the remainder of the life of the court.[3]

The New Judge: Penrhyn Grant Jones

King's successor as Assistant Judge, Penrhyn Grant Jones, was temperamentally completely different to King. Where King was patient, Grant Jones was grumpy. Where King saw good, Grant Jones saw bad. Where King had the patience of a saint for Indian parties, Grant Jones had almost no time for them, particularly Indian money lenders.

Grant Jones had been in consular service in China for 30 years, including eight years as an assessor on the Mixed Court in Shanghai and as Acting Judge of the High Court of Weihaiwei in 1919. With effect from November 30, 1931 he was appointed Assistant Judge of the Supreme Court.[4]

Grant Jones was born on May 28, 1878. He was the eldest son of, Frederick Topham Jones who had been an actor and Elizabeth Grant Jones (nee Fitzgerald). Frederick was the owner of the Royal Sandrock Hotel on the Isle of Wight, a fashionable resort with its own spring. Princess Victoria and the Duchess of Kent had stayed at the hotel, hence the addition of the title Royal. While it was owned by the Jones family, one guest of the hotel had been Rudyard Kipling who stayed there in 1891 when Grant Jones was 12. His father was also rector on the Isle of Wight. Grant Jones was educated at Malvern where he was a prefect. His father was declared bankrupt in 1897 and he lost the hotel.

Grant Jones came to China in 1902 as a student interpreter with the consular service, having passed a competitive exam. Most likely, his father's bankruptcy had meant that he needed to find a stable income quickly. He was promoted to be a 2nd Class Assistant on July 15, 1909. He passed his bar exams,

---

3 Who's Who 1967 Entry for Haines.

4 Biographical date for Grant Jones sourced from: Foreign Office List 1943, p232; *The Times*, April 17, 1912, p4; *Times* July 19, 1945; Inner Temple Admissions Database; *Edinburgh Gazette*, December 21, 1897, p1262 (re father's bankruptcy); 1891 census records for Niton, Isle of White (re Kipling).

being placed in the first class and was awarded a certificate of honour. He was admitted as a barrister of the Inner Temple in 1910 and called to the bar on June 19, 1912. He served in various consular capacities around China, including Chungking, Hankow and Changsha. He was promoted to Consul in 1926 in Harbin and served as Consul there and in Amoy until he was appointed Assistant Judge. He was awarded an OBE in 1928 while in Harbin.[5]

Grant Jones was an old school English judge. He quoted the Old Testament to a condemned man. He did not like Americanisms. In a case claiming money for goods sold and for which a chit was provided, Grant Jones asked if the goods had been sold, the plaintiff responded "Sure!." Grant Jones responded: I don't want any 'sures' in this Court. This is an American expression I don't like."[6]

While sitting as an assessor in the Mixed Court in the 1910s and 1920s, Grant Jones was quoted on a number of occasions commenting on the lack of civil and moral standards in Shanghai. In 1914, he said that flogging should be brought back as a punishment. In 1915, he called Shanghai a "festering sore" on the body politic of China and: "What should be the habitat of a peaceful commercial community has become an Alsatia of rogues and vagabonds, native and foreign." The same year, he said that Shanghai must not become a place of asylum for Chinese and all acts of rebellion against the Chinese government must be firmly suppressed. In 1920, he said on the bench of the Mixed Court: "I have sat here for eight

---

5 Grant Jones was appointed Vice-Consul (Shipping Office) at Shanghai. He was promoted to be a 1st Class Assistant on September 1, 1916. He was Acting Consul in Shanghai in 1920 and in Chunking from 1921 to 1923. He was Vice-Consul at Hankow from 1923 to 1926 and acted as Consul General from 1925. He was officiating Vice-Consul at Hankow from February 1926 and Acting Consul in Changsha from September 1926. He was promoted to be a Consul on 27 August 1926 and served as Consul in Harbin from 1 May 1927 to 23 April 1929 and was Acting Consul General from 1 April 1929. He was in charge of the Consul in Amoy (Xiamen) from January 1930 to November 1931. Foreign Office List Entry for Grant Jones, 1943.

6 *North China Herald*, January 13, 1937, p72.

years, listening to lie after lie."[7]

Ralph Shaw in his book *Sin City* wrote that Grant Jones had a clock stolen from his court while he was sitting as a judge.

> "I was in court once when two Chinese men in blue overalls carrying a ladder pushed their way through the swing doors. They stood at the back of the court and bowed low to Judge Grant Jones. Always a stickler for politeness he bowed back. Then they padded past the benches to stop underneath the court clock - a product of English craftsmanship that was the pride and joy of the court staff, who were inveterate clockwatchers, particularly when they were dying for a smoke or a cup of tea. The two workmen, for that is what they appeared to be, placed their ladder against the wall. One of them mounted it and carefully unscrewed the clock which he handed to his mate. He descended the ladder and carrying ladder and clock in their arms, the two Chinese walked toward the door. There they stood facing the judge. They bowed low. He bowed in return. They left the court with the clock. It was never seen again. For a barefaced act of skulduggery it had no equal - a clock pinched right under the eyes of a stern British judge, who had sent many to jail for lesser crimes.
>
> "Judge Grant Jones took it in good part. He was heard to remark that if he ever set eyes on the two lads again then he would tell them the time in no uncertain terms - and it wouldn't be in seconds, minutes or hours but years."[8]

---

7 Flogging: *North China Herald*, January 24, 1914; Festering sore: *North China Herald*, December 24, 1915, p909. No asylum: *Straits Times*, November 25, 1915, p3; Lies: *Straits Times*, July 3, 1920, p8. The *Straits Times* commented: "the senior beak of Singapore ought to be able to beat that record pretty easily."

8 *Sin City*, by Ralph Shaw, a British journalist in Shanghai from 1937 to 1949. In fact,

A great story, but most likely untrue. A similar story had been doing the rounds of Asia with the clock being stolen from British courts during the 20th century variously in Tientsin, Singapore and Hong Kong.[9]

Perhaps because of his father's bankruptcy, for the entire time he was on the bench, he was in a running battle with Sikh moneylenders. Ralph Shaw wrote that the Sikhs were voracious moneylenders who lent at such extortionate rates of interest that borrowers "were likely to remain insolvent for the rest of their lives." In order to enforce their contracts legally against other British subjects, they had to sue in the Supreme Court.

In one case, Grant Jones said to a Sikh:

> "The extent of your extortion has only been equalled by the amount of the fabrications you have given in evidence. One day I will meet a member of your community who will tell me the truth, the whole truth and nothing but the truth, an occasion which I shall celebrate as the miraculous attainment of the impossible."[10]

In another case, barrister Ranald McDonald appeared for a money lender, Hazara Singh, who already had a judgment for $1,270 against a young British lady. Two judgment summonses to obtain payment had already been heard, but one had been adjourned and the other dismissed. Knowing that he was facing a tough judge in Grant Jones, McDonald, started by saying "there was no more unpleasant or unprofitable task" for a barrister to appear for a moneylender who had already obtained a judgment. But, it would be a sad day for

Grant Jones as a judge of the British court would have had no jurisdiction to try Chinese for the crime of theft. He did have that power when he had been an assessor on the Mixed Court.

9 See: *London and China Telegraph,* July 8, 1902, p591 (Singapore), *North China Herald,* September 3, 1902 (Tientsin), p466, *North China Herald,* September 29, 1917 (Hong Kong).

10 Quoted in *Tales of Old Shanghai,* Cultures.

British justice if a British subject could not find someone to represent him. He then submitted that a "vital matter principle was at stake" and that no matter how sympathetic to the debtor the court may be, his client was "entitled to British justice."[11]

> "My Lord, my client is no Shylock. It is no heart of flint that beats beneath his dusky Eastern skin; all that he wants is a fair and not a harsh order; but to an order of some sort, I submit, he is entitled."

McDonald continued that some suggested that the moneylenders were no better than "pariahs" and should be beyond the pale of the law. McDonald said this was grossly unfair. "Many of them were excellent citizens, who when help could not be found elsewhere took large chances and incurred large losses by coming to the rescue of those in distress." The borrowers accepted the terms with their eyes open. He then asked for an order for payment of $20 per month.

Grant Jones was obviously not impressed. The defendant made $130 per month. After enquiring as to her expenses, he made an order for payment of $5 per month. At that rate it would take more than 21 years to pay off the judgment, without interest.

But Grant Jones was not always disbelieving of Indians. In one case, *First Trust Co v Indar Singh,* the plaintiff was suing for rent. The defendant, Indar Singh, told him: "We do not know who is the landlord, four different companies told us to pay rent. We all stopped payment – Indian, Chinese and Japanese tenants."

Mr Lowe said that First Trust Company had been the mortgagee of the property but had foreclosed on the properties by order of the Chinese court. The company was now the owner of the property and hence the new landlord. Grant Jones

---

11 *North China Herald,* January 22, 1936, p149.

agreed with Singh that First Trust had not shown proof they had now become the landlord and refused to grant an immediate judgment allowing Mr Singh to defend the action.[12]

Grant Jones also had to deal with a number of cases over the internal management of the Sikh temple, or Gurdwara. In one case, he heard a dispute over the Gurdwara Constitution between Basant Singh and Bishan Singh where both of them claimed to be proper representatives of the Gurdwara.[13] All the money of the Gurdwara, its deposit checks and bank passbooks had been handed into court. Grant Jones dismissed the action and vented his frustration with what appeared to be continuous claims brought before the court relating to religious differences. He strongly warned the parties:

> "I admonish both factions to desist from these senseless dissensions which apparently have no foundation in any territorial animosity in India, and I warn them that any further breaches of the peace between them will be visited with the utmost rigour of the law, including sentences of deportation for all concerned therein."

Grant Jones became a judge at the high point of China's drive to bring an end to extraterritoriality. If things had gone according to plan, he may have only served a few years before his position was abolished.

---

12 *First Trust Co v Indar Singh, North China Herald,* 1937.

13 *Basant Singh v Bishan Singh, North China Herald* January 6, 1937, p28.

Chapter 52

Extraterritoriality to End

In 1928, with the Nationalist Party now firmly in power, Britain commenced negotiations on ending extraterritorial rights. In a Memorandum in December 1926, Britain had already urged the extraterritorial powers to institute a policy of "readiness to negotiate on treaty revision and all other outstanding questions as soon as the Chinese themselves have constituted a Government with authority to negotiate."[1]

By the end of 1928, China had entered into agreements with most treaty powers giving it tariff autonomy (that is, allowing China to set its own import and export duties).[2] This prompted the Chinese Government to issue a note signed by Foreign Minister, C.T. Wang, to all the treaty powers on April 27, 1929 seeking an end to extraterritoriality. After pointing out that China had now been unified under one government, the note said:

> "It goes without saying that extraterritoriality in China is a legacy of the old regime, which has not only ceased to be adaptable to the present-day conditions, but has become detrimental to the smooth working of the judicial and administrative machinery of China that her progress as a member of the family of nations has been

1 Negotiations With The Chinese Government For The Abolition Of Extraterritoriality: Memorandum by the Secretary of State for Foreign Affairs to the British Cabinet dated April 27, 1931. The following paragraphs are summary of the key points of that memo.

2 For details, see Tseng Yu-Hao, *The Termination of Unequal Treaties in International Law*, pp335-370.

unnecessarily retarded. The inherent inconveniences and defects of the system of Consular jurisdiction have been most clearly pointed out by the Chinese government on various occasions and also by jurists and publicists of other countries in their official utterances and in their academic discussions. It is a matter of sincere regret that, while many governments which are playing an important role in international affairs are eager and persistent in their endeavor to promote genuine friendship and harmony among nations, such anachronistic practices as only tend to mar the friendly relations between the Chinese people and foreign nationals should be allowed to exist at a time when justice and equality are supposed to govern relations of nations."[3]

Wang pointed out that China had now drafted Criminal and Commercial Codes that would come into force before January 1, 1930 and that numerous foreigners were now subject to the jurisdiction of Chinese courts in China - their governments had not had cause to complain. Wang finally sought agreement that extraterritoriality be abolished at the earliest possible date. Miles Lampson, the British Minster, replied on August 10, 1929 setting out the historical reasons for extraterritoriality in China and stating that since 1902 Britain had committed to relinquishing extraterritoriality at an appropriate time. These had been repeated in 1926. He then said that establishing of legal codes was an important step, but that

C.T. Wang, The Chinese Foreign Minister who almost brought an end to extraterritoriality

3 The full text is set out in Tseng Yu-Hao, *The Termination of Unequal Treaties in International Law*, pp371-373.

it was necessary that the new laws be enforced in practice and not just on paper. He said:

> "In order that those reforms should become a living reality, it appears to his Majesty's government to be necessary that Western legal principles should be understood and be found acceptable by the people at large no less than by their rulers, and that the courts which administer these laws should be free from interference and dictation at the hands not only of military chiefs but of groups and associations who either set up arbitrary and illegal tribunals of their own or attempt to use legal courts for furtherance of political objects rather than for the administration of equal justice between Chinese and Chinese and Chinese and foreigners."[4]

Lampson continued that until these conditions were fulfilled any agreement to relinquish extraterritoriality would be a paper agreement and that extraterritoriality would therefore need to continue for a time.

Unsatisfied with this, the Chinese government took unilateral action. On December 28, 1929, the State Council of the National Government issued a Mandate Abrogating the System of Consular Jurisdiction to take effect from January 1, 1930. The mandate read:

> "In every full sovereign state foreigners as well as its national are equally amenable to its laws and to the jurisdiction of its tribunals. This is an essential attribute of state sovereignty and a well-established principle of international law.
>
> "For more than eighty years China has been bound by the system of extraterritoriality which has prevented

4 Tseng Yu-Hao, *The Termination of Unequal Treaties in International Law*, pp381-384.

> the Chinese government from exercising its judicial power over foreigners within its territory. It is unnecessary to state here the defects and disadvantages of such a system. As long as extraterritoriality is not abolished, so long will China be unable to exercise her full sovereignty. It is hereby decided and declared that on the first day of the first month of the nineteenth year of the Republic (January 1st, 1930) all foreign nationals in the territory of China who are now enjoying extraterritorial privileges shall abide by the laws, ordinances, and regulations duly promulgated by the central and local government of China. The Executive Yuan and the Judicial Yuan are hereby ordered to prepare as soon as possible a plan for the execution of this mandate and to submit it to the Legislative Yuan for examination and deliberation with a view to its promulgation and enforcement."

Read carefully, this mandate did not immediately abolish extraterritoriality. It provided that foreign nationals should abide by Chinese law, but did not announce immediate enforcement of laws against them, rather that a plan would be introduced to bring an end to extraterritoriality. Nevertheless, the mandate clearly laid down China's strong intention to abolish extraterritoriality.[5]

Dr Wang confirmed himself that the mandate was a first step in bringing an end to extraterritoriality. In a discussion with a Chinese writer Edward Bing Shuey-lee, Wang appeared optimistic about a new era of foreign relations coming in 1930. Bing reported that Wang "realized the many difficulties that stood in the path of immediate abolition of extraterritoriality." But Wang said that if the Nationalist government's foreign policy was to be carried out "he must act like a man

5 R. Akagi in *Japan's Foreign Relations* at p406, states that this mandate was "completely ignored" by the Powers.

who is determined to reach his destination." Wang then gave an example saying that if a man wanted to go to Europe, "but kept on delaying his departure he would never get there, but if he boarded the boat he will arrive eventually."[6]

The mandate certainly got the powers' attention. Amid reports that the Judicial Yuan had drawn up plans to implement the mandate, the British Minister, Sir Miles Lampson, arrived in Nanking by gunboat on January 9, 1930 for discussions with Wang on the extraterritoriality. The US State

Sapajou questions whether China will ever reach a final agreement with the foreign powers

6 E. Bing, "Extraterritoriality viewed from a Chinese Standpoint", *North China Herald*, January 7, 1930, p2.

Department issued a statement that US Government did not consider extraterritoriality had been abolished.[7]

Following the issue of the mandate, there were a few scattered incidents where local Chinese authorities took the mandate as the end of extraterritoriality. In Wuchow, Chinese authorities refused to hand over the pilot and coxswain of a British launch on the basis that extraterritoriality had ended. In Hankow, Commander McBride of the British Navy while driving home hit and killed a Chinese boy riding a bicycle, resulting in a dispute over who had jurisdiction to hear the case. The Chinese authorities eventually released him.[8]

By 1931, things moved on quickly, China had completed enacting almost all their legal codes, including a Civil Code made up of 1,225 articles providing detailed regulation of civil and commercial relationships.[9] Not only had the Nationalist government completed the drafting of laws, they had extended their control to most of China. Even in Manchuria, which for a long time had only paid lip service to the government of China, an agreement had been reached with the warlord in control, Chang Hsueh-lian, that recognised the Nationalist Party as the Government of China. Chang had extracted some big concessions for this. He had been allowed to take over the Customs revenue in Tientsin as well as been appointed to Deputy Commander of the Chinese armed forces. When this agreement was reached, Penrhyn Grant Jones was still British Consul in Mukden (Shenyang). He wrote that Japan would

7 "Status of Foreigners in China", *North China Herald*, January 14, 1930, p45.

8 *North China Herald*, February 4, 1930, p169.

9 Introduction to Chinese Laws: Civil Code of the Republic of China, China-American Council of Commerce and Industry, Legal Series 4, p xv and the Civil Code. The Committee drafting the Code worked off previous versions that had been enacted since the process of reform of the legal system had started and also referred to the Swiss Civil Code of 1907, the German Civil Code of 1896, the Japanese Civil Code of 1896, the Code of Napoleon (of France), the Brazilian Civil Code of 1916 and the marriage law of Sweden· The code was divided into 5 books. Book I, governing General Principles, Book II, Obligations, Book III, Rights over Things, Book IV, Family and Book V, Succession. The books were enacted as they were completed between 1929 and 1931. Each book provided detailed regulation of legal relationships and civil and commercial relationships.

not sit idly by and allow the Nationalist government to solidify its control on Manchuria. He predicted, correctly, that Japan would act to safeguard her substantial interests there.[10]

By April 1931, the British Secretary of State for Foreign Affairs, Arthur Henderson, told Cabinet that it would be impossible for Britain to fight against a unilateral abrogation of the treaties by China. The force which would be needed would not be acceptable to either domestic British or Chinese public opinion. The threat of strikes and boycotts against British interests in China, which had been successful in the past, loomed large in deciding that it was better to negotiate the best deal that was possible rather than have one imposed unilaterally.[11]

The world economy also must have had a big influence on British and American decision makers. The Great Depression was biting hard in Britain and even more so in America. Both economies had shrunk by at least 25% and unemployment was a serious problem. No one would have supported going to war, or even deploying troops, as had been done in 1927, to fight to protect rights of foreigners far away in China.

Britain was willing to accept Chinese jurisdiction over British subjects in the new Modern Courts with promises that for at least five years assessors could sit on the courts. The key issue for them was progressive reduction of extraterritoriality so that Chinese would only assume jurisdiction over British subjects in the key treaty ports of Shanghai, Tientsin, Canton and Hankow some time after they had assumed jurisdiction in the rest of China. Two important considerations in relation to Shanghai and Tientsin, in particular, were that if they were to pass immediately under Chinese jurisdiction, there would be a financial panic. Further, it would take some

10 P.D. Coates, *The China Consuls* p486. F.E. Wilkinson in Harbin made the same prediction.

11 CAB/24/221. Negotiations With The Chinese Government For The Abolition Of Extraterritoriality, Memorandum by the Secretary of State for Foreign Affairs, Foreign Office April 27, 1931.

Justice Feetham of South Africa - appointed by the SMC to report on extraterritoriality

time to unwind the systems of municipal government that had been put in place in those cities. Canton and Hankow were considered of secondary importance and the negotiators were authorized to give up rights there if necessary.

The Shanghai Municipal Council in 1929 due to the "public announced policies of the foreign Powers, and particularly America and Great Britain, with the regard to the relinquishment of extraterritorial privileges in China," decided to develop a scheme that would give "full consideration to the aspirations of the Chinese people" but at the same time "afford reasonably adequate protection during this transition period to the great foreign commercial and business interests which have been developed in Shanghai," decided to appoint a South African judge Mr Justice Richard Feetham "thoroughly to explore the subject and develop its practical possibilities."

Feetham had already been chairman of three international commissions, the Feetham Function Committee on constitutional reform in India, the Irish Boundary Commission and the Kenya Local Government Commission. He had earned high praise for his work in India. Lionel Curtis, Lloyd George's main Irish adviser, when recommending him for the Irish appointment said he was "incomparably the best man" and that in India " [in] four months he solved a problem over which the government of India had been struggling with for over 20 years."[12]

12 LG/F/25/2/44

Feetham came to Shanghai in early 1930 and over a period of 18 months prepared a very comprehensive and thorough report which noted the extraordinary position of Shanghai and the Council. The Council relied on independent courts to enforce its bye-laws. It also relied on the continued protection of troops and ships of foreign powers to maintain its authority. Feetham proposed that extraterritoriality continue in the International Settlement until China could form a united and pacified government with a constitutional goverment of checks and balances.[13]

Feetham had also expressed this view to the British authorities before issuing his report saying that a "fixed time limit puts a rope around the neck of the Settlement." However, a fixed time limit was all that Henderson thought they could manage to agree with the resurgent Nationalist Government, noting that "estimating the strength of China political forces" was "a matter which the opinion of Judge Feetham, for all his great ability, is not likely to be of great value."[14]

Henderson summed up the British Government's view of foreign nationals attitudes to extraterritoriality in a concluding paragraph of a memorandum sent to the State Department in Washington:

> "It is not to be expected that the time will ever arrive when the foreign nationals residing in China will agree that the state of the Chinese laws and the arrangements for their administration are such as to justify a relinquishment of extraterritorial rights. They will maintain that the surrender - whenever it takes place - is premature, and there will probably be considerable justification for such a view."

13 J. Chamberlain, "The Feetham Report on Shanghai", 10 Foreign Aff. 145 1931-1932.

14 CAB/24/221, Negotiations with the Chinese Government for the Abolition of Extraterritoriality, June 2, 1931, paras 14 & 15.

Henderson explained, in contorted diplomatese, that extraterritoriality could only exist where one side had the political and military power to impose it on the other:

> "His Majesty's Government, however, believe that the true criterion is not whether the Chinese are fit to assume jurisdiction over foreigners, but whether the Chinese are politically sufficiently stabilised to give effect to their determination to put an end to the extra-territorial system. When that time has arrived, the choice that lies before foreign nationals in China is submission to Chinese jurisdiction with reasonably adequate safeguards duly negotiated and embodied in a treaty or submission without any safeguards at all."

The Americans who were working closely with the British, in principle, agreed with the British position. The French and Japanese were slower in the uptake. Henderson commented they were "somewhat disquieted, their own inclination being to go more slowly." With regard to the French, Henderson view was that their "dilatory policy exposes them to smaller risks." With regard to the Japanese, Henderson said they were less willing to compromise due to their physical closeness to China and the fact that they were "perhaps less averse to the use of force in defence of the existing position" as well as having "special interests of their own, notably in Manchuria." Moreover, they were "apt to flatter themselves that they can manage the Chinese in a way impossible to western Nations."

Cabinet approved Henderson's approach and by June 1931, a draft treaty was finalized. The draft specifically excluded Shanghai for a period of 10 years to allow time to work out special arrangements. The treaty, in the end, was not signed due to the internal break up of the Nationalist Party. In May 1931, Wang Ching-wei and other left wing members of the Nationalist Party had split from the party and formed a new government in Canton opposed to the Nanking government.

Miles Lampson, British Minister to China who signed a treaty with C.T. Wang to end extraterritorially

In a memo to Cabinet dated June 2, 1931 Henderson said that Foreign Minister Wang had "made it plain that he is not in a position actually to sign the Treaty at this moment in view of the political situation in China and the revolt of the Cantonese." Wang feared that the offer regarding Shanghai would be used "as a weapon against the Nanking Government." Wang was however ready to agree on the text between himself and Lampson "for the consideration of the Chinese Government and His Majesty's Government." Henderson recommended following this course because it would have the "advantage of having reached a complete agreement with the Chinese Minister for Foreign Affairs," so that Britain "shall be in a strong position to hold the Chinese Government to the terms negotiated with him." He went on:

> "The only obstacle to implementing the Treaty would be China's own domestic difficulties and not any hanging back on our part. At the same time, apart from the opportunity of careful consideration before signing the Treaty, it will still be possible to make minor amendments in the agreed texts and to take advantage of any improvement in the terms of the Treaty that may be secured by other powers in their own negotiations."[15]

---

15 CAB/24/221.

Cabinet agreed this approach and Foreign Minister Wang and British Minister Lampson signed an agreement between themselves.

Britain had agreed, in principle, to bring an end to extraterritoriality in China.

The United States also on July 14, 1931 submitted a draft text with very similar terms to the British agreement, save that it included a five-year period where extraterritoriality would continue in Tientsin. Negotiations had then broken off for the summer. On September 15, 1931, Wang invited the US Minister, Nelson Johnson, to return to Nanking to finalize negotiations and on September 18, Johnson received instructions to proceed to Nanking but not to mention negotiations on extraterritoriality pending further instructions.[16]

Exactly on the day Johnson was directed to go to Nanking, an event occurred that meant the meeting was never to happen and the end of extraterritoriality was not formally discussed again between China and the United States or Britain until 1942.

16 W. Fishel, *The End of Extraterritoriality in China*, pp185-186.

Part Twelve

The Japanese Empire Strikes Back
(1932 to 1941)

Chapter 53

Major Battles

September 18, 1931.

September 18, 1931 must go down in Chinese and world history as one of those great "What if?" days. If the events that occurred on that day had not happened, would China have abolished extraterritoriality and recovered its sovereignty? Would the Nationalist Party have been strong enough to defeat the communists? Would Mainland China today be as vibrant a democracy as Taiwan is today?

We will never know, for on that day, Japan invaded Manchuria. The pretext for the invasion was an alleged attack on the Southern Manchurian railway by Chinese troops. It is generally now accepted that the attack was set up by the Japanese army to justify their invasion. Chiang Kai-shek ordered Chang Hsueh-liang not to fight the Japanese and Chang pulled back his troops. The Japanese quickly occupied the whole of Manchuria. As part of a peace treaty, they also obtained the agreement of the Chinese to demilitarize Hopei (Hebei) Province surrounding Peking, or Peiping as it was now called.[1]

The League of Nations that had been established at the end of World War I strongly condemned the invasion but was powerless to stop it. The League formed a Commission to investigate. As it was planning to denounce the invasion, in 1933, Japan left the League.

---

1 King (or Jing) means capital in Chinese. When the Nationalists established Nanking as their capital, they changed the name of Peking from "Northern Capital" to "Northern Peace."

The effect of the Japanese action in Manchuria, and later actions in and around Shanghai was to bring to a close to all formal negotiations on the end to extraterritoriality. The Chinese government was not in a position to force the foreign powers to agree to an end to extraterritoriality, and, in fact, the foreign powers' presence in China helped to temper Japanese actions.

Extraterritoriality in Manchuria

After the Japanese occupied Manchuria they set up the "independent state" of Manchukuo on March 1, 1932 with its capital in Changchun.[2] This state, despite its alleged independence,

2 Interestingly, in Manchukuo "state capitalism" (as it is now called) was introduced: "State control was to be the guiding principle of economic development in Manchu-

recognized the extraterritorial rights that had been granted by China. In a note to foreign powers soon after its establishment, Manchukuo stated it would observe, "those obligations incurred by the Republic of China by virtue of treaty stipulations with countries, in the true light of the law of nations, and discharge those obligations with good faith." The note continued that the new government would not infringe upon "the acquired rights of the people of foreign countries."[3]

Britain and America had, however, pledged not to recognize the existence of Manchukuo either *de facto* or *de jure*. So while both sides acknowledged that extraterritoriality remained in place, it was for different reasons.

The first major test of extraterritoriality in Japanese occupied territories came in 1933 when the Japanese authorities, ordered Mr E. Lenox Simpson, editor of the *Harbin Herald* to leave Manchuria. The Japanese said the *Harbin Herald* was publishing pro-Soviet propaganda. Simpson had given an undertaking to cease to do so. When he failed to abide by the undertaking the Japanese sought to deport him. On May 22, 1933, Mr Lun asked the British Prime Minister, Ramsay MacDonald, in the House of Commons if this was true and, if so, what the government was doing about it.[4]

MacDonald replied that it was correct Simpson had been asked to leave. The Consul-General in Harbin had already protested against this breach of British extraterritorial rights and that he had been "instructed to continue to protest strongly, if necessary, against the breach of treaty rights involved." The Prime Minister continued that the "Charge D'Affaires in Tokio has also been instructed to ask the Japanese Government to use their influence to prevent this threatened violation of treaty rights, and the matter is being inquired into by

kuo"; "with all key and military-related industries to be nationalized or conducted by specially chartered companies." *North China Herald*, March 8, 1932, p370.

3 W. Fishel, *The End of Extraterritoriality in China*, p189.

4 HC Deb 22 May 1933 vol 278 cc746-7.

them." Ultimately, a compromise was reached where Simpson moved to Dalian, but the *Herald* was closed down.[5] This was a fudge on the British side. Dalian was still a Japanese colony at the time, so Simpson would have then fallen under the direct jurisdiction of the Japanese authorities there.

The Simpson case and others resulted in questions in British parliament. The Secretary of State for Foreign Affairs, Sir John Simon, was asked:

> "what steps have been taken to ensure that the extra-territorial rights under the treaties between China and Great Britain, which guarantee the liberties of life and the security of property for British citizens in Chinese territory, still hold good in Manchuria in spite of the Japanese military occupation; and what is the position of a British subject in Manchuria at the present time?"

Sir John replied, perhaps a little untruthfully:

> "No special steps have been found necessary to secure the treaty position of British subjects in Manchuria, which remains unaltered."[6]

Sino-Japanese war in Shanghai

Soon after invading Manchuria, in January 1932, the Japanese launched an attack on Chinese forces around Shanghai seeking to create a *cordon sanitaire* around the city. The main goal was to protect the Japanese businesses and Japanese people in and around Shanghai.

To the surprise of the Japanese, the Nationalists committed a large number of troops, over 50,000, to the defence of their positions around Shanghai leading to massive battles. The situation was so tense that the Municipal Council issued

5 HC Deb 14 March 1934 vol 287 at 471-2.

6 HC Deb 26 March 1934 vol 287 c1637.

an Emergency Proclamation imposing a 10pm to 4am curfew, prohibiting public gatherings and banning the publication and distribution of any document "calculated to cause alarm of a breach of the peace."[7]

These battles affected Judge Peter Grain in a direct way when Chinese shells fell on the International Settlement, including in Grain's garden. The *Times* reported:

> "The British and Italian Consuls protested to the Mayor as usual, and got the stereotyped reply to the effect that the Settlement must expect to be fired upon if it is used as the base for an attack on Chinese territory. The legal aspect of this question is likely to receive special attention, as Sir Peter Grain, Judge of the Supreme Court for China, had a shell burst in his garden last night, sharply disturbing his Lordship's slumber."[8]

While the foreign powers had opposed the invasion of Manchuria, they were much more ambivalent about the battle for Shanghai. In private, many supported the Japanese action. If the Japanese were successful in driving the Chinese army back from Shanghai, the situation where foreigners had a free hand in and around Shanghai prior to the Nationalists' successful Northern Expedition in 1927 would in many ways be restored.

Soon after the war started, Stirling Fessenden, as Director General of the Shanghai Municipal Council sent a cable to the *New York Times* explaining that the Settlement could not be neutral in the battle because the Japanese were one of the treaty powers. It was "almost impossible" to get the Japanese to cease landing troops in the International Settlement because their reason for doing so was to defend the Settlement. The Japanese pointed to a precedent from 1925 when the Brit-

7 Proclamation: Emergency Measures dated February 1, 1932, Imperial War Museum, 36(511) [Shanghai]/4.

8 *The Times*, February 24, 1932.

ish had landed troops and extended a cordon of 15 miles outside Shanghai. He concluded that because the Japanese were one of the treaty powers, "talk of neutrality of the Settlement is not based on facts, however distasteful this situation."

The China Association sent a telegram to the British Secretary of State "which contained a confidential passage commenting adversely on the anti-Japanese sentiment as expressed in certain British newspapers and in the communications of the Council of the League of Nations to Japan. These, according to this communication, tended to stiffen the Chinese and to prolong the trouble, and indicated a misunderstanding of the situation."[9]

In the end, the Japanese committed over 100,000 troops to the offensive around Shanghai and forced the Chinese army back. A truce was signed in April 1932 providing that Chinese troops would not be stationed within 20 miles of Shanghai. The Chinese civil government stayed in place. But without the Chinese military to back it, they were in a much weaker position to enforce Chinese rights or challenge extraterritoriality.

Battle for the Hardoon millions

Japanese shelling was not the only thing to disturb Grain's slumber in mid-1932. Two major legal battles also came before the British Supreme Court in 1932 and 1933.

From mid-June, Grain was required to try a case of mind-boggling complexity brought about by the question of the status of Jews from Iraq who had made their way to Shanghai over the years, usually by way of India. As most of these Jews came from Baghdad, they were generally referred to as Baghdadi Jews.[10]

9 CAB/23/70 Minutes of Meeting of the British Cabinet, February 24, 1932.

10 *Ezra Hardoon v Liza Hardoon,* Hearings: *North China Herald* June 14, 1932. p389 and 429 and June 21, 1932. p466; Judgment: *North China Herald,* July 20, 1932. p107; See also S Stein, "Protected Persons? The Baghdadi Jewish Diaspora, the British State, and the Persistence of Empire", The American Historical Review, Vol. 116, No. 1 (February 2011), pp80-108 for a detailed discussion of the case and status of Baghdadi Jews.

The difficulty was that at birth, the Baghdadi Jews were not British. When they moved to and lived in Shanghai, they had no way to acquire British nationality by naturalisation because they were not living in a British territory. Iraq, however, became a British protectorate and most Baghdadi Jews were registered as British Protected Persons at the British Consulate.

Silas Hardoon, a Baghdadi Jew, and one of the richest men in Shanghai, died in June 1931. He owned numerous properties around Shanghai including a massive estate on Bubbling Well Road. His will left all his property to his wife, a Chinese who had converted to Judaism, Liza Hardoon. He left a large personal fortune amounting to at least £4,000,000 (or US$20,000,000) – some reports say it was much higher.

Hardoon had been born in Baghdad in 1860 and moved to Bombay in 1865 where his father naturalized as a British subject. He continued on to Hong Kong and in 1874 came to Shanghai where he was registered as a British subject because his father was working for the Sassoons. In 1907, the question of whether he could be registered came up and Sir Pelham Warren, then Consul-General, directed that he continued to be registered as British. He and Liza later married at the British Consulate.

On July 16, 1931 probate was granted to Liza Hardoon by the British Supreme Court. Three months later, in September 1931, Ezra Abdullah Hardoon, who claimed to be a lawful cousin of Hardoon, filed a caveat against the "pretended will" on the ground that Hardoon did not have capacity to make the will when he signed it. In November 1931, he amended his claim to argue that the estate should be administered according to the laws of Iraq and alleged that the deceased, having been born in Iraq as a Jew, was not a British subject. A defence was filed admitting that Hardoon was a Jew from Baghdad but denying that he was not a British subject and alleging that he had abandoned his domicile in Iraq and was domiciled in Shanghai.

Scenes from the Hardoon case.
H.P. Wilkinson KC returns to the Supreme Court for China for his last appearance.

The trial was extremely high profile in Shanghai and Hong Kong. Six lawyers, including two King's Counsel and one barrister from London, were lined up on the counsel's bench to argue the case before Peter Grain. Ezra Hardoon wanted the best. He convinced Harrie Wilkinson, now a King's Counsel, to come out of retirement to represent him. Who better to argue a case about British nationality than the man who had spent more than 20 years advising the British authorities on the very issue as Crown Advocate? Wilkinson was assisted by a Mr H. Browett.

Liza Hardoon also wanted the best. She hired Mr Eldon Potter KC of Hong Kong with Mr G.H. Wright. At the first day of the trial, Mr Isaac Silas Jacob applied to be joined to the action as the nearest next of kin. He was represented by Mr H.B. Samuel of London and Mr Hartopp.

The key issue in the case was whether Hardoon was a British subject under the Orders in Council. Potter argued that he was. Wilkinson argued that as a British Protected Person, Hardoon was not a British subject and that his estate should be dealt with under the law of Iraq or the Ottoman Empire. Samuels took a more nuanced approach. He accepted that the Order in Council gave the court jurisdiction over the case, but that the court had to decide which law to apply in dealing with the estate. He said that Iraqi law was the most appropriate law.

Grain handed down his judgment in late July on an extremely hot day. The *North China Herald* in a front page editorial saluted the judgment and Grain's stamina. One can almost imagine sweat dripping down his face from under his wig:

> "The judgment was perforce to deal with several important issues, such as domicile and the status of Shanghai. It had to range as far afield as Iraq, whence the late Mr Hardoon originally came. The amount of work involved in writing the judgment must have been great. The mere thought that Sir Peter Grain read it in the present temperatures makes some people tremble with the heat. The stamina and stern sense of duty of the doyen of the British official community could hardly be better proved."[11]

Dealing with Hardoon's nationality first, Grain set out Hardoon's personal history that had brought him to Shanghai. The British Consul-General confirmed that it was the cus-

11 *North China Herald*, Editorial, July 20, 1932. p81 (front page).

tom for the consulate to register Iraqi Jews as British. When the Chinese authorities seized some of his properties in 1927, the British authorities had intervened. Also, Hardoon had sat as a British representative on the Municipal Council and been both a plaintiff and defendant in the British Court. Grain referred to a number of cases to support the fact that Hardoon was British but in particular referred to Privy Council decision in *R v Ibrahim* which confirmed that a British Protected Person was subject to jurisdiction of the court.

Wilkinson KC had argued that special nature of the International Settlement - effectively an extraterritorial enclave - meant Hardoon could not have become domiciled in Shanghai. After considering a number of cases, Grain found that a domicile could be established in Shanghai saying: "This court has now since 1923 been continually finding that British subjects have acquired a Chinese domicile in the Settlement."

Turning to the law to be applied, he then found that the law of the court determined the law of the domicile and accordingly he would apply English law and not Iraqi law. This meant that the case was dismissed and Mrs Hardoon allowed to inherit the fortune. So, Harrie Wilkinson's last case in a court he had first appeared in 42 years before ended with a loss.

Ezra Hardoon filed a notice of appeal. Grain later ordered that Ezra pay security for costs on appeal of $12,000 failing which appeal would be dismissed. The appeal was never prosecuted and Liza inherited the estate in full.

The situation may have been different if Hardoon had died a few years later. In 1933, Iraq became an independent state and was no longer a British mandate territory. Iraqis could no longer claim to be British and therefore enjoy extraterritorial rights. This caused much consternation among the Iraqi community in Shanghai which made representations to the Consul General John Brenan that they should be treated as British subjects. Brenan, in a note to the British Minister, said that it would be very difficult to make such a claim and recommended that they be told they now fell within the jurisdiction of the Chinese courts.[12]

Five years later, K.B. Ezra Hardoon, another cousin of Silas Hardoon, filed a further case against Liza Hardoon on very similar grounds to the first case seeking a declaration that the estate should be divided according to Iraqi law. The case came before Grant Jones who dismissed it on similar grounds to Grain's decision.[13]

Luna Park - Racing around the Court of Consuls

While the plaintiffs in the Hardoon cases had been trying to get the case out of the British courts, in another case, the plaintiffs were trying to get themselves before the British courts rather than take their claim for very large damages against the Shanghai Municipal Council to the Court of Consuls.

As part of a concerted anti gambling campaign the Municipal Council, in 1931, resolved to close Luna Park, a greyhound racing track opened on the eastern outskirts of the International Settlement in Hongkew. The Municipal Council's attitude to Luna Park had, as the *Shanghai Evening Post* put it, been "ambiguous and vacillating." The Council had originally approved the opening of the park. But the increasingly influential Chinese community in Shanghai felt that greyhound racing was a particularly bad form of gambling because it attracted poor Chinese to waste their money. Partly due to Chinese complaints but probably more because of pressure from some consulates, the Council determined to close the park. Rather than taking on the difficult task of working out who to sue and in which court, the Municipal Police took a simple approach. They barred access to the track by placing large numbers of policemen and an anti-riot van at the entrance.[14]

12 FO/219, Letter from Brenan to the British Minister dated February 1, 1933.

13 *K.B. Ezra Hardoon v Liza Hardoon, North China Herald,* December 9, 1936, p417.

14 *Greyhound Racing Association (China) Ltd v Macnaghten & Martin, North China Daily*

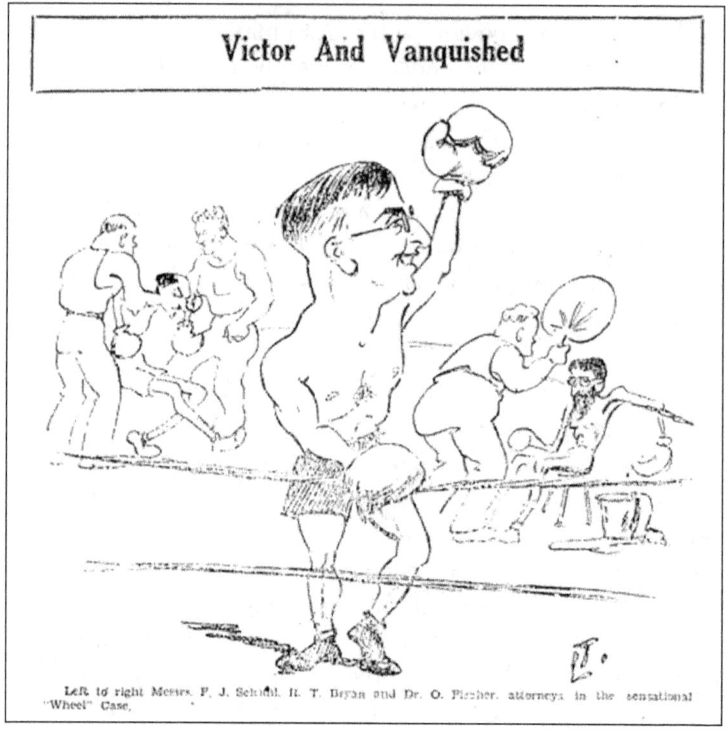

Bryan knocks out Schul and Fischer in the Wheel case

The police had also used similar tactics to close the infamous gambling house The Wheel on Bubbling Well Road (Nanjing West Road), finding that checking the identities of patrons as they entered or left to be a far more effective deterrent than taking the owners to whichever court their current passport required them to be brought before. The police actions did lead to a hard fought case in the Provisional Court against Mr Garcia, the owner of the Wheel, with R.T. Bryan prosecuting and Ferno Schul and Oscar Fischer defending. Garcia, who had until recently been able to hide behind Mexican extrater-

News, February 8, 9, 11 and 14, 1933, March 8, 9 and 10, 1933 (Mossop Law Reports); Ning Jennifer. Chang tells the full story of Luna Park in an excellent article "Pure Sport or A Gambling Disgrace? Greyhound Racing and the Formation of Modern Shanghai" in *Creating Chinese Modernity: Knowledge and Everyday Life 1900-1940*, (PG Zarrow ed).

ritoriality was convicted and sentenced to two years in prison.[15]

The closing of Luna Park led to a closely watched case in the British Supreme Court. The owners of Luna Park sued General Macnaghten, the Chairman of the Municipal Council, and Captain Martin, the head of the Municipal Police, for damages for illegally shutting the park.

The novel feature of the case was that as a claim against the Municipal Council, the case should have been brought in the Court of Consuls. But according to Luna Park's Counsel, Reader Harris, "action had not been brought in the Court of Consuls because, for one reason, there was no appeal from that court … It was known that the British Consular authorities … were supporting the Council and it would be very difficult for the British Consul to say the Council should not have done so and so."

The case was founded on the argument that the Council did not have extraterritorial jurisdiction over a British company. The only authority with powers over a British company was the British Supreme Court. The Municipal Council should have come to the British Supreme Court to seek to close Luna Park and not take the actions it had done. As the heads of the Municipal Council and the Municipal Police, Macnaghten and Martin were liable.

Grain had originally dis-

THE GREYHOUND RACING CLUB

LUNA PARK

8.30—SATURDAY NIGHT—8.30

14 RACES—3rd Meeting (1930)—14 RACES

The George Sadler Stakes—500 Yards Flat

Welfare	Barron's Toss
Nightshade	Black Sheik
Union Lady	Burn Black
Fresh Fancy	Esmeralda

On same card:—
Four 285-yard Flat Races
Two 500-yard Hurdle Races
Seven 500-yard Flat Races

[illegible]

Race-cards on sale from 10 a.m. on Saturday at:—
The G.R.C. Offices, No. 2 Canton Road
Messrs. Kelly & Walsh Ltd., 22 Nanking Road
Messrs. H. E. Brewer, 30 Kiangse Road
Mercantile Printing Co., Ltd., A[illegible] Szechuen Road
Asami Shoten, 32 Woosung Road.
Ah Fong, Photographer, Nanking Road
E. Tai Liang Kee Garage, 58A Hupeh Road
May Wah Garage, Cr. North Szechuen Road and Tiendong Roads.
Lee Lee Garage, all stations
Szechuen Road Garage, 98A North Szechuen Road.
Park Garage, 187 North Szechuen Road.
Far Eastern Garage, 1003-4 Yangtszepoo Road.
Wing On Garage, [illegible] North Szechuen Road.

BAND OF THE 2nd Bn. THE GREEN HOWARDS, by kind permission of Lt.-Col. F. F. I. Kinsman and Officers.

TRAFFIC NOTE:—No cars will be allowed to make a right hand turn off Ward Road. Will those using the Members' Entrance co-operate by proceeding via Haikai (or Pingliang) and Whashing Roads.

Members wishing to make dinner reservations are requested to communicate with the undersigned, No. 2 Canton Road. Tel. [illegible], 10330, 10331, before NOON on Saturday.

DUNCAN E. CAMPBELL,
Secretary & General Manager.

6282

15 *China Press*, August 22, 1929, p8.

missed the case in 1931 on the basis that there was no good cause of action. Grain held that the Association was challenging a decision of the Municipal Council. Such a challenge could only be brought to the Court of Consuls, not the British Supreme Court. In doing so, Grain followed a 1921 decision of the Full Court in *SMP v Rakusen* made up of Skinner Turner and himself. In that case, Rakusen, who was constantly being summonsed for driving offences, had been charged with driving without lights on North Szechuan Road (Sichuan North Road). North Szechuan Road was a municipal road but located outside the International Settlement boundaries. Rakusen had not even bothered to appear to defend the charges but the Magistrate had acquitted him on the basis that the council had no power to make regulations beyond the Settlement boundaries.[16]

On an appeal by the Municipal Police, Turner and Grain held that it was not possible to challenge the validity of a bye-law made by the Municipal Council in any consular court in Shanghai. Any dispute over bye-laws had to be resolved by the consular body in consultation with the Chinese authorities, otherwise, "with a multiplicity of courts there may be a multiplicity of decisions."

The Luna Park appeal was heard by Sir Joseph Kemp, the Chief Justice of Hong Kong, and Grain with Allan Mossop, the Crown Advocate, sitting as an additional judge. In very technical judgments, Kemp and Mossop held that the Rakusen case had only found that it was not possible to challenge legislative acts of the Council in the courts in Shanghai. It was, however, possible to challenge the executive acts of British individuals on the council in the British courts. Put simply, you could not challenge in the British courts the rules the council as a collective body had made, but you could challenge

16 *Rex (SMP) v Rakusen, North China Herald,* December 31, 1921, p929. The arguments in the case are reported in the *NCH* December 10, 1921, p727. See also an editorial by the *NCH* in the December 31, 1921 edition at p883.

in the British courts how British individuals on the council carried out their duties. Kemp and Mossop held, therefore, there was a reasonable cause of action. They allowed the appeal and allowed the case to go to trial. Given the decision of Kemp and Mossop, Grain "felt it unnecessary to record his own views."[17]

Grain then tried the case with a jury of five in February 1933.[18] The damages claimed were for, at the time, an astronomical sum of $2,500,000. The plaintiffs gave evidence regarding the shutting of the Park by the Police and the damage that had been suffered. During the course of evidence, Mr Buyers of the accountants Thomson & Co gave evidence that a 1% "stamp duty tax" had been paid to the Chinese authorities. This immediately elicited the question:

"A British company paying a stamp duty tax to the Chinese government! What for?"

"This payment was paid confidentially and is somewhat of a political matter."

Grain intervened to save Mr Buyers: "I will not compel you to answer."

Relieved, Buyers responded: "I would rather not answer."

The Chinese government would have liked an answer. They immediately wrote to the Greyhound Racing Association asking to whom and how much had been paid.[19]

After this, the defence counsel, Mr A.C. Holobrow, argued that there was no case for either General Macnaghten or Captain Martin to answer. Grain took three weeks to consider this application. He then ruled that there was no case for General Macnaghten as the head of the Council to answer, but Captain Martin as the head of the SMP who had actually carried out the closure, had a case to answer. The jury ought to decide

17 *Greyhound Racing Association (China) Ltd v Macnaghten & Martin, North China Herald,* December 29, 1931, p488; *Shanghai Evening Post,* March 11, 1933 (Mossop Law Reports).

18 The jury members were W.J. Dexter, C.S. Gilson, J. Macbeth, J.S. Flood and R. Hobday.

19 *North China Daily News,* February 11, 1933 (Mossop Law Reports).

if there was trespass on the Plaintiff's property and whether Captain Martin had been acting *bona fide* under the direction of the Council.

Martin's legal team then called evidence as to the problems caused by the park, the large-scale gambling, the fact that gambling was illegal and that the consular authorities had sought to have Luna Park closed. Interestingly, in cross-examination, Captain Martin admitted to having bought shares in Luna Park and that he had made a profit of 45% by flipping them before the park had even opened.

Grain summed up for the jury, virtually directing them to find for Martin. He referred to Luna Park as a "huge gambling club."He said:

> "The Council had to decide how they could stop this intolerable nuisance as soon as possible...I feel with the evidence before me, and also on the facts, that I cannot find that the Council has no power to order their police to take the action that they did ... I find they had the authority to take the course they did to prevent this huge gambling centre being a public nuisance in this Settlement."

Not surprisingly, after an hour's deliberation, the jury returned with a verdict that Martin had been acting *bona fide* and that there were no damages caused by his actions.

The North China Daily News reported the victory for Martin as a victory for commonsense. It also noted that Grain had hinted the case was a "waste of time." Grain may well have thought so. At 68, the oldest age for any judge ever to have sat on the court, he was certainly pondering his future.

Chapter 54

The Last Judges

Soon after hearing the Luna Park case, Peter Grain decided to retire. He left Shanghai in May 1933 on pre-retirement leave. The North China Herald published a fond farewell saying that "[p]robably no man who has served in Shanghai has made so deep an impression on the Community in so short a time, as Sir Peter Grain." His personal contribution to the community was noted in the article as well as in a short article by "Member of the British Bar", who particularly noted:

> "To say that Sir Peter is a man of manifold activities would be understating the case for there are few matters of public or social importance in Shanghai in which he has not figured – no trouble was too much no time was too long if Sir Peter felt he could be of help. Perhaps it is not generally known how many people have looked on Sir Peter as their guide, philosopher and friend and any one, and there have been numbers, who brought their troubles to him was certain of a sympathetic hearing and sound words of advice and, where appropriate, more tangible help."[1]

Grain sailed out of Shanghai on May 16, 1933 on board the P&O ship *Carthage* after 12 years of service in China. He officially retired in December 1933. He died in 1947 in Farnham

1 North China Herald, May 1933.

Common, Buckinghamshire, at the age of 82.[2]

Unlike de Sausmarez's or Turner's retirements, Grain's retirement left the Foreign Office with no obvious internal choice for successor. Given the Japanese attacks the year before and the uncertainty over the future of extraterritoriality, it would also have been difficult to convince any practicing barrister from Home to come out to China. Grant Jones had only just been appointed Assistant Judge and had never practiced as a barrister. In any event, no consular official had ever been appointed directly to the position of Chief Judge. H.S. Wilkinson had been the only former consular official appointed Chief Justice and that was after he had served 16 years as Crown Advocate.

Allan Mossop was, therefore, well placed to succeed where his good friend and mentor, Harrie Wilkinson, had failed: being appointed Judge of the Supreme Court for China. Mossop had now served as Crown Advocate for nine years and in that role had sat as a judge on the Full Court on a number of occasions. He had also served as a Claims Commissioner in 1929 dealing with British claims following the Nationalists attack on Nanking in 1927.

Surely to heartfelt congratulations, tinged no doubt with regret, from Harrie Wilkinson, Mossop continued his rise in the British courts in China and was appointed Judge of the British Supreme Court for China with effect from December 24, 1933. The *North China Herald* commented that "though a local appointment may occasion some surprise, in the present instance, it will be generally popular not only with the British Bar, but the practitioners of all courts in Shanghai, who are constantly exchanging legal courtesies and most certainly with the whole of the British community."

2 *The Times*, Obituary May 7, 1947; There was some debate as to whether his service in Zanzibar would be pensionable. The Foreign Office originally considered it was Foreign Office service, but it was later concluded it was service for the Government of Zanzibar. Nevertheless, in the end, he was granted a pension for this service as well. See: CO 618/57/6.

Following Mossop's appointment as Judge, Victor Priestwood, who had worked as Mossop's assistant for eight years and been Acting Crown Advocate for eight months in 1930 when Mossop was on leave, was appointed Crown Advocate. Priestwood was born in May 1902 in Lancashire. He studied at Keble College Oxford and was called to the bar of the Inner Temple on January 29, 1920. He passed his bar exams in April 1922. He was the second son of John George Priestwood, a solicitor who had practiced in Shanghai and regularly appeared before the courts. John Priestwood had been a partner with the Russian spy barrister, William Levinson.[3] In February 1924, at the age of 22, Victor had sailed from Birkenhead in England intending to reside in Shanghai permanently. He was admitted before the British Supreme Court and joined first his father and later Harrie Wilkinson as his assistant. After Wilkinson retired, Priestwood continued to work with Mossop.[4]

Mossop first sat as Judge in February 1934. The hearing was attended by almost all the members of the British Bar and representatives of the American, French and Chinese Bar Associations. His wife and Victor Priestwood's new wife, Gwen, were also in attendance. Speaking on behalf of the British bar, Mr Lipson Ward welcomed him as Judge saying that from Mossop's time as Crown Advocate "we remember you as a man of high judicial mind, of unimpeachable integrity and great courtesy." Mossop in reply said that all lawyers were "highly sensible to the fact that the administration of justice is indeed, the keystone of the entire arch of sound government, and that without an honestly and efficiently administered system of justice no community can hope to survive and prosper." He thanked those present for their kind words.[5]

3 See Chapter 42.

4 Priestwood acted as Crown Advocate in 1934 and was appointed to the substantive position in 1935. Foreign Office List Entry for Priestwood, 1939; Embarkation record for *Sarpedon* February 17, 1923; Letter from Mossop to Davidson November 1, 1933, FO 656/219 Item 46.

5 *North China Herald*, February 21, 1934 (Mossop Law Reports).

Around the time of his appointment, Mossop had to deal with one minor, but important issue for the court and its lawyers. Improvements in long distance communications meant that reports of court cases were no longer so newsworthy. International news and even photographs could be sent by telegraph, meaning reports of court cases had lost their interest to readers of local newspapers. The members of the bar had made numerous complaints that the *North China Herald* was no longer reporting cases accurately. This was a particular problem because the *North China Herald* remained the official gazette for British court cases. There was no other official collection of case reports.

Mossop, while Crown Advocate, had addressed a complaint to Grain concerning this. Grain took it up with the editor of the *North China Herald.* Grain and the editor agreed that the *North China Herald* would follow judgments exactly as given, but that its daily sister, the *North China Daily News,* would be allowed more flexibility in reporting. But the accuracy of reporting continued to be a concern. Finally in 1936, when Mossop was Judge, he and the editor of the *North China Herald* agreed that proofs of all judgments would be sent to Mossop for approval.[6]

Changes in the US Court

At almost exactly the same time Mossop was appointed Judge of the British Supreme Court for China, down the road in the United States Court, Milton Purdy's term of office came to an end in February 1934.

At the time, Purdy was no longer an employee of the State Department. About half a year earlier, the United States Court for China and its staff had all been transferred from the State Department to be under the Department of Justice as part of a re-organisation of government services. In March 1933, Con-

6 See FO656/221, Miscellaneous local correspondence of the Court 1933 to 1936 for various pieces of correspondence on the issue.

gress had passed a resolution requiring the President to investigate what re-organizations could be made of the executive branch. In June 1933, President Roosevelt issued an executive order which, among other things, transferred the United States Court for China, the District Court for the Panama Naval Zone (which had been under the Navy) and the District Court for the Virgin Islands to the Department of Justice.[7] For the State Department, this meant that the court's roles as "a part of the machinery for conducting foreign relations of the United States" and "indirectly an agency of the Government of China" had come to an end.[8]

One of Purdy's last cases was quite extraordinary and almost reads like an April Fool's joke. A Japanese lady, Mitsuko Shiga, who was described as a "petite cabaret dancer," sued her jealous American boyfriend John B. Penniston. Shiga was claiming for the loss of her wardrobe when Penniston had burnt all her clothes. According to Shiga, she had met Penniston when she suffered a leg injury and had been working temporarily as a masseuse in a bathhouse.

Penniston was an interesting character. He sported long hair and a long beard - in the modern world, one would say he looked like a hippie. He was at the time working as a writer for an English language newspaper in Shanghai, the *China Press*. He had self-published a number of works of philosophy both in America and in Shanghai. He also had a theory that earthquakes were caused by shocks from outer space. He had recently published a book, "My Philosophy" where he used

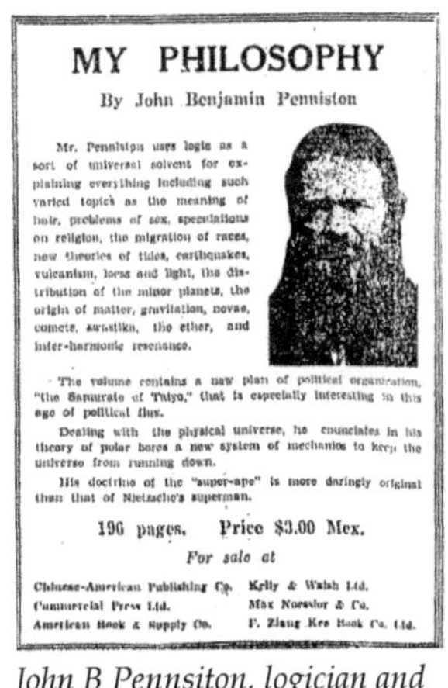

John B Pennsiton, logician and philosopher

7 Executive Order 6166, dated June 10, 1933.

8 Quoted in E Scully, *Bargaining with the State from Afar*, p184.

"logic as a universal solvent for explaining everything" including "problems of sex".[9]

His powers of logic had not helped him in his relationship with the beautiful Miss Shiga. Penniston had come home to the apartment they were sharing and found she was not home. In a fit of jealous rage, he had soaked all her clothes in Benzine and burnt them. He also took pawn tickets for kimonos from her bag and burnt these as well. Shiga returned home with what the *North China Herald* specifically chose to describe in inverted commas as a "girl friend" to find the process of incineration complete. Shiga's total claim against Penniston was for $5,000. This was a large claim. To put things in context, Purdy's salary as a judge was only $10,000 per year, or about $800 per month. Shiga's Chinese tailor told the court that Shiga had spent $1,400 on clothes. Other clothes she had bought cost US$1,600. She claimed another $1,000 for lost time, because she could not work (as a cabaret dancer anyway) without clothes, as well as $1,000 for lost documents, "my mother's picture" and "my diary." Purdy questioned if a cabaret dancer's wardrobe could be worth $3,000. Her lawyer, Major Holcomb, promptly suggested that Purdy, perhaps, had not been attending cabarets. Purdy gave judgment for Shiga for $1,200.[10]

In early March 1934, a special presentation was made to Purdy in the United States Court by the American Bar Association. Most members of the bar and Consul General Cunningham attended. Mr R.T. Bryan, President of the Association, read out a resolution which described Purdy as having been "an upright, fearless and impartial judge who has administered the law with favour to none and justice to all." The resolution continued that the members "particularly admire

9 Hiruste philosopher has Theory for both China and Japan Problems", China Press, January 24, 1933, p1 (with photo); J.B. Penniston, "The Cause of Earthquakes", China Press, June 7, 1935, p10

10 *Shiga v Penniston, North China Herald,* January 24, 1934, p146.

his profound understanding of human nature and psychology," and noted that he had upheld the "prestige of the United States Court for China with credit to himself and honour to his Government." Purdy then thanked all those present for their kind words and asked for the same understanding they had shown him during his term of office to be shown to his successor, Mr Helmick. After the ceremony, all the lawyers and staff of the court posed for a photograph with Purdy on the bench. Purdy himself remained in Shanghai and became a president of a local finance company. He retired in 1936 and died in Honolulu in February 1937 at the age of 71 during a visit there.[11]

Purdy's successor, Milton Helmick, had been a judge in New Mexico since 1925. He had graduated in law from the University of Denver in 1910 and at one time had served as the Attorney General for New Mexico. Helmick had been appointed the new Judge by President Franklin D. Roosevelt six days before Purdy's term of office came to an end. The Senate, however, delayed confirming him for two months, giving "law breakers in China a field day," according to an Associated Press report. The AP report continued:

> "For the last two months American legal machinery throughout China as been paralysed. Lawyers say the situation is unparalleled in American jurisprudence. The court docket is choked with civil and criminal cases, awaiting a judge to hear them."[12]

While the situation was not without parallels – Lebbeus Wilfley and Charles Lobingier had both been away for longer periods - there were probably now many more cases that

---

11 *North China Herald*, March 7, 1934, p369. A picture of the ceremony is published with the article. Obituary, *North China Herald*, February 17, 1937, p285, *New York Times*, February 14, 1937.

12 *New York Times*, April 29, 1934.

needed to be dealt with so that the absence of a judge was more keenly felt.

Helmick finally arrived three months after Purdy had stepped down on Monday, June 4, 1934 and was met by an official reception committee including Dr George Sellett, the District Attorney, and R.T. Bryan, the President of the Far East Bar Association. He stayed with his wife at the Cathay Hotel (now the Peace Hotel) on the Bund. The next morning, he walked along Nanking Road to Kiangsi Road (Jiangxi Road), turned left to get to the American Consulate that was now located in the former Kalee Hotel directly opposite the Trinity Cathedral. He got straight down to work dictating letters. After that, he met with members of the Bar Association and the Press.[13]

The first session of the US Court for China under Helmick was on Monday, June 11, 1934 before a packed court room. Mr Bryan on behalf of the American Bar Association and Dr Hua-chuen Mei on behalf of the Chinese Bar Association welcomed Helmick. He thanked the bar for their greetings. Then Helmick, it seems without a trace of irony, said:

> "I have learned that the bar of this court is famous for its probity and high ethical standards and for its support of the judiciary."

He then turned to the pending cases and disposed of four civil cases over the administration of an estate, a claim on a loan, a landlord and tenant dispute over the sale of furniture and a mortgage claim by a British bank against an American. When the cases were finished, the Marshal, Mr T.R. Porter announced the court would adjourn until the following Monday. Helmick countermanded this saying, with a smile, that he would sit the following day.

Norwood Allman, who appeared before Helmick for the

13 *North China Herald*, June 6,1934, p 346 and June 13, 1934, p357 for details of his arrival and first hearing.

entire time he was on the bench in Shanghai, described Helmick as "without a doubt the most popular of all with Americans as well as with other nationals, especially the Chinese. Because Judge Helmick always viewed cases from human angles and flavored common sense with a sense of humour, I, like the other lawyers, enjoyed trying cases before him."[14]

Thomas Sellett had tendered his resignation as District Attorney in early 1933. He had, at the request of the State Department, stayed on for another year until the new Judge was appointed. In May 1934, on Helmick's recommendation, Felthan Watson, a young lawyer from Helmick's home town of St Louis was appointed the new District Attorney. Watson had been born in 1902 and was active in the Democratic Party in Missouri. He had never held public office before this. On taking his post, he was described by Mr W.T. Collins, the Clerk of the Court, as a "brilliant young lawyer in his early thirties." Watson arrived in Shanghai in August following his formal confirmation and immediately started work. [15]

Which law to apply?

Later that year, Helmick had to determine in two cases whether to apply the District of Columbia Code or the old Consular Regulations. He made clear his disdain for the Consular Regulations and his preference for the DC Code. In the British Court, Mossop also had to decide a tricky case of which law to apply when enforcing a judgment of the US Court against a former American citizen who had become British.

The first of Helmick's cases related to what interest could be charged on loans made by American companies in China. It also showed the problems of the wholesale change of judges in the court, leaving no institutional memory of previous cases. Helmick said that "it is strange that after all these years" the question of what interest could be charged had not

14 N. Allman, *Shanghai Lawyer*, p107.

15 *North China Herald*, May 30, 1934, p306; *North China Herald*, September 5, 1934, p 351.

been considered.[16] In fact, Milton Purdy, soon after taking office in 1925, had ruled on exactly this issue.

The District of Columbia Code provided that the maximum interest rate could be 12%. The Plaintiffs who had lent the money at a rate greater than 12% argued that the District of Columbia Code was not suited to China and that under the act establishing the Court, the laws of the United States did not need to be applied "where such laws are not adapted to the object." Helmick in his opinion said that the court should be very slow to use this exception because it challenged the separation of powers. He ruled:

> "Habitually to test adaptability too freely tends to put this tribunal in the anomalous position of legislator and court."

He therefore found that the District of Columbia Code applied and ordered that the maximum interest that could be charged be 12%.

Nine years before, Purdy had reached the exact opposite conclusion as to the applicability of the DC Code. He had found that the legislature had not intended that rules apply outside Washington DC and that as a matter of practicality it could not work in an extraterritorial jurisdiction. An American moneylender when "making a contract with a British, French, Italian or Brazilian Citizen would be compelled to ascertain the interest rate in each country."[17] Strictly speaking, Purdy was wrong. In extraterritorial China, an American money-lender would need to do this anyway. If they wanted to sue on a loan made to a non-American, they would need to ensure they complied with the law of the borrowers' country

16 *Finance Banking Corp Ltd v Luebbert's Pharmacy, Fed Inc USA, North China Herald,* July 12, 1934, p 111.

17 *International Banking Corporation v Barnes, North China Herald,* November 14, 1925, p304.

so they could enforce it in the borrowers' courts.

Soon after this, Helmick presided over another bitter battle between lawyers where he needed to decide which law to apply. This time, the case was over a lawyer's favourite thing: money. Cornell Franklin had been in partnership with Walter Chalaire, a US attorney who had come to Shanghai in 1922. Chalaire was a World War I hero having made front page news for shooting down (with his British observer) at least two German fighters in a dogfight. He was also described later as one of the handsomest men in New York.[18]

Chalaire had decided to return to New York to practice in the late 1920s and sold his share in Chalaire & Franklin to Franklin. Chalaire made the big mistake of agreeing that payment be based on future profits. He and Franklin had agreed that Franklin would pay 60% of the profits made by the firm until 50,000 taels had been paid. Franklin had paid 2,225.88 taels up to April 30, 1930 but no more after this. The question that Helmick first had to determine was whether the three years limitation period under the DC Code applied or whether the six-year period under the old Consular Regulations applied. In his decision Helmick again made it clear he preferred the DC code. He said in relation to the Consular Regulations that "it is true Congress in creating the United States Court for China endowed it with the doubtful benefit of existing Consular Rules and procedure," but only so far as practicable. The Biddle case had made it clear DC law could be applied and Congress had sought to create in the court "something in the image of a Federal Court." On this basis, he should apply federal procedural rules and accordingly the action was statute barred. Franklin could, therefore, keep all the money he had made.

Chalaire appealed to the Ninth Circuit in San Francisco. Franklin was represented by former District Attorney for Chi-

---

18 Dogfight: *New York Times*, October 6, 1918 and *Helena Independent*, September 22, 1918, Front Page; Handsomest: *Reading Eagle*, February 17, 1934, p3.

na, Frank Hinckley, who was now in practice in San Francisco. The Ninth Circuit overturned Helmick's decision holding that the Act creating the US Court for China required the Consular Regulations to be applied unless they had been expressly modified or changed. The limitation period was therefore six years and judgment should be entered ordering Franklin to pay the balance of the 50,000 taels. Franklin unsuccessfully sought leave to appeal to the United States Supreme Court.[19]

Allan Mossop faced a slightly trickier question in the British Supreme Court in a case heard in Tientsin.[20] Mrs Rabbetts had originally been British. She had married a US citizen and become American. She had then divorced in 1927 and become British again when she married Mr Rabbets, a British citizen. In 1924, while she was American, judgment had been granted against her in the United States Court for China for $5,500. No attempt had been made to enforce the judgment between 1924 and 1930. In the US court, judgments were enforceable for 12 years. The issue that Mossop had to decide was: what was the period for enforcement of a judgment of a US extraterritorial court in China in a British extraterritorial court in China?

The first step was to decide how to enforce the judgment. There were no special rules governing enforcement of judgments of other extraterritorial courts. So, even though both courts sat in the same country and were physically very close, Mossop had to apply the law of England for enforcement of foreign judgments. Under these rules, a foreign judgment may be sued upon as a debt. The limitation period for a debt claim is six years. This created three possible dates when the limitation period could expire. First, six years from the judgment of the US Court in 1924, that is in 1930. Second, applying the US rules for the enforcement of judgments: 12 years from

19 *Walter Chalaire v Cornell S Franklin, North China Herald,* September 12, 1934, p392 and September 19, 1934, p437; *Chalaire v Franklin* 81 F. 2d 105, Wilbur, Mathews and Haney, Circuit Judges. The petition for certiorari was dismissed on May 18, 1936.

20 *Greenfield v Rabbetts, Peking and Tientsin Times,* October 20,1934 (Mossop Law Reports).

the judgment in the US court, that is 1936. The third was, six years from when Mrs Rabbetts came back under the jurisdiction of the British Court, that is 1933. Mossop held that he must treat the case as if Mrs Rabbetts had been in England all the time and there had been a judgment against her in America. In that case, the limitation period would be six years from when the judgment was granted and this was the period he would apply in China. He therefore dismissed the application to enforce the judgment.

The final farewell

In spring of the next year, 1935, Mossop had the sad duty to bury his old friend and mentor Harrie Wilkinson. In late March 1935, Wilkinson contracted pneumonia and was admitted to the Country Hospital (now Huadong Hospital on Yan'an Road). After a brief illness he died on April 1, 1935, at the age of 68. Sadly, his wife, Marjorie, was not with him; she was in Hong Kong at the time.[21]

Having been born in Asia – in Yokohama in 1866 - it was perhaps fitting that he died in Asia. Harrie's funeral was held at Bubbling Well Cemetery (Jing'an Park) on April 3. His wife who had flown from Hong Kong, Allan Mossop and the British Consul-General, John Brenan, were the chief mourners. Judge Grant Jones and Registrar Haines were in attendance as well as many of the members of the British bar in Shanghai. Dean Trivet read a short service. Mossop, Brenan and the Crown Advocate, Victor Priestwood, were among the pall bearers to carry his coffin to the grave.

Harrie had appointed Mossop as special executor to deal with his assets in Shanghai. Mossop, now a judge, renounced the appointment and Victor Priestwood dealt with his probate. Their years in Asia had left both Harrie and his father well off. Harrie's total estate in Shanghai was valued at the

21 *North China Daily News*, April 2, 1935 (re death) and April 4, 1935 (re funeral) (Mossop Law Reports).

very substantial sum of $288,000. About half was made up of stocks and shares and the other half included a number of lots of land that had been left to him by his father.[22]

As we shall see in the next chapter, Wilkinson's estate may have been valued at its peak.

22 FO917/3358 Hiram Parkes Wilkinson probate file.

Chapter 55

Predators

Milton Helmick, the new Judge of the United States Court for China, was called upon to deal with three very complex difficult cases in 1935 and 1936. The first two were brought about by a financial crash; the third, it seems, by a desire to remarry. In one of the cases, Helmick had to answer the tricky question of what was an American corporation. In the other two cases leading American citizens of Shanghai and Tientsin were on trial.

While the rest of the world had been going through a depression in the early 1930s, in China and in Shanghai in particular, there had been a mini bubble. The bubble finally burst in late 1935, leading to a sharp fall in land and stock values. The crash caused the collapse of two American registered financial houses.

Attack on a Russian American bank

In Harbin, an American registered bank, the Thriftcor Bank, became insolvent in October 1935. The Thriftcor Bank was incorporated in Nevada. It had its headquarters in Harbin with a branch in Shanghai. The bank had been founded by a Russian whose daughter had been born on an American boat while crossing the Pacific Ocean, making her American. The bank, whose main customers were Russians, flew an American flag on top of its offices in Harbin. Directly above the main door the name was written in Russian with English being written much higher up above the second floor windows.

It had been refused registration as a United States company by the American Consulate in Harbin.

Thriftcor was one of the few remaining independent banks in Manchukuo. The Japanese had since 1931 been tightening their hold on Manchuria. This had included earlier in 1934 installing Pu Yi, the last Emperor of China (ignoring Yuan Shikai), as the Emperor of Manchukuo. Pressure was being put on foreign companies to sell out or to take on Japanese partners. Almost all other banks in Manchuria had effectively been forced to bring in Japanese partners.[1]

In October 1935, Thriftcor became insolvent and needed to be put into liquidation. On October 5, 1935 Walter Adams the US Consul-General in Harbin telegrammed the US Ambassador in China, Nelson Johnson, saying that there was "much excitement in Harbin over the suspension of Thriftcor Bank which remained closed yesterday." He said that appointment at once of a liquidator by the US Court for China was necessary and asked if the US Court wished him to take any action.[2]

Ambassador Johnson reported to Secretary of State Hull that Helmick had said to him on October 4 that he had already told H.D. Rodger, the lawyer for Thriftcor (and its vice-president), that there was no American interest in the bank, registration with the Consulate had been denied and Helmick saw no reason for the US Court to be taking action. Johnson said he agreed with Helmick's view and asked for confirmation from Department of State that he should proceed in this way. Hull wrote back stating that the State Department "was doubtful whether American authorities in China could properly refuse to recognize the jurisdictional status of the bank as an American citizen if the question were submitted for judi-

1 Oral History Transcript of George Constantine Guins, p323-324, University of California, Bancroft Library: "Trading Conditions in Manchukuo"; *North-China Daily News,* July 23, 1935 (Mossop Law Reports)

2 Foreign Relations of the United States, 1935, pp1101 et seq.

cial determination." However, this was a matter for the court and if Helmick was willing to maintain that the court did not have jurisdiction, then Johnson could proceed to tell Harbin to take no action. Hull, however, added that if it was thought the American court would have to take jurisdiction at some point, it should do so as soon as possible.

Rodger telegrammed the bank in Harbin to say that the court had declined jurisdiction. Consul General Adams in Harbin was very concerned that this would look like weakness on the part of the Americans by allowing the local courts to take over the liquidation. He asked for permission to put out a statement that America had declined jurisdiction. Helmick agreed to this. He said that this was not a new question. A few months before, he had already made a decision in another case ruling there was no jurisdiction for "lack of substantial American interest," but the case received no publicity.[3] Adams put out the statement in eight Harbin newspapers and told Thriftcor to stop flying the US flag.

While this solved the Thriftcor problem, it caused big problems for the genuinely American-owned National City Bank in Harbin. The refusal to accord Thriftcor protection triggered a run on the bank. This was exacerbated by the *Harbin Times* (described by Adams as being "Japanese controlled" but "Russian edited"), which published an editorial questioning the status of other American enterprises in Manchuria. It said that the US government had allowed Thriftcor to fly the US flag for many years but once troubles hit, abandoned it. Adams wrote a formal letter to National City Bank confirming its registration and, therefore, right to US protection. The US Ambassador complained about the editorial to the Japanese embassy in Peiping and was told that the "Japanese Consul General in Harbin will take measures to prevent the publications in Japanese papers of attacks connected with

3 I have not been able to find any record of the decision to which Helmick was referring.

the Thriftcor bank."

Frank Raven – A bird of prey

Back in Shanghai, the attacks on American finance companies were not coming from outside. Rather, they were rotten to the core from within. In May 1935, in what was described as "the most severe blow to American business prestige in the Far East since the beginning of Chinese-American business relations,"[4] four finance companies, all under the American Oriental Banking Corporation, and all controlled by Frank Jay Raven, closed their doors. Bewildered investors, many who had lost their life savings, milled outside the doors of the companies. Affixed to the doors was a simple sign "Closed by Order of the Board of Directors."

Frank Raven, fraudster

The closure of the finance companies was bad for its investors and did, indeed, deal a serious blow to American prestige. It was, however, a bonanza for lawyers. As soon as the companies shut almost every lawyer in town filed claims against them. At the time, Helmick was in Peiping trying a case. Norwood Allman was also in Peiping appearing before Helmick. Allman's office in Shanghai telegraphed him to obtain various restraining orders from Helmick against the bank officers and to start some claims. Allman was able to do this, "sitting right in the lap of the court, as it were." Allman had

4 *New York Times*, February 1, 1936.

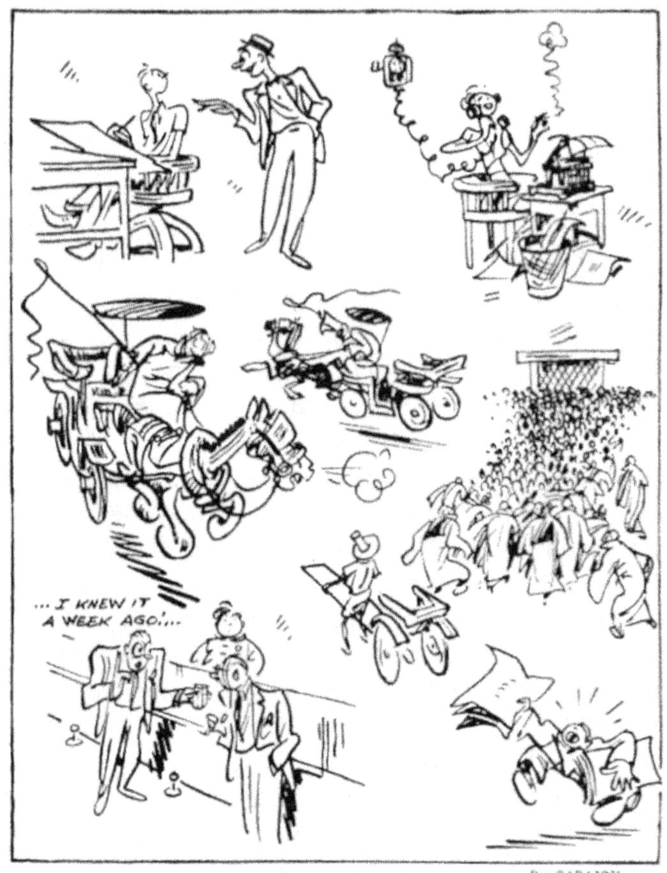

THE NEWS THAT ROCKED THE MARKET By SAPAJOU

Sapajou on the collapse of AOCB

one further trick up his sleeve. Chinese postal law allowed for the sender to re-route mail that had not yet been delivered to another address. His firm arranged for all mail from their clients to be sent to his office.[5]

5 N. Allman, *Shanghai Lawyer*, p135.

Helmick flew back to Shanghai the same day. He wanted to appoint an American lawyer as the liquidator of the group, but could not find a lawyer who had not either acted for the Raven Group or was not now acting against them. Finally, he appointed Mr Frank Hough of the R.C.A. Victor Company and a "prominent and reputable businessman" to liquidate the Raven Group.[6]

Hough was also not impressed by Allman's trick of re-routing the mail, particularly, as Allman recalled, "in all the excitement it completely slipped my mind, and the minds of my partners as well, to notify Mr Hough." When Hough found out, "he was furious. He phoned the office, accused us of trickery and demanded the mail." After he cooled down, compromises were reached in most cases. However, as the mail contained payment drafts and other documents, possession was nine-tenths of the law.

Norwood Allman's tricks were the least of Hough's worries. On taking over the companies, Hough found that the Raven Group had been effectively insolvent since 1932 and Raven and the top management had known about it. He later estimated that the companies would only pay seven cents in the dollar on liquidation.

This prompted a criminal investigation by Felthan Watson, the US District Attorney. The investigation revealed a scandal on a grand scale.[7] Frank Raven, a church-going municipal councilor and hero of the American community was, quite simply, a fraudster.

The case was so big that Watson asked for Thomas Sellett,

---

6 N. Allman, *Shanghai Lawyer*, pp134-135. Scully, *Bargaining with the State from Afar*, p190-1. Scully notes that some Chinese scholars have argued that this delay was deliberate to allow Raven to hide his remaining assets.

7 This section is based on the following reports: *North China Herald*, May 29, 1935, p338 "American Oriental Bank Closes Doors" *North China Herald*, September 4, 1935, p383 "Embezzlement Charges over AOFC"; *United States v Raven and Brown*: *NCH*, January 1, 1936, p28; *NCH*, January 8, 1936, p58; *NCH*, January 15, 1936, p106; *NCH* January 22, 1936, p149; *NCH*, January 29, 1936, p190; *NCH* February 5, 1936, p233; *NCH*, February 12, 1936, p281; *Oakland Tribune* February 19, 1936, p16.

the former District Attorney, to be appointed a special assistant to prosecute the case. Sellett came on board from October 10, 1935.[8]

Dr Sellett called back to help the prosecution of Raven and Brown

The fraud was very simple. The Raven Group and in particularly the American Oriental Finance Corporation (AOFC) would use client money or shares to gamble on the stock market. When customers bought shares fully paid, they would be issued notices confirming their holdings of fully paid stock. AOFC, however, would not necessarily buy the shares. When they did, they would buy through a margin account held with their brokers in San Francisco, E.A. Pierce. With a margin account, you do not have to pay the full price to buy shares. For AOFC, Pierce allowed them to purchase shares with a 25% margin. This meant they needed only to have funds available to cover 25% of the value of the shares. In addition to this, there were occasions when AOFC received orders to buy shares and instructions from other clients to "short" shares. They would just offset the orders in their books, meaning there were no actual shares purchased for the customers who were long. For a little gravy on top, they still charged both clients cable charges for telegraphing E.A. Pierce in San Francisco, even though no cables were ever sent.

Raven, J. Warner Brown, the President of the companies, and Alfred Driscoll, the Company Secretary, were all charged with 15 counts of embezzlement, theft and related charges.

8 *North China Herald*, December 4, 1935, p409.

Mr R.T. Evans of Tientsin, Warner Brown's defence attorney

Halfway through the case, Watson dropped the charges against Driscoll in return for him giving evidence against Raven and Brown. The case commenced straight after New Year in 1936. Watson and Sellett had worked very hard in preparing the case. More than 30 witnesses were called and over 300 exhibits prepared. Before the trial started, a further 16 counts were added bringing the total number of charges to 31.

Before the trial commenced, Raven and Brown made an application for a jury trial. Mr R. T. Evans, a senior American lawyer from Tientsin, for Brown made the first submissions. He said first that jury trials were not prohibited by the statute establishing the US Court. He conceded that the Ross case had held that US citizens did not have a constitutional right to a jury trial outside the US. However, the Ross case had been decided in 1890 when there were very few US citizens in Yokohama. Now, in Shanghai, there were at least 800 male US citizens in China who could act as jurors. The jury pool would be even larger if women could serve. The reasoning in the Ross case should no longer apply and Brown and Raven should be entitled to a jury trial. Cornell Franklin for Raven supported this application pointing out that there were now 4,000 US citizens subject to the jurisdiction of the court.

Dr Sellett, in reply, said it appeared that Evans and Franklin were arguing that the mere growth in the US population in Asia altered the legislation governing the court. But even in Hawaii (which was not yet a state) and the Philippines (which was a colony) there were no jury trials and there was a much larger population of Americans in both places. In any event, while there may be a large population of Americans in Shanghai, the court had to sit in Tientsin, Hankow and Canton and could sit in smaller towns such as Foochow, Amoy or Yunnanfu. There may be difficulties in finding sufficient jurors in these places.

Evans pointed out that Sellett's latter arguments were a fallacy. The supposed difficulties "did not seem to appear to bother the British courts." There, if necessary, witnesses would be brought from distant places for trials.

Helmick refused the application. He said that if he "had been the first judge of the US Court for China he would, of course, have made the matter the subject of exhaustive study. But after 29 years of established policy, he did not feel he could make any rule offhanded or lightly which would establish the precedent set up."[9] If he was mistaken, the matter could be decided by a higher court. He added he thought that any judge "would prefer to divide the responsibility with a jury of trying a case," but that was not sufficient to change established practice. The case therefore went on without a jury.

The trial itself was a grueling four-week slog, as any white-collar crime trial is, particularly where there are well-paid defence attorneys. Numerous witnesses were called to give evidence about paying money to buy shares through AOFC; that they received statements that the shares were "fully held" and that they had never approved any margin trading. In addition to Driscoll, who was testifying under immunity, the three main witnesses for the prosecution were the liquidator, Mr Frank Hough, Mr CC Curtis of E.A. Pierce & Co who came from San Francisco to give evidence, as well Cletus Joseph Haley, who had been treasurer of AOFC in 1932.

Hough gave evidence about the dire financial situation of

9 *North China Herald*, January 1, 1936, p28.

the entire Raven group of companies with numerous cross loans between the companies. Mr Curtis from E.A. Pierce was brought from San Francisco. He confirmed that almost all trades were done on margin and if required, E.A. Pierce would call on other shares held on behalf of AOFC to cover any margin losses. Driscoll, the insider, gave evidence as to how secret codes were used to identify accounts held by Raven and his family for trading as well as by other businessmen who used the trust to hide their deals. He said that Raven had attended many meetings regarding the financial situation of the companies. Haley, who had only been treasurer for a short time, told the court that he had been given the title of treasurer but no real authority to act as treasurer. He was not allowed to sign documents. All he had received was a name card. His evidence was, however, vital. He said that when he was at AOFC, he had written a report setting out his concerns about how the company had been margin trading with client shares. He had given a copy of the memorandum to Brown and, he said, discussed it directly with Raven.

Brown chose to give evidence in his own defence. Raven, claiming ill health, did not. Brown may have been better off if he had followed Raven's lead. He ended up giving evidence for a total of 22 hours over five days. Watson grilled him in cross-examination. Brown made a very poor witness and ensured his own, as well as Raven's, conviction. When questioned about whether it was right to pledge other people's property to cover your own loans, he was evasive or did not answer. On the "matching" of orders, he said that he had told staff this should not be done, but when asked to name one staff member he had told this to, he could not do so.

Brown also said that he had given a copy of the Haley memorandum to Raven and discussed it with him. Raven was furious with this. During a break in the trial, Raven accosted Brown in the coffee shop downstairs demanding to know why he had said they had discussed the memo. The

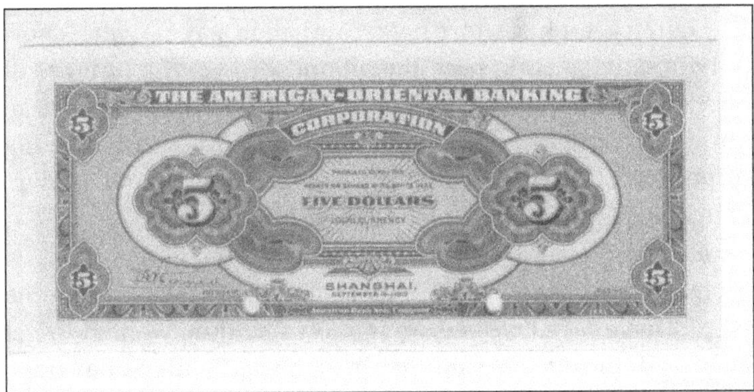

A now worthless AOCB bank note

conversation was overheard by others. Back in court, Watson asked Brown if, in fact, he was angry with Raven because Raven had decided not to give evidence. He asked Brown if he had told Raven: "I am not going to take the damn brunt of this affair myself." Brown effectively convicted Raven there and then with his answer by saying that other than "that bad word," yes, this is what he had said.

Sellett summed up the case for the prosecution, focusing on Raven's personal involvement, and the fact that even though his name was not on many documents he was clearly deeply involved. He added, somewhat snidely, that while Brown had perjured himself every 15 minutes in the witness box, having seen him for many days in the witness box: "I don't think that, from your observation, Your Honour will conclude that Brown was a mastermind." It was clear that Raven was the mastermind and should be convicted.

The main defence put forward by Franklin and Evans on behalf of Raven and Brown was that the group of companies was solvent and that if the bank had not closed, then all the other companies would not have closed. Franklin bravely argued that in the case of Raven there was no evidence of his direct involvement in any fraudulent dealings.

Helmick took a short break and then gave a very short judgment convicting both Raven and Brown of a number of offences. He adjourned sentencing until the next day. At 10 am the court was packed with a large crowd outside trying to peer in. The US marshal sat between Raven and Brown. Helmick asked Raven if he had anything to say.

He did. He showed just what a scoundrel he was.

Despite, having chosen not to give evidence - where he would have faced cross-examination - he now wanted to get even with Brown. He said that Brown was "a man of average ability, fundamentally and basically honest." He had made many mistakes, as they all had, but, Raven claimed, Brown had never told Raven of any of the matters that he said he had. He said he had never seen the Haley memorandum or spoken to Haley, finishing: "if you convict me on the two reports and the evidence of those two witnesses, which I know, and they know, to be entirely untrue, you are sentencing, me an innocent man to the penitentiary." Raven sat down but stood up again when he saw Helmick was about to address him.

Helmick sentenced Raven to five years in McNeil Island. Brown had nothing to say. Helmick sentenced him to two years in McNeil Island.

Brown and Raven both filed appeals. The appeals included the ground that they had been deprived of their right to a jury trial. On this point, Helmick said that it was a settled policy since the Ross case that there would be no jury trials in United States extraterritorial courts. The Ninth Circuit in San Francisco had reviewed a number of convictions from the United States Court for China and never commented on the lack of a jury. He added:

> "It is possible that this question which appears so unsubstantial to us in China who are so familiar with the uniqueness of the jurisdiction may appear substantial to the Appellate Court at Home, but this court ven-

tures to forecast, not merely to guess, that the Appellate Court will not overturn the long-sanctioned and hitherto unchallenged procedure of this jurisdiction. If this prediction turns out a mistake, it will be a very bad mistake indeed, but the risk must be taken unless the Court abdicates the duty imposed on it by the letter and spirit of Rule VI."

Raven and Brown both left Shanghai on February 19, 1936 aboard the *President McKinley* for Seattle and then McNeil Island arriving in early March. Brown withdrew his appeal before he left and, it appears, that Raven did also, Brown was released after nine months in prison, two days before Christmas in 1936. Raven was granted parole three months later in March 1937.[10]

Doctor, poison thy wife?

Just after the Raven trial, United States District Attorney Felthan Watson, travelled to Tientsin to investigate a case that also involved a leader of the American community and also made international headlines. He returned in May 1936 with Judge Milton Helmick for the trial. Watson was assisted by Mr A.R. Morrison, an American attorney in Tientsin. Mr B.C. Eastham defended.

One of the scions of the American community in Tientsin was accused of attempting to kill his wife by poisoning. The case had shades of the Carew case 40 years before in Yokohama, including strong hints of infidelity, although in this case the poisoner was a doctor and the husband of the victim. As in the Carew case, proving and then deciding if there had

10 The *New York Times* reported on February 9, 1936 that Brown had withdrawn his appeal. I have not been able to find any record of an appeal hearing for Raven. Raven's case was not cited in a subsequent case, *Casement v United States*, where the lack of trial by jury was challenged suggesting the issue had not been raised in the appeal court by them. Parole: Records of Prisoners Received at the United States Penitentiary McNeil Island, Entry Nos. 12020 (Brown) and 12021 (Raven).

been a poisoning was very hard. Helmick openly said in court he would have very much liked to have had the assistance of a jury to decide guilt or innocence.[11]

Dr John Colbert, a medical doctor, was accused of attempting to murder his, much younger, fourth wife. Colbert was a leading member of the Tientsin foreign community and a member of the Rotary Club. He was also deeply involved in getting medical treatment for poor Chinese children. He had served as a surgeon and physician for the French and American armies in World War I. After the 1923 Kanto earthquake in Japan, he had organized a relief effort to sail to Yokohama. His prosecution was a great surprise to many.[12]

His third wife had died in Tientsin six years earlier in suspicious circumstances. Colbert had been very friendly with the fourth Mrs Colbert just before the third Mrs Colbert died. Before the fourth Mrs Colbert became ill, Dr Colbert had a very close relationship with a Grace Thomas, a teacher at the Tientsin British School. The question left unanswered in the court was: was Grace Thomas meant to become the fifth Mrs Colbert?

The alleged poisoning, as would be expected from a trained doctor, was much more complex than the arsenic poisoning that Mrs Carew carried out. Mrs Colbert was an avid tennis player. Her husband had started treating her for exhaustion, which he diagnosed as anemia. She was treated at home for most of October 1935 before Dr Colbert called a British doctor, Dr J. W. H. Grice, to also treat her. Dr Grice did not agree with the diagnosis of anemia and convinced Mrs Colbert to move to a hospital. Once in hospital away from her husband, her condition improved markedly. At one point, Dr Colbert gave

11 *United States v Colbert*, *North China Herald*, May 20, 1936, p316; May 27, 1936, p358. and June 3, 1936, p404.

12 Rotary: Proceedings of the 25th Annual Convention of Rotary International; Earthquake: Joshua Hammer, *Yokohama Burning*, p219; War service: John W. Colbert: A Register of His Papers in the Library of Congress, Manuscript Division, Library of Congress, 2009.

Dr Grice an ampule of medicine to give to his wife. As soon as the injection was started, she complained it was making her unwell. Grice then became suspicious and had the remainder of the ampule tested. The substance was found to be blood poison. Mrs Colbert recovered and returned home. Dr Grice visited her at home and found her condition had worsened. She said she was taking some tablets given to her by her husband. Dr Grice took away one of these tablets without Mrs Colbert noticing. This was also tested and found to contain pure acetanilide, a poison.

Dr Grice reported his suspicions to the American consular authorities who began an investigation. The investigation found that Colbert had purchased very large quantities of acetanilide and antifebrin, both poisons, in September and October 1935. During the investigation, Colbert told District Attorney Watson that Mrs Colbert was his third wife. Only at trial did it come out that she was, in fact, his fourth. He had been married twice before he had married his deceased third wife. He had divorced his first and second wives and was still paying alimony to his second wife.

Watson and Morrison called evidence from Dr Grice, a number of nurses, Russian pharmacists, a German doctor and an American doctor, all to prove that the treatments Colbert was giving his wife were unnecessary and the substances were poisonous. One doctor gave evidence that Mrs Colbert was not anemic. Some witnesses also said that Dr Colbert had told people that his wife was dying.

This was about the best case you could possibly have to prove a poisoning. However, there was a serious difficulty. While it could be expected that Dr Colbert would defend his treatments, it could not be expected that his wife and her mother would. But they both did. They both gave evidence at the trial that they had complete faith in Dr Colbert and the treatment he had given. Mrs Colbert said: "I am convinced of my husband's innocence and am backing up for all I am worth." She also said that she was friends with Grace Thomas as well and had no problem with her husband's relationship with her. Mrs Colbert's mother and a number of other friends also testified that they were happy with Mrs Colbert's treatment and that Dr Grice could not have removed the capsule unobserved. A French doctor, Dr Lataste gave evidence to support Colbert's diagnosis.

In his closing speech, Morrison asked for the heaviest sentence possible for "this menace to society," and said that the evidence pointed clearly to Colbert trying to poison his wife. Mr Eastham for the defence argued that the prosecution had not proved that Mrs Colbert was poisoned and had only produced "a parody of a motive." Dr Grice had been slow to report a poisoning and even in court had not been willing to say if he thought Dr Colbert was poisoning his wife.

The next morning, Helmick gave his verdict. He first said that he was in the "unenviable position of sole juror." He considered that Dr Grice had been fully justified in his suspicions and the prosecution had been fully justified in bringing the case. He said that while he harboured a "strong suspicion" of guilt of the defendant, he must give the defendant the benefit of the doubt. He acquitted Colbert saying, however, he did so "with some misgivings, but realizing that if an infallible decision cannot be reached the law holds that it is better to make a mistake in favour of the accused than against him."

Following the verdict, the crowd in the courtroom sat in complete silence and then slowly filed out. Colbert's friends congratulated him. But this was not the end of the matter. Five days later, Colbert was attacked in his office. A foreigner "with a hat lowered to cover his forehead and a handkerchief covering the lower part of his face," walked into his office and tried to stab him in the heart. Colbert warded off the blow and then the foreigner struck him in the head, knocking him out. Mrs Colbert, who had heard about the incident by phone, accompanied her husband to the hospital. A very strange conclusion to a very strange case. Who was this assailant? Mrs Colbert herself? Someone she paid? Someone else all together?

Change in DA

Soon after the Colbert case Felthan Watson was called to Washington to serve as a special assistant to the Attorney General in 1936.[13]

To replace him, Leighton Shields, also from Missouri, was appointed the last US District Attorney for China. Shields was much more experienced than Watson or even Thomas Sellett had been. He had already practiced law in St Louis for 28 years. He was born in 1883 and at the time of his appointment he was in his mid-50s. He had graduated from Harvard College in 1903 and Washington College of Law at St Louis University in 1905. He was a political player in Missouri. He had attended Harvard with President Franklin D. Roosevelt and been a member of the Glee Club with him. In 1934, Roosevelt appointed him counsel of the Reconstruction Finance Corporation in Washington DC. He then appointed him District Attorney for China.[14]

Shields, initially, had a quieter time than Watson. It was not for a number of years that he had to deal with a major case, a murder so gruesome he sought the death penalty. For now it was the British courts and prosecutors that were dealing with some very violent deaths; one judicial execution; and, perhaps, one extra-judicial execution.

Leighton Shields, New US District Attorney for China

13 *New York Times*, October 22, 1936.

14 RFC: Harvard Alumni Bulletin - Volume 59 - Page 678; "Washington Side Show" *Pittsburgh Post-Gazette*, July 21, 1934, p2.

Chapter 56

In the Shadow of the Gallows

It was not only murder cases in Tientsin that attracted international attention in 1936. In Shanghai two murder cases in the same year were extremely high profile both in China and worldwide. Both cases involved British policemen. The first drew attention for the almost unbelievable nature of the crime; the second for its equally almost unbelievable conclusion.

Throw the beggar in the river?

Before and during their trial in early 1936, Frank Raven and Warner Brown had been held in the foreigners' section of Ward Road Gaol. Newspaper reports at the time said that Raven and Brown were in very comfortable rooms with private bathrooms allotted to them.

Ernest Peters, a British sergeant of the Shanghai Municipal Police debunked this. Raven and Brown were in very uncomfortable cells with a shared communal bathroom. Peters knew the cells were uncomfortable because he, along with British Probationary Sergeant William Judd, had occupied the very same cells for some time while awaiting trial for murder of a Chinese beggar, Mau Te-piau. Peters and Judd had allegedly thrown Mau in a river in Hongkew at 3.30a.m. on a cold winter's night of December 1, 1935.[1]

They were prosecuted in the British Supreme Court before Judge Allan Mossop and a jury of 12 almost immediately

1 Trial transcripts: *R v Peters and R v Judd, North China Herald,* February 12, 1936, p276 and February 19, 1936, p321. Peters recounts the trial in his book, Shanghai Policeman.

Kenneth Bourne, son of Frederick Bourne, ordered an immediate investigation into Mau's death

after the Raven case finished.[2] It was an extraordinary case for many reasons. First, the prosecution had not been initiated by the British authorities because of any complaint by Chinese officials. The Municipal Police themselves had moved quickly to prosecute Peters and Judd as soon as allegations were made against them. Even before Mau had died, Assistant Commissioner Kenneth Bourne (son of former British Judge Sir Frederick Bourne) authorized an investigation and prosecution. Second, the prosecutors really believed in the guilt of both men. Victor Priestwood, the Crown Advocate, assisted by John McNeill, prosecuted the case with great vigour, clearly believing Peters and Judd were guilty and doing all that he could to get a conviction. Third, the case does not seem to have raised any particular anger in the eyes of Chinese officials, perhaps because the victim was on the lowest rung of society. (There were a number of complaints and protests in the Chinese press relating to the case, Shanghai's extraterritorial status and the arrogance of foreigners, particularly foreign policemen.) Fourth, unlike all other cases, we have a long account written by one of the accused, Peters, giving his side of the story. Fifth, Peters had a Japanese girlfriend, Sumiko, who he planned to marry. This last point was never mentioned by Peters to anyone so never came out at the trial. It is an interesting fact. He cannot have been a complete racist; yet perhaps he never mentioned it because having a Japanese girlfriend would have played out badly before an all-white upper class Shanghai jury.

2 The jury members were N.L. Sparke, H. Standring, E.S. Hine, C. Trickett, G.D. Smart, R.V. Yarrow, H.K. Strachan, K. McKelvie, E.A. Dearn, C.S. Kemp, K.R. Plowright and H. Walton. There was some amusement in court when Mossop asked Dearn if his deafness would prevent him sitting on the jury. Dearn replied strongly, "I am not deaf!"

The evidence against Peters and Judd was damning. Peters was assigned to the charge room of Kashing Road Police Station on that night. Kashing Road Police Station was located just off Kashing Road (Jiaxing Road) right on the border between the International Settlement and Chinese Territory in Chapei. This was a tough area to police. Since 1932, the Japanese controlled the Chinese territory and foreign police were sometimes detained by the Japanese military for seeking to enforce the law against Japanese.[3]

Peters was required to report for duty at 12 midnight, but had arrived late at 2.30 am because, he was to admit later in court, he had been with a lady friend. When he arrived on duty, he was told that two Chinese constables had called in that a Chinese beggar was sick on Point Road (Zhoujiacui Road) where it met Shinkeipang Road (Xinjiang Road). Judd had just come in for a coffee break half an hour before he was meant to. Peters told him to warm up with a coffee and then told him to go with a Russian sergeant, Boris Makovetsky, to see if there really was a sick beggar. Peters said later that he was concerned that in other cases he had called an ambulance and the call had turned out to be a false alarm. Peters then countermanded his order to Makovetsky and told him to look after the charge room while he and Peters went to check on the beggar. He ordered up the station car and the Chinese chauffeur, Doo Sung-foo, came along and took them. They found the beggar who was foaming at the mouth.

They decided to take him to the hospital and put him on the running board, the step that was built outside the doors of many cars in the 1930s. As Peters put it, "anyone who has seen and smelled a Chinese beggar will realize why we did not put him inside the car. Diseased and filthy, it was bad enough having to handle him, and anyway we made him quite comfortable."[4]

3 E. Peters, *Shanghai Policeman*, p146.

4 E. Peters, *Shanghai Policeman*, p176.

Judd got in the car while Peters stood on the running board and held on to Mau. When they reached Fearon Road (Jiulong Road), according to Peters, Mau appeared to be in a better condition and began to move about. Peters told the chauffeur to turn around and drive along Fearon Road. The road ran along the west side of Hongkew Creek and led to Chapei back near Kashing Road. According to Peters and Judd, they intended to take Mau outside the International Settlement to drop him off. The police practice of the time was to "deport" beggars back to Chinese territory. When they reached the Yuhung Road (Yuhang Road) Bridge they told Doo to stop.

Up to this point, the evidence of the prosecution witnesses and Peters and Judd essentially matched. After this, the stories differed. The chauffeur, Doo, told the court that Peters and Judd then threw Mau directly into Hongkew Creek. Doo physically demonstrated in court how Mau had been thrown and how he heard the water make a noise which sounded like a "wah" or a "piah." Another Chinese witness, Zung Ching-sung, a Chinese hawker who lived across the creek, said that he had seen a man struggling in the river and had called for help. He had taken down the number of the car he had seen leaving the scene. This matched the number of the police station car. Mau was fished from the river but died six days later from pneumonia.

Peters and Judd were very ably defended by two British barristers: Ranald McDonald for Peters and Hugh Reeks for Judd. The defence faced a serious challenge. There was a very strong case against Peters and Judd. When first challenged about what had happened that night, they did not say what they had done with Mau. Peters had also committed a serious breach of regulations by leaving the charge room. The evidence of Doo, the police chauffeur, could not really be challenged. The evidence of Zung who admitted to an opium habit was easier to challenge. Be that as it may, Mau had been fished out of the river soon after Peters and Judd were alleged to have thrown him in. Mau had been in their charge and very soon after he had been found in a freezing river.

On the other hand, Priestwood and McNeill also faced a serious challenge. One of the great difficulties in prosecuting police officers is that they know how the system works. They have seen numerous people they considered guilty get off because they have worked the system. They also know that the smaller the lie the better the lie. If you lie about what happened, make sure that it is only a small lie. You can tell the truth about everything else and appear credible and can more easily remember the details of the small lies. With competent lawyers, and Peters and Judd had very competent lawyers, this can get you an acquittal.

Having said that, I have no idea if they were telling the truth or not. From the transcripts of the trial, the evidence of all the prosecution witnesses seems credible. Peters and Judd did not seriously challenge their stories. So what was Peters and Judds' story? It was very simple, and for that reason it was very effective. They said that having decided to return Mau to Chinese territory when going along Fearon Road, they had seen a beggar boat. Peters in his book described the creeks of Shanghai as "being infested with beggar boats. The Police near the waterways go off duty at night and the beggars seize the opportunity to bring their boats close to the shore, tying them along the embankments even in the most central parts of the city, and then going off to do their begging."[5] The beggar boat that Peters and Judd had seen was "about 20 foot long, dilapidated, cloth covered in the centre." While the streets were part of the International Settlement, the rivers were Chinese territory. This seemed the simplest way for them to resolve the problem of what to do with Mau. They told the driver to stop. Peters told the jury:

"We then both walked to the creek, looked at the boat

5 E. Peters, *Shanghai Policeman*, p19.

> and decided that it was quite safe to put him there. We then went back to the beggar. I held his left arm and Judd his right and we walked him to the railing alongside the creek. There we sat him down … We then lowered him on to the rear portion of the boat."

They said nothing more. They made no suggestion that perhaps someone else had then thrown Mau off the beggar boat or that Mau was not the beggar they had picked up.

Priestwood attacked Peters aggressively in cross examination firing off question after question at him. As he later explained to the jury, "questions must be put as quickly as possible, otherwise witnesses will have time to think up another lie." The questions came so fast that McDonald objected that he "could not take down the answers." Priestwood retorted: "I am not interested in that." Mossop told Priestwood to slow down enough that Mossop could take notes.

McDonald and Reeks then took over. They put the jury between a rock and a hard place. McDonald and Reeks had already met with Peters and Judd in prison and made the very tough decision on tactics. Peters recounts telling McDonald that he had nothing to hide:

> "Mr McDonald looked at me very straight in the face for a few moments and then finally said:
>
> > 'Look here Peters, you must understand this is a very serious business, and as your counsel, I wish with your permission, to ask you something … When we are in court, I want to stick out for murder or nothing. That is to say, if you killed this man, then you must pay for it; but if you did not, then I as your lawyer for the defence will do all in my power to see you are acquitted.'
>
> "I agreed with everything that he said, because I knew that I had not done this thing, and I did not want to

cringe behind any pleas of manslaughter. So after a long talk about my character in the Royal Tank Corps and the case in general, he left me, and I returned to my cell with the words '*Murder or nothing*' ringing in my ears."

This was the tactic in court. In both their closing speeches, Reeks and McDonald made it clear it was an all or nothing verdict. Murder and the gallows. Or, acquittal and freedom. On the evidence, there should have been no question of manslaughter or any other verdict arising. Peters and Judd either threw Mau in the river and killed him or they did not. McDonald emphasized that if the jury was satisfied beyond reasonable doubt, they had to convict but if they had any doubt they should acquit. He then suggested that "there were sinister figures behind the prosecution." Priestwood leapt to his feet to challenge him on this. McDonald quickly said that no foreigner was involved. McDonald went on that Peters had covered up to seek to protect himself because "like Samson of old he had dallied with Delilah" but this did not amount to murder. He concluded by leaving the "issue of life and death" in the hands of "good men and true."

Reeks, on behalf of Judd, took another tack, appealing at first to logic rather than emotion. There was no reason to believe the accused had any malice towards Mau. A crime of this nature could only be "committed by a man or men deprived of all sense of social justice and a total disregard of the laws of humanity." The Crown case was that they had committed the crime before the eyes of a Chinese policeman, yet afterwards had never said anything to him to seek to silence him. He then turned to emotion, referring to Judd's father and mother in England "and possibly a little friend at the back of the court" were awaiting a verdict.

Judge Allan Mossop then directed the jury, emphasizing the importance of reasonable doubt. He took them through all the evidence before reminding them that it was for the prosecution to prove the defendants guilty and not for the defendants to prove their innocence.[6]

The jury retired.

Peters and Judd, who were being guarded by SMP policemen and were being given relatively special treatment, were taken out of the court to the top of the steps facing Yuenmingyuen Road. The steps led down to the consulate gardens. McDonald said nothing to them and only "made some encouraging signs." Reeks told them that he thought the judge had "dwelt rather too much on manslaughter" and that "although we should be alright in the end, it was always best to prepare for the worst."

Peters did not want to hear this. "I began to realize the grim reality of all that I had been through. And still the issue was uncertain. My great fear was manslaughter and a sentence of imprisonment ... I can not describe my feelings as we waited. [Judd] and I kept out thoughts to ourselves and spoke encouraging words to one another."

A reporter from the *China Press* came up the stairs looking for a quote. He left soon when he realized there would be no information. "It was about time," Peters recalls, "or he might have received a little help down those steps."

The jury returned after 41 minutes. Anyone who has seen a jury trial knows this is one of the tensest moments anyone can experience. The questioning to the jury seems to take an eternity. The accused must sit there while the question is put to the jury as to whether they are guilty or not guilty. Time seems to stop still.

Once in a trial in Hong Kong, I was seated directly in front of and in touching distance of an accused who was facing serious prison time while the verdict was read out. When the foreman uttered the words "Not Guilty" I have never heard a

6 The best record of the summing up is in Peters' book, *Shanghai Lawyer,* p222 to 225.

greater exhalation of breath from sheer relief in my life.

Newspapers reported that Peters and Judd sat impassively waiting for the verdict. Almost certainly, their breath was held in the same way. Mossop asked first what was the verdict for Peters. "Not Guilty" replied the foreman to cheers from the 150 so people in court. The clerk had to shout "Be Quiet" three times before the verdict for Judd could also be read with the same result. Mossop then discharged both men and excused the jury from service for 10 years. As soon as they left the court, Judd and Peters were surrounded by wellwishers congratulating them and celebrations continued into the night.

They both, however, faced disciplinary charges for their admitted breaches of discipline during the trial. Both resigned from the force. They were able to collect their own superannuation contributions, but the Council did not pay them the Council's contributions. Peters returned to England after the trial. Judd stayed on working as a clerk at Clarke's Detective Agency.

The trial and the verdict did not attract any protest from the Chinese authorities. There were two letters to the editor of the *Shanghai Evening Post.*[7] One from "Anglo-Saxon" bemoaned the weakness of the jury system and, in particular, noting that Frank Raven had been convicted by the United States Court in a trial without a jury. This drew a response from "A Chinese" who said that he or she had been "agreeably shocked" by the fact that Peters and Judd had been prosecuted and had during the trial told his Chinese friends that what China needed was English-style justice where policemen would be prosecuted for killing a beggar. Then came the anticlimax and the judge's caution about "malice" and intentions. The writer went on that of the Chinese papers only the *Shunpao* had carried an article critical of the acquittal. No other paper even mentioned it because:

7 "Juries and Justice", *Shanghai Evening Post*, February 14, 1936; "The Jury System", *Shanghai Evening Post*, February 15, 1936 (Mossop Law Reports).

"we Chinese are accustomed to this form of English justice as we accept the Sun rising from the East."

This was not entirely correct. Some of the Chinese press had been scathing. The Modern Daily News noted that victim was a "beggar of a semi-colony, while the culprits [were] policemen of a great power." The editor of Lung Yu wrote sarcastically that he expected the verdict contained the expression: "The deceased lost his life because he could not swim."[8]

John Brenan, the British Consul General was also dismayed saying in a note to the Foreign Office that British juries were most reluctant to convict a white man on Chinese evidence.[9]

What was the truth? On a cold December morning, I retraced the route Peters and Judd had followed that fateful night. The bridge near to where Mau was found is still there. On three corners, the same buildings that were there in 1935 remain almost exactly as they were. Standing there, it was hard to believe that Peters and Judd (or any other human being) could have, in cold blood, thrown Mau in the river. Chapei, which was Chinese territory, was only a short drive away - a couple of hundred metres. On the other hand, Peters in particular was in a foul mood. He had had a fight with his girlfriend. He had travelled on the running board of the police car in the freezing cold keeping a dirty filthy struggling Mau in place. Peters may have wanted to kill him; but why Judd? In any event, I am certain that he and Judd did not gently lower Mau onto a beggar boat as they describe. They had most likely manhandled him roughly over the side.

What was the truth? It is hard to say. What can be said is that three questions went unanswered during the trial, because neither side wanted to ask them.

8 Modern Daily News, Feb, 15; Lung Yu, Issue 83, both from SMP file on Peters and Judd.

9 P.D. Coates, *The China Consuls*, p170.

First, Doo said that he heard a splash. Did he? It was a cold night. He had most likely left the car engine running and had his window closed. Priestwood did not ask how he heard the splash. Doo said he had heard the splash – it was for the defence to challenge this. McDonald and Reeks did not want to challenge him by asking a question they did not know the answer to. Perhaps he had, in fact, switched off the engine and wound down his window.

Second, was there a beggar boat there? Was there anyone else on that beggar boat who might have thrown Doo off or forced him to leave? Beggar boats were not charities. Mau may have been asked for money if he wanted to stay or been told to get off. In his weakened condition he could have been thrown off easily or, if he tried to stand up, fallen into the river. Again, neither side needed to know the answers. For Peters and Judd in particular, going for "Murder or Nothing" they could not suggest that Mau had not been made safe. This would open the door to the jury to consider manslaughter.

Third and most confusing, Zung, the hawker, at the committal hearing before Registrar Haines had said he had seen two foreigners in uniform shining torch lights on the creek before the police car had driven off.[10] This did not come out at the trial. But, as evidence coming soon after the incident, it was probably true. What were Peters and Judd doing shining their torches on the river? Zung did not mention this in his evidence at the trial; there was nothing Priestwood and McNeill could do about it. They were not allowed to ask leading questions to get the evidence from him. Reeks and McDonald could have cross-examined on it, but again it did not support a "Murder or Nothing" case. Reeks had, in fact, cross-examined Zung strongly on the point in the committal hearing, so it was not something he would have forgotten. If Mau had been safe, why would Peters and Judd have needed to shine

10 *R v Judd & Peters, North China Herald* (committal hearing), December 18, 1935, p493 and December 25, 1935, p533.

their torch lights on the river?

Divine intervention?

Later the same year, Priestwood and Reeks were back in court in another high profile case where a policeman was accused of murder. This time, Priestwood had a much easier case to prosecute; Reeks had it tough. The policeman was not white, but Sikh, and there was no doubt that the victim had been killed by the accused. Atma Singh hacked another Sikh policeman, Bawa Singh, to death in the bathhouse of the Pootoo Road Police Station (on the corner of Pootoo Road (Putou Road) and Gordon Road (Jiangning Road)) in the northwest of the International Settlement.[11]

The killing was especially vicious. Sergeant Simms and Sergeant Peterson had heard terrible screams coming from the bathhouse. They went inside and found Bawa Singh lying on the floor. The floor and walls were splattered with blood. Bawa Singh had a deep chopper wound in his forehead and both his forearms had been almost severed. Bawa Singh was taken to hospital where he had both arms amputated and an eye removed. He died soon after of hemorrhage and shock.

Atma at the time was 32. He had been in the Shanghai Municipal Police for 12 years and had a clean record. He was put on trial before Penrhyn Grant Jones, as Acting Judge, and a jury of twelve Englishmen.

Atma Singh had clearly killed Bawa Singh. He was the only other person in the bathhouse at the time and there was a bloody chopper on the table. He did not deny the killing but pleaded that there had been extreme provocation. Atma's wife, Sha Dur, had complained that Bawa had been spreading rumours that she had been seen going into the house of another Sikh constable. That morning, Atma had gone home

11 *R v Atma Singh, North China Herald,* November 25, 1935, p330

around 4.30am and found his wife weeping. She said that Bawa Singh had come to their house and woken her up. She had demanded he leave or she would blow a police whistle. Bawa had left. Atma had gone to the police station looking for Bawa. He found him in the bathhouse. Atma asked Bawa if he had been to his house. Bawa said yes, "and it was not the first time he had been ... he had been there many times before." This suggestion of improper relations with his wife drove Atma into a passion and seeing a chopper on the table he attacked Bawa.

Atma claimed at this trial that he had "hit him only to hurt him, not to kill him." Bawa had insulted his wife: "Without respect, life is not worth living."

Given Bawa's horrific injuries, Reeks had a hard job to convince the jury to bring back a verdict of manslaughter.[12] He relied on the fact that the attack had occurred openly; Atma, he said, should not be "bracketed with traitors and those who plot death secretly." He then played on the Sikhs' martial character and loyalty, saying the Sikhs as a race "were slow to speak, quick to strike, brave, attached to their officers and the best fighters in the East. They were the ruling tribe in India until they met us. They are not bred to stand insult."

Grant Jones in summing up said that the presence of a person in a man's house is certainly sufficient to arouse justifiable indignation: but was it sufficient provocation to justify murder? He then reviewed the law and, taking advantage of the fact he had a jury to decide the case, said: "Well, Gentlemen you are men of the world, men of common sense, and I prefer to leave it – possibly you may call it shirking on my part – but I propose to leave the matter to you." After five minutes deliberation, the jury convicted

12 The jury members were J. Prentice, P.T. O'Neill, G.L. Atchison, E.A. Richardson, G. Pickering, A.A. Williams, V.H. Bourne, R.L. Reade, A.J.G Parkhill, W. Canning and S.R. Owen and one other. The case report only listed 11 names.

Atma of murder. Before passing sentence, Grant Jones said to Singh:

> "You will recognize, I think, the righteousness of the saying contained in an old Book: 'Who-so sheddeth man's blood, by man shall his blood be shed'."

Grant Jones put on the black cap and sentenced Singh to death telling him in the time-honoured words that he would be "hanged by the neck until he was dead."

The British Ambassador - in mid-1935 the legation in Peiping had been upgraded to an embassy - was required to approve the sentence. Singh and Reeks, must have had a justifiable hope for a reprieve. There was provocation here. Three years earlier, Katherine Hadley, a British of Lithuanian descent, had been convicted of murdering her common-law husband, Captain Youngs, in an apparent drunken rage. After her appeal had been dismissed, Sir Miles Lampson, as almost one of his last acts as British Minister had commuted her death sentence.[13]

Reeks and other members of the British community considered the sentence of death to be harsh. Reeks circulated a petition that Atma be granted clemency that received a large number of signatures. Justice in the British China, however, was not colour blind. Perhaps because of the brutality of the killing and perhaps to send a message to other Sikh policemen, the British Ambassador, Sir Hughe Montgomery Knatchbull-Hugessen, confirmed the sentence just before Christmas 1936.[14]

13 *Straits Times,* August 31, 1933, p2 and *Straits Times,* December 28, 1933, p6. The appeal court was made up of Grant Jones (presiding), Acting Chief Justice John Wood of Hong Kong and C. Haines, Acting Assistant Judge. Hadley was transferred to England to serve her sentence. Daily Sketch, October 12, 1935. A picture of Hadley arriving in England is shown on the front page. Hadley had been acquitted of murder three years earlier in Tientsin. For more on her background see C.S. Hagen, *Tientsin at War,* Part VIII - Broken Moons (www.cshagen.com).

14 "Death Sentence Confirmed", North China Herald, December 30, 1936, p536

Singh was scheduled to be hanged on December 29, 1936. Mr H. Plumb, a hangman with 12 years experience, was brought from Hong Kong.

Hanging is a complex business. The executioner must work out the exact length of rope to be used based on the prisoners weight and height. This is modified depending on the physique and muscularity, particularly of the neck. The goal is for the fall to break the prisoners neck; killing him instantly. If the calculation is wrong, the prisoner can either be slowly strangled or decapitated.[15]

Darshan Singh, Singapore's former Chief Executioner, in order to calm those he was about to execute, would quietly say to them just before hanging them: "I am sending you to a better place than this." Darshan Singh had been trained by Singapore's last colonial hangman, Mr Seymour. Presumably this was the formula that had been passed down by all British hangmen to each other.

Plumb brought a rope with him from Hong Kong. In order to try out and stretch the rope, he conducted a test the day before the hanging using a sandbag attached to the rope. The sound must have been chilling to Atma Singh who had been placed in the condemned man's cell directly next door.

We can imagine the scene in Ward Road Gaol on that fateful day. Singh is pinioned by Sikh guards and brought into the small execution chamber. The rope is in position hanging above the trapdoor over a steel bar. The trapdoor had been specially designed to open directly into the prison's mortuary below. Plumb orders Singh to stand on the trapdoor. He places the noose around Singh's neck, firmly fixing the knot next to his ear. Singh, as a good loyal Sikh, presumably takes this all stoically, accepting it as God's will. The witnesses must have felt sick to the pit of their stomach. When everything is ready,

15 A Shadrake, *Once a Jolly Hangman*, p16. The quote below is from p21. *Singapore Free Press and Mercantile Advertiser*, December 31, 1936, Page 1 for the subsequent quote from Plumb.

the executioner tells Singh the last words he will ever hear:

"I am sending you to a better place than this."

The next words from Plumb were an anguished cry:

"My God! That's a Terrible Thing."

Atma Singh woke some time later in the police hospital. The rope had broken. Singh was still breathing and had been rushed for medical treatment. His neck had been stretched two inches (six cm) by the hanging and he had suffered a concussion. His first words were to ask for some water. He then said: "I thought you were going to hang me." Due to the damage to his throat he was kept on a liquid diet for over two weeks.[16]

Sir John Brenan, the Consul-General, as Sheriff, immediately convened an enquiry. Cyril Haines, the Registrar of the court, assisted Brenan. Plumb, the Governor of the prison and a number of other witnesses were examined. Two ships' captains also gave evidence as experts on ropes.

There was some suspicion that the Sikh warders guarding Atma Singh may have weakened the rope. But they had been locked in the condemned man's cell with Atma and had no access to the execution chamber. The explanation was, in the end, remarkably simple. In Hong Kong, the rope was thrown over a round wooden girder when a prisoner was hanged. In Ward Road Gaol, a steel "I" shaped girder had been installed. This was intended to be used with a specially designed shackle. Plumb was not provided with a shackle, so he followed the procedure he had always used in Hong Kong. Some months before, he had executed another prisoner in Shanghai and used the same method as well. He had simply tossed the rope

16 The *China Press*, January 1, 1937, p1 and January 15, 1937, p9

over the steel beam.

The enquiry found that the edge of the beam had cut the rope. Fragments of rope were found on the beam and the place the rope had broken matched where the rope had passed over the beam. The ships' captains confirmed that they considered this was the cause. One said that he thought the rope used for Atma's hanging, while satisfactory, was not as strong as the rope Plumb had used in the execution some months before.[17]

Sir John Brenan, asks, why did the rope break?

As soon as the enquiry finished, in order to allay suspicions, Brenan immediately announced: "The Consular Court and the rope experts found the break in the rope was due to a cause not foreseen. The rope was not tampered with by anyone." Brenan stated that the enquiry's conclusion was that the rope had been cut by the sharp edge of the beam to which it was attached.[18]

British officials now had to decide whether to hang Atma again. One suspects many of them would have believed in divine intervention. Grant Jones, having quoted the Old Testament when sentencing Singh, must surely have had doubts. At Grant Jones' suggestion, the Foreign Office consulted the Home Office in London as to the usual procedure in England. The Home Office reported that the only case of an unsuccessful hanging in England had occurred in 1884. In that case, Mr Lee had been reprieved but only after he had been unsuccessfully hanged three times![19]

17 HO 144/2304 Report by Brenan to the British Ambassador, January 4, 1937, p6. The steel beam was soon after replaced with a round wooden girder.

18 FO656/351 Letter dated January 25, 1937 to CAG Hong Kong from British Supreme Court; *The Emporia Daily Gazette*, December 30, 1936, p4.

19 HO 144/23046 Home Office Memorandum dated January 4, 1937 under initials J.H;

Singh was to be a little luckier. Brenan and the British Ambassador were against carrying out a new execution. Grant Jones supported a reprieve.

The only question was how to reprieve him. There was no specific provision in the Orders in Council as to how to deal with a failed hanging. The Foreign Office considered that a pardon may be necessary, but this created a problem that there was no power to impose a conditional pardon in China, meaning that if Singh was pardoned he may have to be released from prison. The Home Office suggested that because under the Orders in Council, the British Ambassador in Peking had approved the execution, there must be an implied power for him to withdraw the approval and substitute a different sentence.

This was done and Atma's sentence was commuted to life imprisonment. Singh was later transferred to Lahore Central Jail in the Punjab.[20] In British India at the time, life did not mean life. Due to the lack of space and harsh conditions, normally a prisoner sentenced to life imprisonment only served 14 years. Singh should have been released at the latest in 1950, but most likely, given that World War II and Indian Independence in 1949 both intervened, he was released well before that.

Atma Singh had been saved by a broken rope. His wife, Sha Dur, thought it was a higher power telling newspapers:

> "His delivery comes from God. Ever since he was sentenced, I have firmly believed he would not die. God has looked upon a good man and God has saved him."[21]

No higher power was protecting anyone in North China.

telegram from Sir Hugh Kutschbull-Hugessen (Peking) to FO for Grant Jones' suggestion on same file. The file only refers to the "Judge." Mossop was on leave at the time so I have assumed these are references to Grant Jones.

20 FO656/231 Petition from Atma Singh transmitted to the Registrar of the Court by the Superintendent of the Central Jail, Lahore, September 21, 1938.

21 *Emporia Daily Gazette*, December 30, 1936, p4.

Chapter 57

The Badlands of North China

In the mid 1930s, tensions were very high in North China. Peiping (as Peking was now known) was almost completely surrounded by Japanese troops. Since occupying Manchuria, the Japanese had slowly been extending their control of provinces north of Peiping. Using their rights under the Boxer Protocol, they had also stationed large numbers of troops on the railway line between Tientsin and Peiping. A large legation guard was stationed in Peiping. The foreign powers also had substantial troop presences in Peiping. Tensions between Japan and China and Japan and foreign powers were high.

As a result, North China was not a safe place for women, foreigners and even, Japanese soldiers. The British courts and consuls in the space of a few years had to deal with the murders of a Japanese solider and a young British girl, the attempted rape of a French girl by a British solider and the incarceration and ill treatment of British Indians for attempted arson.

Problems after Midnight in Peking

In June 1936, in the badlands in Peiping - a strip of virtually unregulated bars and entertainment venues near the city wall - the actions of three British soldiers heightened the already high tensions between Britain and Japan. The soldiers, Herbert Cooke, T.D. Parrish and Ralph Hunt, from the embassy guard were accused of killing a Japanese officer, Kisaku Sasaki, in the street, and assaulting another Japanese, Mr Onishi, in a Korean bar, The No. 27.

Given the importance of the case, Victor Priestwood, the Crown Advocate, flew from Shanghai to Peiping to prosecute at the preliminary inquiry. Japanese officials, including Mr Okamura, second secretary of the Japanese embassy, were present.[1] British Vice-Consul, Nicholas Fitzmaurice conducted the enquiry.

Priestwood at the beginning of the hearing, said the charges were manslaughter for the killing of Sasaki and causing bodily harm for the assault on Onishi. Priestwood offered no evidence against Parrish. The hearing went on for two weeks and numerous Japanese, Chinese and Koreans were called to give evidence, all needing translation into English.

One particularly testy exchange showed the tensions at the time between the Japanese and British. When a barboy from the Korean bar was giving evidence in Chinese, the British interpreter, Mr G.W. Creighton, the Assistant Chinese Secretary at the Embassy, motioned him to silence.

Mr Okamura said loudly, "Let him speak."

Priestwood chastised Okamura: "Excuse me, Mr Okamura, I am in charge of this examination and intend to conduct it."

Okamura responded "Please let the Chinese Chief of Police interpret. Mr Creighton is interrupting the witness and I object. I have the right."

"You have no right," retorted Priestwood coldly.[2]

At the end of the hearings, Fitzmaurice held that there was insufficient evidence to try Cooke or Hunt for the killing of Sasaki. Cooke was remanded for trial for assault and causing bodily harm of Onishi. As the charge no longer was that of unlawful killing, which would have required a trial in the Supreme Court, Priestwood withdrew from the case, leaving the prosecution to the local British consular staff. Cooke was tried in the British Magistrate's Court in Peiping, but acquit-

1 *Hong Kong Daily Press*, July 1, 1936, p4; *The Times*, June 25, 1936.

2 *Singapore Free Press and Mercantile Advertiser* (1884-1942), July 2, 1936, p9.

ted on the basis that the magistrate believed he had not been present when Onishi was attacked.

The Japanese Residents' Association organized an "indignation meeting" and asked the British Embassy for a "just solution." In a lament at the weakness of extraterritorial jurisdiction, they complained:

> "We Japanese residents placed our trust in the conscience of the British authorities and hoped for a fair trial, but we find we have been betrayed and our lives are placed in jeopardy."[3]

They also telegraphed to the Japanese Army headquarters in Tientsin and the Ministries of War and Navy in Tokyo. Three British soldiers were fired at in a drive-by shooting on their way back from the cinema.

A spokesman for the Japanese Embassy criticized the verdict, resulting in a question in the British Parliament as to what was being done about it. The Secretary State for Foreign Affairs, Mr Eden, replied that the matter had been brought to the attention of the Japanese government. A follow-up question was asked as to whether the "procedure followed in this investigation was similar to that well-established in this country?" Perhaps showing that the workings of extraterritorial courts were no longer as high a priority as they may have been in the past, Eden replied:

> "I should like to have notice of that question. The procedure was that of the Consular Court, but it was the normal and proper procedure in the circumstances."[4]

Not long after Cooke's acquittal, in January 1937, a 19-year

3 *Straits Times*, July 7, 1936, p9.

4 "Japanese Anger at Acquittal", *Straits Times*, July 6, 1936, p9; HC Deb 20 July 1936 vol 315 c9

-old British schoolgirl, Pamela Werner, the adopted daughter of Edward Werner, a former British consular officer (and barrister) was brutally murdered in Peiping. Her body was found beneath a watchtower of the city wall. Her stomach had been sliced open and all her internal organs removed. Her death was investigated by the British authorities and a number of hearings were held into her death in the British Consular Court in Peiping without reaching any satisfactory conclusion. No suspect was prosecuted, although a number of Americans suspects were identified. Her father continued to investigate the killing for the rest of his life.[5]

The same year, a British army officer, Lieutenant Wilson, attacked a 19-year-old French girl on the roof of the Peking Hotel. He was charged with rape in the British Consular Court, the same court that was also responsible for the coronial inquests into the killing of Pamela Werner and had tried Cooke and Hunt. After a preliminary hearing, Consul Archer dismissed the case against Wilson on the basis that a jury would not have convicted.

Archer, nevertheless, sent a detailed report on the case to Judge Allan Mossop in Shanghai. He wrote that he would not normally send a long report with the case record. However, the French girl had after the acquittal, for reasons Archer attributed to "youth, French nationality, and ignorance of British judicial procedure," accused him of letting Wilson off because he was a British army officer. Further, and probably the true reason, he said he was sending the report because the Consulate and Court was "under criticism for alleged lack of energy and even integrity in connection with the still unsolved murder of Pamela Werner." Archer lamented "the singularly unfortunate accident that I should have been called upon to hear and decide another serious case affecting safety

5 Paul French has told the story of the killing and investigation of Pamela Werner's death in his book, *Midnight in Peking*. He concludes that she was killed by a number of Americans who lured into Peking's Badlands to sexually assault her. This is challenged by some.

of young women in Peking."[6]

Archer and his Vice-Consul, Nicholas Fitzmaurice, who was sitting as coroner in the Pamela Werner case may have been singularly unlucky. Their handling of the Sasaki case may have been the cause of Pamela Werner's death. A year later, Sir Edmund Backhouse, a noted China scholar, wrote to the British Embassy that he had received information the murder of Pamela Werner had been carried out by the Japanese as revenge for the acquittal of Cooke and Hunt. Backhouse may have been a fantasist. He wrote memoirs where he claimed to have engaged in sex orgies in the Forbidden City and even to have had sex with the Empress Dowager herself.[7]

Nevertheless, his story is given some credence by Mr Creighton who interpreted at the trial of Cooke and Hunt. Many years later he wrote that the killing of Pamela Werner was a "Japanese revenge act" against the British consular authorities for the acquittal of Cooke and Hunt. He continued: "After all they easily could have found out that Werner was still living in Peking, was a former British Consul, so if they couldn't get Fitzmaurice's hippopotamic wife, then why not get the Werner girl?..."[8]

Extraterritoriality tested: The China Eastern Railway Zone

The Japanese were certainly, at the time, aggressively asserting their rights in Manchuria where two British subjects, both Indians, suffered the wrath of the Japanese police in the China Eastern Railway Zone. The railway had originally been built by the Russians from east to west across Manchuria to connect Vladivostok to the rest of Russia. A spur line, the South Manchurian Railway had been built from Harbin to Dalian.

---

6 FO656/231, Letter from British Embassy in Peking to Mossop, dated September 9, 1937.

7 See: *Decadence Mandchoue: The China Memoirs of Sir Edmund Trelawny Backhouse.*

8 Letter from Archer to Howe dated February 11, 1938; Letter from Creighton to P.D. Coates April 29, 1989 SOAS PP MS 52. Both reproduced on http://www.pamelawerner-murderpeking.com, a site dedicated to researching the Pamela Werner murder.

The Japanese had taken over most of the South Manchurian Railway following their victory over Russia in 1905. The Railway Zone was a sixty-metre wide strip of land on either side of the railway line. The zone had been created when the line was built to allow for effective management of the line and to provide security. In cities, this meant that properties built near the railway fell within the zone.

The Japanese were prepared to allow extraterritoriality to continue in Manchukuo. But they took a different view in relation to the CER, asserting that they had sole jurisdiction over all people in the zone. Despite this, in most cases, they allowed other powers to exercise jurisdiction in the zone over their own subjects as well.

In mid-1937, the difficulties of this *modus vivendi* came to the fore in a case where two Indian employees of a British shopkeeper in Mukden (Shenyang), Motwani and Lahkati, were arrested for suspected arson by the Japanese police. They were detained in a cell with 14 other prisoners and were made to sleep on the floor sharing only one blanket. After numerous protests by the British, they were released. The British Consul in Mukden, P.D. Butler, wanted to put them on trial in the British Consular Court and issued a warrant for their arrest. In order to avoid "political complications", Butler ordered the warrant only be executed outside the zone.[9]

Butler faced the difficulty that the Japanese police would not assist the prosecution in the British court. Butler had written to the acting Japanese Consul-General in Mukden, C. Yoshimura on June 7, 1937, requesting Japanese police and fire brigade officers to give evidence in court. In a formal letter to Butler the next day, Yoshimura rejected this request stating: "I regret that I am unable to comply with this request, as a ques-

9 FO656/231 Official correspondence in this section: Letter from Butler to JL Dodds, Charge d'Affaires, British Embassy Tokyo, 11 June 1937; Letter from Yoshimura to Butler dated, 8 June 1937; 231 Telegraph dated 5 June 1937 from Butler to Supreme Court; Telegraph dated 7 June 1937 from Judge of Supreme Court to Butler; Letter from Butler to JL Dodds, Charge d'Affaires, British Embassy Tokyo, 11 June 1937.

tion of principle is involved."

Butler had no evidence on which to base a prosecution. Foreseeing this possibility, he had telegraphed the Supreme Court in Shanghai asking if he could rely on a letter "from the Japanese Consul embodying an outline of the Japanese police case against the men who have been examined by them and of whose guilt they profess themselves convinced."

Mossop immediately responded that the "letter from Japanese Consul would not be admissible as evidence," and that any preliminary examination must be held in "strict compliance with provisions of China Rules of Court, 1905." Butler had to release the men who, though under no immediate threat of arrest by the Japanese, chose to leave Mukden to avoid further problems. Butler in a letter to the British Charge d'Affaires in Tokyo described the outcome of the case as "highly unsatisfactory" as the attitude of the Japanese authorities had made a proper judicial investigation of the case almost impossible.

Even after this, the Japanese police continued to exercise their claimed rights in the zone by arresting and beating the Chinese employee of the British insurance company who had come to investigate the fire.[10]

These difficulties of protecting extraterritorial rights in Japanese-occupied territories were only a very small taste of what was to come.

10 FO656/231 Price & Co memorandum dated June 3, 1937.

The Shanghai Club building opened in 1910 .The home of the British elite in Shanghai. Lawrence Kentwell was refused membership due to his mixed race

The entrance to the former American Club in Shanghai. DA Leonard Husar received his bribes here. The author is at the bottom right corner.

HD Rodger

Reader Harris

Norwood Allman

Ranald McDonald

Photos by Ah Fong.

They're off! Greyhounds leaving the Starting Boxes in a Race at Luna Park, Shanghai.

Capt Martin, head of the Shanghai Muncipal Police and General McNaghten, sued in the British Supreme Court for closing Luna Park, a greyhound racing track.

Silas Hardoon, one of Shanghai's Richest men. His death led to a probate battle in the British Court

Lisa Hardoon, Silas' Chinese wife inherited his fortune

Walter Chalaire, former partner of Cornell Franklin, and WWI flying ace. His claim- against Franklin went all the way to the US Supreme Court.

A photo taken in 1934 when Judge Milton Purdy left the bench of Purdy (seated on the bench) and the members of the US Bar. The photo includes Ferno Schul (1st left), Cornell Franklin (2nd left), Thomas Sellett (4th left), HD Rodger (5th left), Stirling Fessenden (6th left), Chauncey Holcomb (7th left), Hua-chuen Mei (6th right) and Norwood Allman (3rd right).

The Kalee Hotel – Home of the US Consulate and US Court in the 1930s

Allan Mossop and Penrhyn Grant Jones in full robes at Trinity Cathedral in 1936

The US Court for China on circuit in the 1930s. The judge appears to be Milton Helmick. Norwood Allman is second from right.

The British Supreme Court for China in the 1930s

Frank Jay Raven

J. Warner Brown

Crowds mill outside the AOBC offices when its closure is announced

Sgt Ernest Peters and Sumiko. Peters was accused of throwing a Chinese beggar in a river.

John Colbert, doctor accused of trying to murder his wife

A beggar boat on a river in Shanghai. Peters claims to have placed the beggar on a boat like this.

FOREIGN SECTION, MUNICIPAL GAOL, WARD ROAD (3rd Floor, Interior)

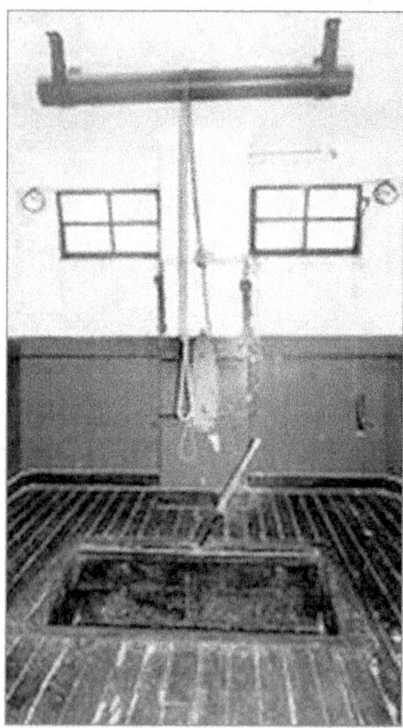

The gallows at Ward Road Gaol

A warder looks through the hole made by Japanese shelling of Ward Road Gaol in 1937

McNeil Island Penitentiary where Americans were imprisoned from the 1930s. Frank Raven, Warner Brown and Gerald Casement were all imprisoned here.

Bilibid Prision in the Philippines, where Americans were imprisoned In the 1910s and 1920s.

HJIMS Idzumo in Shanghai in 1937. The China Printing and Finishing Factory where Maurice Tinkler was bayonetted is top left on the Pudong side.

Bombing and death on Nanking Road (1937)

A bomb-damaged house, flying the German Swastika, on Hungjao Road (1937)

Kenneth Piper and his wife, Jane, ordered to pay rent for a house of Hungjao Road despite the danger of war.

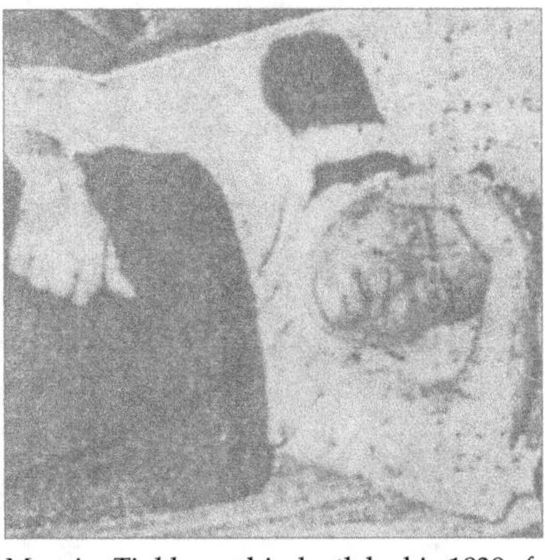

Maurice Tinkler on his death bed in 1939 after being bayonetted by Japanese soldiers. 76 years before when Charles Richardson has been cut down by a samurai, British gunboats bombarded Kagoshima.

Japanese electric fences surround the Tientsin British Concession in 1939

Seaforth Highlanders on patrol in Nanking Road in 1939

HMS Peterel, the last British gunboat in Shanghai in 1941. The Picture shows her when she had been damaged on the Yangtse and purposefully grounded for repairs.

USS Wake after her capture as the Japanese gunboat Tatara

The very last British or American court hearing in China. The US Court for China in Kunming which tried Boatner Carney in January 1943.
Top row, left to right: 1. Captain Edwin Kessler, US Attorney; 2. Major Bertrand Johnson, Special Judge; Lieut. Lincoln C. Brownell, Defense Counsel; Raymond P. Ludden, US Consul, Kunming. Bottom row: 1. Stanley A. McGeary, Marshalll; Mrs L.D. Tayler, Recorder; Alfred T. Wellborn, Clerk of the Court

Boatner Carney

Carney in Kunming in 1937, part of the Flying Tigers. General Chennault is on the right.

Chapter 58

Dark Days

The years from mid-1937 onwards were dark days in extraterritorial China. In the late summer of 1937, Japan occupied the whole of China's eastern seaboard leaving foreign concessions completely surrounded by Japanese-controlled territories, making them, as they were called at the time, "solitary islands."

The war had started in July 1937 when Japanese troops garrisoned near Fengtai, on the railway line between Tientsin and Peiping, skirmished with Chinese troops on a number of occasions. Fengtai is near the Marco Polo Bridge and the incident is now referred to in English as the Marco Polo Bridge Incident. Matters were heading to a diplomatic resolution after numerous negotiations between the Chinese and Japanese governments. But on August 9, a Japanese officer in Shanghai was killed. Japan launched an all-out invasion of China from the North as well as from Shanghai. Very quickly, Japan occupied large parts of North and Eastern China.[1]

In Shanghai, there was intense fighting throughout the Chinese part of the city between Japanese and Chinese troops outside the International Settlement and French Concession that went on for five months. The Japanese battleship the HJIMS *Idzumo* shelled Chinese positions from its position in front of the Cathay Hotel (Peace Hotel) on the Huangpu River. The Chinese returned fire with their shells often missing and falling on the International Settlement. The war was the

1 For more on the Japanese invasion, see I. Hsu, *The Rise of Modern China* (4th ed.), pp578-585 and E. Drea, *Japan's Imperial Army: Its Rise and Fall*, pp.191-206.

Shanghai Doomed City

DESTRUCTION IN SHANGHAI.—Land, air and sea fighting by Japanese and Chinese in Shanghai, China, is fast reducing the "Paris of the Orient" to ruins. This map shows location of (1) Cathay and Palace hotels, (2) Japanese cruiser Izumo, (3) Japanese Consulate, (4) Pootung, with American and British warehouses, and (5) Japanese barracks at Hangkew. All were bombed.

2. Is in fact the location of the hotels, and
3. Is the location of the Idzumo and consulate

main topic of news in all the city's and, indeed, the world's newspapers. One newspaper carried a map of the city under the heading "Shanghai Doomed City."[2] Because of the intense urban warfare that was seen, a later book on war called Shanghai "Stalingrad on the Yangtze." During the war lo-

2 Shanghai Doomed City, *Daily Gleaner*, August 26, 1937, p5.

cal papers all carried reports on difficulties for travel out of Shanghai; battles all around the city; and, Japanese victory parades through the streets of the International Settlement.

Officials of the courts evacuated their families from Shanghai. United States District Attorney Leighton Shields, who was in Japan at the time with his family, was advised to stay there. This was not due to over-cautiousness. British and Americans were attacked during the fighting. On August 26, the official car of the British Ambassador, Sir Hughe Montgomery Knatchbull-Hugessen, was strafed by two Japanese fighters between Nanking and Shanghai and the Ambassador shot through the chest. He survived but was evacuated to Hong Kong after being hospitalized for a month. Two months later in October, a British Embassy car with the Union Jack painted on its roof was attacked by Japanese fighters, but no-one injured. In December 1937, the USS Panay, a Yangtze River gunboat, anchored near Nanking was attacked and sunk by Japanese warplanes.[3]

In order to reduce attacks on Japanese nationals by Chinese fighters, the Japanese took complete control of the Hongkew and Yangtzepoo sections in the north of the International Settlement. They installed barricades on the bridges across Soochow Creek and refused access to the area to all citizens of other nations, including the non-Japanese police of the Shanghai Municipal Police. Police officers and firemen who tried to enter the area were repeatedly attacked by Japanese troops. Ward Road Gaol was located in the middle of the area. Shells whined overhead during most days and nights and on a number of occasions the gaol took direct hits killing a number of prisoners. The Municipal Council decided it was no longer practicable to carry on the prison and tried to remove Chinese prisoners back to Chinese territory. After 500 prisoners had been released this

3 Staff and Shields: *New York Times*, August 20, 1937; Sapajou, *Five Months of War*, p47 (Ambassador) and p90 (Embassy Car) – text and photos; "Japanese insist Panay was sunk by Accident", New York Times, December 26, 1937.

way, the Japanese refused to allow further releases.[4]

The British also sought to protect their prisoners. On August 21, 1937, the 14 convicted British prisoners in Ward Road Gaol were removed from the gaol. Eight of them had their sentences remitted and were freed. The remaining six prisoners - one European and five Indians - were sent to Hong Kong, where the European prisoner was kept. The Indian prisoners, including Atma Singh, now serving a life sentence for killing Bawa Singh, were sent on to India. All other foreign prisoners were also removed from the gaol in August and the prison did not accept any new prisoners until November 1937. The foreigner section of the gaol only returned to full operation in March 1938.[5]

The war and the practical problems of where to send convicts were brought home in a case in September 1937 before Milton Helmick in the United States Court for China. Stephen Kyau, a China-American from Hawaii, was tried for assaulting a British SMP policeman. While the hearing was going on, "Japanese airplanes droned overhead dropping bombs on Chinese positions just out of the International Settlement." Kyau was convicted and sentenced to six-month imprisonment, but Helmick was forced to suspend the sentence because there was no safe jail in the city to hold Kyau.[6]

During the fighting, the Japanese also made demands to effectively take over the running of the Shanghai Municipal Council and Shanghai Municipal Police by appointing Japanese to all senior positions. Cornell Franklin and Stirling Fessenden, who were now respectively the Chairman and Secretary General of the Municipal Council, were deeply involved in negotiations with the Japanese to save the Settlement.

4 *Shanghai Under Fire*, pp48-49 for text and pictures of the damage to the gaol.

5 Memo from Allan Mossop, Judge of the Supreme Court to Sir Archibald Kerr, British Embassy, Shanghai dated August 4, 1938, CO129/573/8; Shanghai Municipal Council, Gaol Branch Report, 1939, p2.

6 "New Mexican is Law for U.S. in China" *Clovis New Evening News*, September 1, 1937, p1.

Stirling Fessenden defends against Japanese attacks

Franklin and Fessenden, as wily lawyers, were able to stave off these requests by referring them to the consular body.[7]

The Japanese were not yet ready to fight the other foreign powers and made no attempt to occupy the International Settlement as a whole, but from time to time, they sealed off sections of the city after attacks on Japanese nationals. On December 7, 1937, the Japanese army closed a large section of the Nanking Road area following an attack on a victory parade on that road.[8]

The Japanese occupation of Eastern China meant that life became harder for foreign policemen in Shanghai. Guidelines for the Shanghai Municipal Police issued in 1938 required that a Japanese police officer should be present at all raids where Japanese may be arrested and, chillingly warned that the "officer in charge of the raiding party is responsible for any unlawful entry into the houses of innocent persons." Helpfully, the Guidelines stated that "Japanese residences may be eas-

7 House of Lords Debate 15 February 1938 vol 107 at p655; Foreign Relations of the US, Vol IV, 1938 p118 et seq..

8 *North China Herald*, December 8, 1937, p368.

ily distinguished by the painting of a cherry blossom on a wooden block at each doorway."[9]

End of extraterritoriality off the table

In December 1937, Japan captured Nanking, the Chinese capital, and massacred over 100,000 civilians in what has become known as the Rape of Nanking. The Nationalist Government moved to Chungking. The Japanese established a "Provisional Government of China" in Peiping in December 1937, but moved the government to Nanking the following month as the "Reformed Government of the Republic of China." The Chinese courts outside the foreign concessions all came under control of this puppet government. However, in Shanghai, still under British and American control, the Special District Court remained independent from the Japanese-controlled Chinese government of Kiangwan (Jiangwan) and continued to be loyal to the Nationalist Government.[10]

The Japanese attacks meant that the question of ending extraterritorial rights in China was taken completely off the table. United States Secretary for State Cordell Hull said the invasion made it necessary for American armed units to remain in China and that to pull them out would look like weakness. He added, "the Chinese themselves, although previously eager to have extraterritorial rights annulled were anxious for us to stay, since they felt that withdrawal of our troops would appear like abandoning China to her fate..."[11]

Just before Christmas in 1937, the British Secretary of State for Foreign Affairs was asked in the House of Commons "whether negotiations are taking place, or are contemplated, with China for the abandonment of British extra-territorial jurisdiction, or whether the British Government will be willing

9 *Shanghai Municipal Police: Guide and Regulations 1938* (D0335), Complied by Inspector WH Widdowson, Printed by the Municipal Gaol Printing Department.

10 "District Court Guarded by Police, Military", *North China Herald*, April 12, 1939, p57.

11 Cited in W. Fishel, *The End of Extraterritoriality in China*, p197.

to give favourable consideration to the matter?"

Viscount Cranborne, the Parliamentary Under-Secretary of State for Foreign Affairs, replied, very clearly: "The answer to the first part of the question is No, Sir. The second part does not, therefore, arise."[12]

Nor did the Japanese seek to abolish extraterritorial rights in China for foreign nationals. In 1938, the British Prime Minister, was asked in the House of Commons "whether his attention has been drawn to the official declaration by the Japanese spokesman in Shanghai that the Japanese Government intends to abolish extra-territorial rights in those portions of China which are in Japanese occupation; and whether he is in a position to make any statement on the matter?" Mr Butler responded on behalf of the Prime Minister that the Japanese government had advised that the Japanese spokesman was misunderstood:

> "The Japanese Government had no intention of using the present situation in China as a pretext for denying the extra-territorial rights enjoyed by Great Britain and other Powers vis-á-vis China. They consider that this is a question which solely concerns the Powers and China."

The spokesman's statement was explained as meaning that:

> "should individual foreigners contrive to endanger the safety of the Japanese forces or to impede the conduct of their military operations, these forces will naturally take the necessary actions against them."[13]

12 HC Deb 22 June 1937 vol 325 c1048W.

13 HC Deb 13 July 1938 vol 338 p1294.

The Sino-Japanese war and the courts

The war brought a number of problems to the British and American courts. The United States Court faced the particular problem of how to deal with companies that were incorporated as American companies but were in reality Chinese-owned and controlled. This was less of a problem in the British courts because of the 1919 Order in Council that required the senior management of a British company to be British.

Things became particularly problematic when Chinese sought to transfer their interests in properties to American companies so as to put them out of reach of the Japanese. Soon after occupying the area around Shanghai, the Japanese military authorities announced that they would not recognize any transfers of properties by Chinese to foreigners after August 13, 1937.[14]

Under the principles of extraterritoriality, this declaration should not have been binding on foreign courts. No foreign power could tell another what to do. However, Milton Helmick, Judge of the United States Court for China, later explained that "there was such supine acceptance of the Japanese fiat in all quarters that conveyances from Chinese to foreigners were regarded as transfers in fraud of creditors." Helmick explained this supineness as being based on "the earnest wish of the United States not to risk the lives of its sailors and marines or maybe provoke a war with Japan by assuming protection of property ostensibly American but actually Chinese." The US consular authorities adopted an almost Jekyll and Hyde personality. On the one hand they would insist on Americans' right to trade but on the other hand would do their best to refuse to recognize certain transfers.

One transfer that was effected and that particularly annoyed the Japanese was the transfer of the *Shunpao* (*Shenbao*), a Chinese language newspaper, from its owner I.K. Shih to

14 Milton J. Helmick, "Cases before the Court" Far Eastern Survey, Vol. 14, No. 21 (Oct. 24, 1945), p304 at p305.

American lawyer Norwood Allman. Shih, who was only 20 years old, had inherited the paper from his father Shih Liang-Tsai who had been assassinated in 1935, most likely on the orders of Chiang Kai-shek.[15] The *Shunpao* had been founded by a British tea merchant, F. Major, in 1872 and had always had an independent editorial policy. After the Japanese invasion, the younger Shih, as Allman put it, "wanted to keep it that way. He did not want to capitulate to the Japs, nor was he ready to die." He shut the paper down for a while but this put the employees out of work. Shih came to Allman for advice. Allman told him that "it would be the better part of valour for him to leave Shanghai until conditions change." Allman agreed to take over the newspaper. He set up an American company to do so and, as he put it, "neither I nor this American company ever advanced any claim to owning the paper, it was well known to everyone in Shanghai that I was publishing and editing the *Shunpao* for the Chinese owner, but on my own responsibility." These actions led to the *Shunpao* being bombed on a number of occasions and to Allman being placed on a Japanese blacklist.[16]

Most cases where a company was transferred from Americans to Chinese were dealt with by the consular authorities, who usually refused to recognise the transfer. However, one particular tricky case came before Helmick in the US Court. William Hunt, a former consular officer and entrepreneur, had entered various debt guarantees with China Merchants Steam Navigation Company. China Merchants was largely owned by the Chinese government and operated vessels along the coast or on the inland waterways of China. After the war with Japan started, Hunt announced he had taken

15 Norwood Allman in his book is very coy about the reason for the elder Shih's death, referring to him being "mysteriously murdered." Frederick Wakeman shows convincingly that he was in fact assassinated on orders of Chiang Kai-shek. Allman was writing during WWII when Chiang was an ally of the US and presumably did not wish to weaken support for him. See F. Wakeman, *Policing Shanghai,* 1927-1937 p257-259.

16 N. Allman, "Shanghai Lawyer", Chapter 17, especially, pp245-247.

over all the assets of China Merchants because it had defaulted on its debt. Many suspected that the transactions were a sham designed to keep the shipping company out of Japanese hands. The US consular authorities refused to recognize the transfer.[17]

Helmick said he never dreamed that the issue would end up in his court. But in 1938, China Merchants filed an application for an injunction to prevent Hunt from seizing their ships in areas of China the Japanese did not control. Helmick noted drily: "Apparently China Merchants had no objection to Hunt taking over in areas where the Japanese were menacing." To Helmick, it was clear "that both sides wanted the same decision - an adjudication that Hunt was the lawful owner of China Merchants," made by the United States Court for China.

The application for an injunction was a neat trick to give the US Court jurisdiction. Normally, Hunt would have been required to bring a case in court to have his ownership under the contracts confirmed. However, this would have required him to bring a case in a Chinese court. The Special District Court in Shanghai was still under Nationalist control so he could have filed there or in a part of China the Nationalists controlled. Or he could have also brought a case in a court in Japanese-controlled China. A judgment from a Nationalist-controlled court would be useless against the Japanese. The outcome of an application to a Japanese-controlled court could be easily predicted.

A way had to be found to make Hunt a defendant so that the US Court could have jurisdiction. This was done by seeking an injunction against him. Helmick suspected collusion, but "it would have been a painfully delicate thing to suggest to the Chinese Government, which was the virtual plaintiff,

---

17 *The China Merchants Steam Navigation Company v William Hunt*. The details of his case are from, M. Helmick, "Cases Before the Court", *Far Eastern Survey*, Vol. 14, No. 21 (Oct. 24, 1945), pp. 304-306.

that the United States Court for China would not hear its suit and action on moral grounds, and besides I had no evidence of collusion."

Helmick confessed to doing the "unusual thing of conferring with Consul-General C.E. Gauss about it." Gauss was not particularly shocked and suggested that the parties were entitled to bring some kind of test case. Helmick allowed the case to proceed and both parties produced their contracts which were dated in 1936 and 1937. It was suggested, of course, that they may have been backdated, but one of the contracts was also with Hong Kong & Shanghai Banking Corporation whose manager confirmed the date of the contracts. Helmick, in his judgment, held that Hunt was entitled to do what he wanted to enforce the contracts and refused the injunction. He doubted, however, "whether the decision did anyone much good." He did not make a finding that Hunt now owned the ships, nor did the decision get the State Department to offer Hunt extraterritorial protection. It did, as he wrote later, show the dates on the contracts were not backdated. The decision was later cited as a "worthy example of American judicial firmness in the face of the Japanese unilateral declaration."

Consul-General Clarence Gauss, unusually consulted by Judge Helmick on a legal question

Does Piper have to pay?

One case in the British Supreme Court related directly to the fighting between the Chinese and Japanese. Kenneth Piper had rented a large house at 21 Granada Estates on Hungjao Road (Hongqiao Road) intending to live there with his wife and two children aged seven and two. Hungjao Road was located outside the International Settlement boundaries but was treated as part of the Settlement by the Municipal Council because it was an extension of a road from the Settlement. Such niceties did not impress the Japanese and Chinese armies which fought pitched battles from August to December 1937 in the area. The area was sealed off with barricades and residents were refused access by the Settlement authorities. Houses owned by foreigners were not immune from attack. This was partly due to a Chinese anti-aircraft battery being located near to the Granada Estates attracting Japanese fighter planes trying to destroy it. On 14 October, one house at 140 Hungjao Road owned by a German, Mr Wilhelm Moller, and flying the German Swastika on its roof, was directly hit by a bomb.[18] Piper moved out of his house when the war started in August 1937. By February 1938 the fighting had died down, but the British Consul-General still warned that it was not safe for British subjects, particularly women and children, to live in the area. In June 1938 Granada Estates, the landlord, sued Piper for rent for February to May 1938. No claim was made for rent for November 1937 to January 1938.[19]

Piper was not a rich man; nor was he a poor man. He had done well for himself in life. He came from a modest family background in England. He had been a scholarship boy to the Blue Coat School in Horsham for indigent families. He came to Shanghai in the 1920s. His wife's father, Cecil Dawson, had served in the Chinese Customs for many years. In 1910, Dawson had been awarded the Imperial Order of the Double Dragon, Third Class and in 1915, the Order of the Excellent Crop.[20]

Piper was a senior Chartered Accountant in the Union In-

18 *Five Months of War*, p97, North China Daily News & Herald Ltd, 1938.

19 *Granada Estates v Piper, North China Herald*, June 1, 1938 (Mossop Law Reports).

20 Biographical details on Kenneth Piper from an email dated 27 June 2012, from his son, John Piper. John was my neighbour in Australia for more than 20 years. Dawson awards: *London Gazette*, September 27, 1910 and *Edinburgh Gazette*, April 23, 1915.

COMPARING NOTES

surance Society of Canton Office in Shanghai, located at No.5 the Bund. Piper enjoyed the life in Shanghai, going out to cabarets with his wife regularly. While he never became fabulously wealthy, he had a nice little cabin yacht which he sailed with the, reluctant, involvement of his son, John, in Pootung. His first house in Shanghai had been a small place in Verdun Gardens next to the French Club. He had then moved a little further down to 1273 Avenue Joffre (Huaihai Road) in a very nice neighbourhood. The house in Granada Estates was his next upgrade.

Piper defended the claim on the basis that the premises were unsafe to live in and that "occupation and or enjoyment of the premises has been and still is further prevented by the restriction of normal access to the Hungjao area, including the closing of all access by the Japanese authorities on various occasions, curfew regulations, lawless acts and looting, guerrilla fighting and lack of any normal policing or maintenance of order."

All good reasons, one would think, not to pay rent. But when the case came before Allan Mossop in the British Supreme Court, Mossop disagreed. English law had always given strong protection to landlords. Relying on a 300-year-old case from 1647, *Paradine v Jane*, Mossop held that even if a tenant was expelled by a trespasser, the tenant had to pay rent. Mossop did say that Piper may have a claim for loss of quiet enjoyment and stayed the judgment for one week to allow Piper to decide if he wished to bring a claim. It appears that he did not. Piper moved with his family to Amherst Avenue (Xinhua Road) in the International Settlement, near to where J.G. Ballard, author of *Empire of the Sun*, lived. His son, John Piper, recalls playing with J.G. Ballard as a child. John, who had been sent to a British boarding school in Tsingtao for safety's sake, says he never lived in the house in Granada Estates but does recall visiting the very large house where he saw "an army of gardeners weeding the lawns."

British spies for Japan?

The Sino-Japanese war also brought espionage cases before the British courts in China. In two cases, the Chinese government requested British citizens, Miss Kathleen Weston and Peter Prevot, be arrested and tried for spying on behalf of the Japanese against China.

Weston was accused of working with a German, Karl Rein, to gather information about Chinese troop movements. Weston and Rein had travelled from Canton to Hankow by car, leaving on May 8, 1938 and only arriving on 21 May, taking almost two weeks to complete a trip that should normally take three days. Upon their return to Canton, Rein and Weston were arrested by the Chinese police. Weston agreed to be detained at the British Consulate until evidence to support a charge could be brought. In the end, the Chinese authorities said they believed that Weston did not have knowledge of Rein's activities and allowed her to be released.[21]

Prevot was arrested by Chinese military police as he tried to leave Hankow by plane to Hong Kong, where he had been born. He had posted a letter addressed to himself in Hong Kong that discussed the relations between the Nationalists and the Communists; troop movements; and, the war between China and Japan. After interrogation by the Chinese police (which he had strongly objected to as a breach of his extraterritorial rights), he was taken to the British Consulate. The Chinese pushed for him to be prosecuted, but the Consul in Hankow could not find an offence to charge him with. He cabled Victor Priestwood, the Crown Advocate, for advice. Priestwood advised that a charge under Article 89(1)(a) of the Order in Council for committing acts likely to breach the peace would be appropriate. Prevot was charged and pleaded guilty. He was ordered to be deported to Hong Kong by plane, which he was.[22]

21 FO656/231 Report from British Consulate, Canton to British Ambassador, May 31, 1938.

22 FO 656/231 Correspondence and Newspaper clippings regarding the Prevot case, in

Tinkler, Failure, Solider, Spy - Hero

Spying was not the only activity that could get foreigners in trouble with the Japanese or Chinese authorities. In June 1939, the British in Shanghai and Tientsin were to find out exactly what was meant by the explanation given in British Parliament as to the Japanese position on extraterritoriality:

> "should any individual foreigners contrive to endanger the safety of the Japanese forces or to impede the conduct of their military operations, these forces will naturally take the necessary actions against them."

In Shanghai, it was one individual who would suffer; in Tientsin, it was the entire British community.

Former Inspector of the Shanghai Municipal Police, Richard Maurice Tinkler, was by 1939 a failure in life. He had resigned from the police force in 1930 after having been demoted back to be a sergeant in the uniformed division for various misconduct offences. He had drifted for the next nine years before washing up ashore on the Putong side of the Huangpu River as the Labour Superintendent of the China Printing and Finishing Company's Lun Chong Mill. The mill was owned by a British company and workers came over to the plant from the Shanghai side by boat. The land gates, which led on to Japanese-occupied territory, were locked. Tinkler stayed at the plant and kept detailed notes on Japanese ship movements which he passed on to the British consulate.[23]

The mill was facing serious communist agitation. As a result of a labour incident, Tinkler ended up in an altercation with Japanese troops. This brought him back into a British court in Shanghai for the last time, as a hero.

particular, report from Consul General in Hankow British Ambassador dated July 22, 1938.

23 For details of Tinkler's fall and resignation see R. Bickers, "*Empire Made Me*", pp191 to 197; for details of the labour agitation and his death, see pp277 to 288.

A dead hero, but nevertheless a hero.

And, Tinkler did, literally, appear in court. Following his death at the Shanghai General Hospital, Registrar Cyril Haines, as coroner, convened an inquest at the hospital to identify his body. Mr Robert Cowan, director of the China Printing and Finishing Co formally identified him. Haines then ordered an autopsy.

Earlier the previous day, Japanese troops had been called to the mill due to labour unrest. Tinkler had met them with a loaded revolver which he had waved around. He also fired one warning shot into the ground. His colleagues had tried to get him to go back indoors and to put the gun away. Tinkler had been a solider in World War I, and had killed many men. As a former soldier and policeman, he well knew that the only thing that can happen from challenging a superior force was that, at the very least, you would get a beating. He had certainly given out some beatings when he was in the police force.

The Japanese soldiers knocked the gun out of his hand. They then gave him his beating. Unfortunately, they did this with rifles to which bayonets had been fixed. Tinkler was bayonetted three times in the stomach. He was first treated by a Japanese naval surgeon at a Japanese military hospital, but when his condition worsened he was transferred late at night to the Shanghai General Hospital where he died after emergency surgery.

His death caused an uproar in the British community and the British Government ordered their Ambassador in Tokyo to take the matter up with the Japanese government.

A Japanese spokesman, explained that the Japanese military respected extraterritorial rights but in diplomatese conveyed the clear message: "Keep out of our way." He said:

"in any case of a person threatening the safety of the

Japanese forces in occupied territory it was only natural that his extraterritorial rights would be limited … It would not be a question of application to the law but of direct action necessary to maintain the safety of the Japanese Forces. It would be an act of law but a summary act."[24]

The spokesman continued that after investigations, a treaty foreigner would be handed over to his consular authorities.

The inquest into Tinkler's death reconvened on June 15, 1939 at the Police Court before Coroner Haines.[25] Mr John McNeill instructed by the China Printing and Finishing Co appeared on behalf of the company and Tinkler's next of kin. The hearing continued for five days with evidence from his colleagues who had been at the plant and the doctors at the General Hospital who had treated him. No Japanese came to give evidence at the inquest, despite being invited to.

Haines delivered his verdict on June 21. He made brief findings saying that the evidence disclosed "a most deplorable story" and that the "bayonetting of Tinkler after he has been disarmed" was "entirely unnecessary and unjustifiable." He criticized the Japanese Naval Surgeon for failing to appreciate the gravity of Tinkler's injuries.

He then gave his verdict. Almost 80 years previously when Charles Richardson had been killed by a Japanese samurai outside Yokohama, British gunboats had shelled and almost destroyed Kagoshima to obtain justice.

Times had changed.

The extraterritorial boot was now well and truly on the other foot. Haines could only find that Tinkler had died:

"as a result of injuries inflicted on him by persons not

24 "Mr RM Tinkler Dies", *North China Herald,* June 14, 1939, p454 at p455 col 2.

25 Inquest: *North China Herald,* June 21, 1939, p518 to 519; Verdict: *North China, Herald,* June 28, 1939, p562.

subject to the jurisdiction of this court."

He dared not even state that Tinkler had been killed by Japanese soldiers.

Produce the bodies

In Tientsin, things were getting far uglier between the British and Japanese than a dispute over the death of a labour supervisor. During the year, in both Tientsin and Amoy, the Japanese had blockaded the British Concessions to force the British to agree to hand over Chinese silver that had been stored in banks in the concessions. In Tientsin, the Japanese also demanded the right to supervise criminal trials against Chinese.

By June, things had heated up. Four Chinese who were suspected by the Japanese authorities in Tientsin of having assassinated, on April 9, 1939, Cheng Shi-kang, manager of Tientsin branch of the Federal Reserve Bank and Customs Commissioner. The Chinese suspects had fled to the British Settlement in Tientsin and were detained by the British at the Municipal Council gaol.

For the Japanese it was very important that they punish the alleged killers. The Japanese were intent on establishing Chinese-led governments in the areas they controlled. Cheng had come over to work for the Japanese puppet government in Tientsin. At the time Cheng was killed, the Japanese were assiduously pursuing Wang Ching-wei, the major rival to Chiang Kai-shek in the Nationalist Party to lead their reformed government. They had to do everything in their power to show Chinese they were wooing that they would be protected.[26]

The Japanese-controlled government of Tientsin made a request to the British authorities for the suspects to be handed

26 Lynn Pan describes the pursuit and agreement with Wang in "Old Shanghai: Gangsters in Paradise", Chapters 9 and 10.

Japanese troops blockade the British Concession in Tientsin

over for trial. Evidence was provided to show their complicity in the murder but the British did not think it sufficient. The Japanese became frustrated at the refusal of the British to hand over the suspects and in early June 1939 the Japanese consul at Tientsin demanded that the suspects be delivered to the Japanese authorities by June 6, 1939.[27] The demand concluded with the following words:

> "Failure to give a reply on June 6 would mean independent action."

The suspects were not handed over and the Japanese started to enforce a blockade of the British Concession as well as the French Concession which was next door to the British Concession. The Japanese stated that it was necessary to blockade the French Concession to ensure the British concession remained isolated.[28] The British and French concessions were completely surrounded. Barbed wire was put up in the streets around the concessions and electrical fences placed

27 *Argus*, Saturday June 3, 1939, p9.

28 *Illustrated London News*, 24 June 1939. There are also pictures of the blockade.

around the non-urban areas. Anti-British protests were stirred up and the Chinese servants of British in Tientsin were encouraged to leave their employers.

The matter was dealt with at the highest levels between the British and Japanese governments. The British Prime Minister even faced intense questioning over the affair in the House of Commons.[29]

A Dutch cartoon shows British Prime Minister Chamberlain in a Japanese headlock

By August, after receiving further evidence from the Japanese, the British authorities made a decision to hand the suspects over to the puppet authorities for trial. This was met with an immediate protest by the Nationalist government in Chungking that the suspects should only be handed over to Nationalist Chinese authorities.

Seeking to save the suspects, Professor Norman Bentwich, Professor of International Law at Jerusalem University and the former British Attorney General of Palestine, and Marjory Fry, a human rights campaigners based in London, instructed British barrister Hugh Reeks to make an urgent application to the British Supreme Court in Shanghai for a writ of *habeas corpus* to be issued against the British municipal gaol in Tientsin for the prisoners to be brought before a judge of the British Court. The writ of *habeas corpus* is an ancient writ designed

29 HC Deb 19 June 1939 vol 348 cc1794-8.

to prevent illegal detention. *Habeas corpus* means in English "produce the body." A person may apply to the court to seek an order that the person or persons detaining a person be required to bring the person before the court to decide if their decision is legal or not. A first hearing of the application came on before Allan Mossop on August 12, 1939. He ordered that the application be heard later in the week.[30]

By this time, the war in Europe had broken out and local newspapers were completely full of news of war in Europe and the German invasion of Poland.

Grant Jones heard the application. On August 17, 1939 he handed down a decision rejecting the writ. In his decision, he did not consider any of the political aspects of the case, but relied on case law that the person making the application must have some standing and that a "mere stranger or volunteer could not do so." He also said that there should have been an affidavit from the Chinese prisoners or someone with authority to act on their behalf. There was no such affidavit in this case. The applicants had relied on the case *Re Gooloo and Invokwana* where the British and Foreign Anti Slavery Society had been able to bring an application. Grant Jones noted that no similar society had made an application in China.[31]

Professor Bentwich and Ms Fry were, however, not going to give up so easily. They made an immediate application to the High Court in London for a writ of *habeas corpus* against Lord Halifax, the Foreign Secretary, the British Consul-General at Tientsin, the chairman of the British Municipal Council, and the gaoler of the municipal prison. This time the application was made on their behalves and, presumably to avoid the standing issue, on behalf of the "China Campaign Committee." Justice Cassels granted leave for the summons to issue and a full hearing was held a few days later with Sir Walter Monckton KC appearing for the applicants and the Solicitor-

30 *North China Herald*, August 13, 1939, p452.

31 *North China Herald*, August 23, 1939, p321.

General, Sir Terence O'Connor KC, for the Foreign Secretary. The Solicitor-General pointed out the absurdity of the idea of the four Chinese suspects being brought to London to determine the question of the legality of their detention saying:

> "The application for the production of these four men here is very little short of a fantasy ... I cannot say what percentage of the Home Fleet might be necessary to secure such production."

Cassels decided that, under Britain's treaties with China, the court had no power to make an order for *habeas corpus* when the suspects were not British citizens and had never resided in the British Settlement. They were being detained for the purposes of handing them over for trial in the Chinese District Court and this could not be considered illegal. He therefore dismissed the application.[32]

Bentwich and Fry would not give up, and on September 1 they made a new application to Grant Jones having obtained the authority of the Chinese suspects. Grant Jones ordered there be a full hearing on September 11. Unfortunately for the Chinese, they were handed over and executed before the final hearing could be held. The Japanese blockade was lifted.

Priestwood terminated

The pressures of being Crown Advocate in Japanese-occupied China also appeared to have got to Victor Priestwood. Soon after the Chinese suspects were executed, he was terminated. The Consul-General, Herbert Phillips, and other officials had felt uneasy for some time with Priestwood's performance, and particularly that he was prone to excessive drinking. Between April and June 1939 there was correspondence between the Shanghai Consulate, the British Embassy and the

32 *The Times*, August 22 and 23, 1939.

Foreign Office about what to do with him.[33]

Phillips, said that when he had first arrived in Shanghai in 1937 he had been asked to make a confidential report should Priestwood show signs of "alcoholic excess, but although at times I have had my suspicions no sufficient evidence has been forthcoming which would justify making an unfavourable report." He added that he did not consider Priestwood a satisfactory type and that he had "no particular reliance on his judgment." He complained that Priestwood had on several occasions become ill and remained "in his house incommunicado" for up to two weeks and would not respond to correspondence delaying "important public business." Phillips, perhaps most damningly, added he never saw Priestwood socially.

Phillips noted that if Priestwood lost the position of Crown Advocate he would lose the £900 per year he was paid as well as the "prestige of the post." He therefore suggested that Allan Mossop, as Judge of the Supreme Court, be consulted but added that "since I have been here, there have been no important cases in the Supreme Court and therefore the Judge does not see so much of the Crown Advocate's work as the Consul-General does."

Priestwood had been Mossop's assistant when Mossop was Crown Advocate. Mossop was not going to be part of the execution team. Phillips reported that Mossop "confessed that he had heard that from time to time Priestwood had bouts of drinking, but that never been sign of it in the court where his work was satisfactory." Mossop had no grounds to seek his dismissal. Mossop did tell Phillips that "socially speaking Priestwood had an inferiority complex which made him shun the usual parties."

The British Ambassador, Sir Archibald Clark Kerr, reported this to the Foreign Office who after discussions, in a typi-

33 For correspondence regarding Priestwood's termination see FO371/23523.

cal British ambush fashion, decided that "Priestwood being the drinker he apparently is, is bound to put his neck in the noose before long, whereupon we can pull it tight and we can dispose of him with a clear conscience." The Foreign Office gave instructions to Clark Kerr that "you, and particularly, Phillips, might therefore keep an eye open for his next lapse and utilize it as above."

The terms of Priestwood's contract were checked. It was found that he could be terminated on three months notice. On June 3, Clark Kerr telegraphed the Foreign Office that "there have been further difficulties with him and his delay in dealing with official correspondence is such that I feel his retention is not in the public interest." Clark Kerr recommended Priestwood be terminated. This was agreed to. Priestwood was then terminated on three months notice to avoid, in particular, "scandal at Shanghai which would ensue if he were terminated at once on disciplinary grounds or with three months salary in lieu of notice."

To be fair to Priestwood, the demands on the Crown Advocate had become very high. The Crown Advocate's Journal for the period 1934 to 1938 shows him dealing with all range for matters, including cases before the court; numerous questions from Indian money lenders as to the legality of their activities (not surprising given Grant Jones' attitude to them); extraterritoriality in Manchukuo; claims against the Japanese and Chinese governments for damage caused in the 1937 war; British nationality issues; questions from the British Shipping Office; numerous letters to and from the British Registrar of Companies; dealings with the Shanghai Defence Force; dealings with the Office of Works on issues regarding British government premises all around China; numerous delegations from the Sikh Gurdwara; and, leasing properties to British companies.[34]

34 FO 656/3 . The Journal sets out on a case by case basis the work done by the Crown Advocate.

The job had clearly outgrown the part time position and part time remuneration that was given. The position of Crown Advocate had also become far more administrative than courtroom based. The legal questions he faced with the Japanese occupation of China had never been faced by previous Crown Advocates. Priestwood may well have descended into bouts of depression and drinking. He may also have just had enough, but was not willing to deal with the loss of face, and loss of income, in quitting.

It was a bad time for Priestwood. Victor had truly become a loser. After losing his job, he lost his marriage. His wife, Gwen, who in a later letter to her mother referred to him as "old pie face," had decided to leave him. She moved to Hong Kong with her mother and instructed lawyers to prepare divorce papers.[35]

There was no farewell and no valedictory article in the newspapers for Priestwood. In late 1940, he slipped out off Shanghai, apparently unnoticed, for good, travelling to England via Canada. He arrived in England in early 1941 and joined the Royal Air Force on 28 February 1941 as a probationary pilot officer in the Administrative and Special Duties Branch.[36]

New Crown Advocate

The recommendation from all concerned was that John McNeill, who had acted as Crown Advocate in 1937 when Priestwood was on leave, was the best man to replace Priestwood. McNeill was appointed Acting Crown Advocate from September 23, 1939, when Priestwood's notice expired, and was formally appointed Crown Advocate on January 1, 1940.[37] McNeill, like Priestwood and Wilkinson before him, had

35 Divorce: Personal letter from Gwen Priestwood to her mother and sister, April 4, 1942. Thank you to Richard Wheeler, her nephew, for providing this letter to me.

36 Arrival in UK, Merchant Shipping Act Return for M/S Axel Johnson, January 18, 1941; RAF: *London Gazette*, 28 March 1941, pp1815 to 1816.

37 Biographical data on John McNeill: FO List, 1943, p255; *North China Herald*, September 27, 1939, p532; thepeerage.com, p6828; Inner Temple Admissions Database.

a father who had practiced before the court. John McNeill was the younger son of Duncan McNeill who was a barrister who practiced in Yokohama and then Shanghai for more than 30 years from the early 1890s to 1926. This included a period from 1901 to 1903 when he was Acting Crown Advocate when Harrie Wilkinson was on leave to avoid a conflict of interest while his father, H.S. Wilkinson, was Chief Justice. Duncan McNeil, it will be recalled, had been forced to apologise to Chief Justice Wilkinson after accusing him of making an unjust decision.[38]

The McNeills came from the ancient Highland family, the McNeills of Colonsay. One of their forebears Lord Colonsay had been Lord Advocate of Scotland. John McNeill was educated at Charterhouse and Trinity College, Oxford where he studied Classics and took an honours degree in Litterae Humaniores (Greats). He also gained a half blue for fencing. During WWI he signed up to join the army despite not having finished his studies and in December 1917 he joined the Guards Brigade. In the spring of 1918 he obtained a commission in the Royal Highlanders, Black Watch, and served in France and Germany with the first Battalion.

After demobilisation he returned to Oxford and in 1923 was called to the bar of the Inner Temple and then practiced in London. In 1926, just as his father was leaving, he moved to Shanghai where he joined a local law firm, Hansons. He served on a number of Committees of the Municipal Council, including the Health Committee, Band and Orchestra Committee and various Hospital Committees. He was joint editor, with Dr Wei Wen-han, of an English translation of the Chinese Code of Maritime Law.

McNeill took over as Crown Advocate at a time when things were going to get even tougher than they had been for Victor Priestwood.

38 See Chapter 30.

Chapter 59

Live by the Gunboat...

THE LAST TWO YEARS of the effective exercise of extraterritorial rights in China by Britain and the United States were a very difficult time in China. War had broken out in Europe at the end of 1939. It was clear that war between Japan and the Western powers was coming to China sometime soon. The foreign settlements saw an exodus of foreign residents. John McNeill's wife and daughter had already left Shanghai during the war in 1937 and Allan Mossop's wife also appears to have left.

In Shanghai, this exodus had an immediate effect on the Municipal Council's revenues, the finances of which were also being stretched by retirements by officials keen to cash out their superannuation while they could. The Council started trying to collect rates from Chinese residents who continued to hold land in the settlements under fangtan title deeds. Approximately one-fifth of the land in the International Settlement was owned under such deeds. Mr Justice Feetham when he had prepared his report on extraterritoriality had expressed surprise that Chinese owners were not taxed by the Council. When the Council tried to tax them, Chinese landholders brought a suit against it in the Court of Consuls to determine whether owners of land under fangtan title deeds could be taxed. The Council was also forced to levy a 40% surcharge on rates with effect from 1 January 1940. This upset the Japanese residents in particular and at a special meeting convened to pass the resolution W. J. Keswick, the Chairman of the Council was shot and wounded by a Japanese, Mr Y. Hayashi.[1]

Despite all this, the British and American courts continued to function handling many dark cases that came about from living in the shadow of impending war. The war meant that the British Supreme Court for China could not celebrate its 75th Anniversary in September 1940.[2]

Soldiering on

Perhaps the people with the most difficult job in Shanghai during this time were soldiers in the British and American military forces stationed in Shanghai, purportedly to defend the International Settlement. This must have been a soul-destroying post. Even though the Japanese had relaxed some of the pressure they had put on in 1937 and the situation was less tense than it had been then, the only enemy the British and American soldiers could possibly be fighting was the Japanese. It was clear that they were outgunned and outmanned. What made matters worse is that they did not even have a defensive line. The Japanese were just as entitled to enter the International Settlement as the British and Americans. Fully armed Japanese troops regularly passed by British and American soldiers on guard duty.

This pressure led to a number of tragedies. On November 4, 1939, Private David Eckford of the Seaforth Highlanders was on sentry duty in blockhouse E at the corner of North Thibet Road (Xizang North Road) and Kaifeng Road just north of Soochow Creek. North Thibet Road was on the edge of the International Settlement. Eckford was on duty with Lance Corporal Davis and three other privates. Eckford had drunk about six bottles of beer and was drunk. Davis told

1 The fangtan case went on for a long time. See *Fang Chiao-Ho, Hu Tsing-Pang, Fang Ven-Tuck, and Tse Zay-Tsing v S.MC., North China Herald,* March 12, 1941, p419 for one hearing. "Japanese Shoots W.J. Keswick", North China Herald, January 29, 1941, p166.

2 The North China Daily News did on 4 September 1940, p3 publish an article commemorating the 75th Anniversary. John McNeill was quoted saying there would be no celebration due to the war.

Eckford he was placing him on report for being drunk on duty. Soon after this Eckford shot Davis. Eckford admitted that Davis had been killed by a shot from a gun that he was holding but denied that he had intended to kill Davis. He said that he merely intended to scare him. The British Army could have court martialled Eckford, but instead chose to hand him over to the Supreme Court for trial.[3]

The case was the first case to be prosecuted by John McNeill after his formal appointment as Crown Advocate. Mossop tried the case with a jury of 12.[4] Eckford pleaded not guilty. Despite Eckford's admission that the fatal shot had come from his gun, the case lasted for three days. McNeill called more than 10 witnesses including the other privates who were in the blockhouse at the time of the shooting. The evidence from those who were there was all to the effect that Eckford had immediately admitted to shooting Davis and had, in fact, been the one to turn himself in by calling headquarters. Eckford then gave evidence that he had drunk about six bottles of beer that day while on duty. Davis had asked him if he was drunk and if he had any more beer with him. Eckford had told him that he had one more bottle and Davis had told him to "go get it." The other privates on duty also said they heard Davis tell Eckford to "go get it."

McNeill alleged that it was more likely Davis had told Eckford he was putting him on report and told him to get his rifle so he could be sent to headquarters. Eckford then said that he got his rifle, put a bullet in the chamber making sure that Davis could see him do this, and then pointed it at Davis with the intention of "giving him a fright because he had been bullying me." He then said, "I'm going to shoot you dagger."

3 *R v Eckford*, *North China Herald*, January 17, 1940, p102 (trial) and North China Herald March 6, 1940, p385 (appeal); for Eckford's reprieve *Singapore Free Press and Mercantile Advertiser*, April 3, 1940, p1. Eckford's Home Office file (HO 144/23208) held at the National Archives is closed until January 1, 2023.

4 The jury members were A.G. Davies, F.F. Sullivan, R.H. Box, G.T. Gambling, G.A. Morris, J. Watson, R.V. Thomas, H. Stephenson, R.B. Moller, P.R.M. Wallis, N. Boniface and P.J. MacKellar.

The gun discharged, killing Davis.

Mr K. E. Newman, defending Eckford, was left with a very difficult case to put to the jury. He only had the desperate plea that "if Eckford's story had not been true, he could have made up an endless number of infinitely better stories." He asked the jury to believe Eckford. The jury did not. They returned a verdict of guilty of murder but with a recommendation for mercy. Mossop then, for the last time, in the British Supreme Court for China, passed a sentence of death.

Eckford appealed. The appeal was heard six weeks later in late February before the Chief Justice of Hong Kong, Atholl MacGregor, Mossop and Grant Jones. The key argument on Eckford's behalf was that in the summing up, Mossop had misdirected the jury on the burden of proof as to Eckford's intention. This was soundly rejected by the Full Court. Eckford then applied to the Chinese Ambassador, Sir Archibald Clark Kerr, for a reprieve. Hundreds of British and American residents signed a petition supporting a reprieve, citing his youth, his good record and "the abnormal service conditions under which British soldiers in the northern defence sector, especially in war time, have to work."[5] His sentence was commuted to life imprisonment with hard labour. He was sent to England to be imprisoned.

The Seaforth Highlanders was certainly not such a happy place because between Eckford's conviction and appeal another private, Private Roy, killed himself with an officer's gun. Registrar Haines, sitting as coroner, held an inquest and determined that the killing was suicide and not accidental.[6]

The last British troops were pulled out of Shanghai towards the end of 1940. The British government knew that it was impossible to defend Shanghai against the Japanese and that the Settlement was only allowed to survive because the Japanese were not yet ready for war with the Western powers.

5 *Singapore Free Press and Mercantile Advertiser*, March 16, 1940 p3

6 *Inquest on David Roy*, North China Herald, February 21, 1940, p303

Marine kills baby

US Marines, however, remained until almost the end of 1941, bringing a very sad case before Milton Helmick in the US Court. Private Gerald Casement was charged with the murder of his stepson, Floyd "Skipper" Sebastian. Casement, who was from Nebraska, was only 22 at the time. He had studied at high school for one year and joined the marines at 17 or 18. He had already served in North China and recently been transferred to Shanghai. Against regulations, he had married in Shanghai. Skipper had been born some time earlier to another man. Casement was normally required to live on base, but when he got leave he would return home to the one-room apartment he shared with his wife and Skipper. They had a Chinese maid who stayed overnight if necessary.[7]

Casement was given liberty on March 12, 1941 at 1.45pm. He first went on a drinking spree with his buddy, Homer Triplet. They had three or four bottles of beer at the Marine Club and then went to "Spud Johns" around 6.25pm. A Russian waitress, Miss Dulepova, gave evidence that they were both drunk and stayed until 9.00pm. The Chinese Amah said that Casement came home drunk that evening. "Missie" was in hospital, but Casement told the amah she could stay and sleep on the floor if she wanted. She went home, planning to come back in the morning.

The next thing anyone saw of Casement was when the watchman of the compound where they lived saw a marine leaving the compound on Seymour Road (Shaanxi North Road) before sunrise with a package under his arm. The watchman saw him entering the Jewish School Compound (now part of the City Education Bureau Compound) where another watchman also saw him. A bundle was later found in the compound with the badly beaten body of Skipper wrapped in it. The amah came in at 7am and found both

7 *United States v Casement*, North China Herald, April 9, 1941, p66.

Skipper and Casement missing. On the orders of Missie, she reported the baby missing to the police. The police showed her a photograph of the body that had been found and she confirmed it was Skipper. Casement was arrested at the marine barracks and blood-covered clothing recovered from his room.

After a coronial inquest, Casement was arraigned on a charge of first-degree murder. At the beginning of the hearing, Casement told Helmick he had no money for a lawyer. Mr H.G. Nelson was appointed to act for him. Skipper had been killed in what could only be described as an act of sheer brutality. Dr Dana Nance gave evidence at the inquest that Skipper was a healthy and sound child who had died most likely by suffocation. He said Skipper had been killed about two hours after his last meal and had been badly beaten:

> "There were numerous signs of external wounds on the body, including bruising of both cheeks, especially the left one, abrasions on the side of the forehead, laceration on both lips, with blood stains on them as well as around the nostrils and gums, bruising of the right thigh as it had been gripped roughly, scratches on both knees and injuries to the private parts. Dirt or brick dust was ground into the skin in the forehead."

Casement, when faced with the damning evidence of the watchmen and the doctor, had no choice but to give evidence. He fell back on the defence of all scoundrels: "I don't remember." He claimed: "I thought of the child as my own. I never beat him." He also tried to shift the time he got home to later in the evening, so that it could not have been him who killed the baby. He explained that he had woken up and found Skipper dead in bed next to him. He did not admit that he had hidden the baby. Mrs Casement, as was her right as a spouse, refused to give any evidence.

No motive was offered for the killing, a point Mr Nelson was to make in his closing speech, but perhaps unspoken in the court was the suggestion that Casement had killed the baby in a fit of jealous rage when he found himself home alone with the child of his wife's former lover. The frustrations of being a soldier in a city everyone conceded could not be defended must have contributed to his anger. Nelson also claimed that Casement's alibi was good and that "the Amah knows more about the crime than we do, she knows more than she told."

The District Attorney, Leighton Shields, summed up saying the case against Casement was damning and concluded that the only thing to do with Casement was to "send him to the chair."

Helmick adjourned the trial until the next day. The next morning, before a packed courtroom in a very short judgment, Helmick convicted Casement of second-degree murder and sentenced him to imprisonment for the term of his natural life on McNeil Island.

The sad case of Mr Turner and Mr Kau

In the last unlawful killing case to come before the British Supreme Court, Mr E.C. Turner was prosecuted for the accidental killing of Kau Kwang-sung, a coolie working at his house. By 1941, western Shanghai faced a serious law and order crisis. The overlapping jurisdictions of the SMP, Chinese police and Japanese police made proper policing almost impossible. In 1940, an agreement had been reached to improve policing, but still with the ever-declining economy and war ravaging China, crime was at an all-time high. Mr Turner lived at 377 Haiphong Road (Haifang Road). He had lived in Shanghai most of his adult life and had been senior architect with the Shanghai Municipal Council for 22 years from 1904 to 1926 when he had retired. He had designed the new council headquarters on Foochow Road. By May 1941, his house was being regularly robbed by thieves. In response, Turner set up .22 calibre rifles as booby traps in his garden to keep away marauders. On May 18, Kau Kwang-sung, a grass cutter's coolie working at his property was shot and killed by one of the booby traps. Turner was arrested and committed for trial before Grant Jones in July 1941. Turner pleaded guilty to unlawfully killing Kau. Mr Jones appearing for Turner then spent close to a day pleading for a light sentence. He told Grant Jones that Turner had already paid $1,500 for Kau's burial and to buy his eldest son a larger plot of land so he could provide for the family. A trust fund had also been set up for the family and in total $7,000 had been paid.[8]

Jones, in his speech, said many residents in Shanghai faced the same problem Turner had and wondered what they could do to protect themselves. Grant Jones in response read out the Offences Against the Person Act which provided that "spring guns, man traps or other engines" could be placed to protect dwelling-houses between sunset and sunrise, but not during the daytime.

Jones closed his mitigation by saying that Turner was in the "autumn of his life" and "was a man who had been in retirement for 15 or 16 years and who had occupied himself with gardening and music – that is not the stuff that a criminal is made of."

All very true, but Turner had caused the death of a man. Grant Jones taking into account all the factors, including his plea of guilty; the compensation paid; that Turner's house had been "infested by a plague of thieves;" and, his unblemished record, sentenced Turner to four months imprisonment. Not a long sentence, but still the British courts had moved on from the days when Captain Drake was sentenced to three months imprisonment for the manslaughter of 23 Japanese.

8 *R v Turner*, *North China Herald*, July 16, 1941, p189.

One final scandal for the US Court

Having started life with a number of scandals, it is perhaps fitting that the life of the United States Court for China ended with a scandal. Mr Sam Titlebaum, the deputy Marshal of the court was charged with a number of counts of embezzlement in August 1941.[9] Titlebaum, who was 32, had only been appointed Deputy Marshal at the beginning of 1941. He was a close friend of the Marshal, Mr Charles Richardson Jr, who had recommended him for the job. He had previously worked as an announcer and radio commentator on a local radio station. As Deputy Marshal, he had gained some local fame when, together with Inspector Crighton of the SMP, he had arrested Jack Riley, Shanghai's "slot machine king," on charges of illegal gaming. Riley had been avoiding arrest and for good reason. He was in fact "Fahnie Albert Becker" and had escaped from prison in the US 16 years earlier where he had been serving a 25-year sentence for armed robbery. He had literally run away from prison while chasing a fly ball during a prison baseball game and just kept on going - all the way to Shanghai. After his arrest in Shanghai, Riley had forfeited his bail of $25,000 and had to be tracked down. At his trial, Riley was sentenced to 18 months imprisonment at McNeil Island despite a request to go to Ward Road Gaol.[10] Presumably, he hoped that if he was not

9 *United States v Sam Tittlebaum*, Nos 1 and 2, *North China Herald*, September 3, 1941, p385, September 10, 1941, October 15, 1941, p104. See also *North China Herald* of August 14, 1941, p287 for a statement by the US District Attorney.

10 *United States v Riley*, *North China Herald*, April 9, 1941, p66; *Miami Daily News Record*, March 28, 1941, p6 re Riley's escape in America. See also F. Wakeman, *The Shanghai Badlands: Wartime Terrorism and Urban Crime, 1937-1941*, p106 for more on the life of Riley.

sent back to the United States he could avoid going back to prison for his armed robbery conviction.

Titlebaum was accused of 12 counts of embezzlement, including taking six .38 Colt revolvers and 1,500 rounds of .38 pistol ammunition. He had been caught because he sold two of the guns to a Chinese policeman who immediately tried to register them in the International Settlement. His arrest caused an immediate problem for Leighton Shields, the District Attorney, who was left with only one female Marshal in his office.

What, in the past would have been an even bigger problem was that there was no judge available to try the case. Helmick was in the United States on leave. This was no longer an issue. An amendment to the act creating the court had finally been passed in 1935 allowing for special judges to be appointed. On August 25, by telegraph, President Roosevelt appointed the US Commissioner, Nelson Lurton, to be a Special Judge of the Court, a position Lurton had also held in 1938.[11]

Titlebaum was brought before Lurton three days later. He pleaded not guilty to the charges. Inspector Crighton was in charge of his case and had brought Tittlebaum to court from Ward Road Gaol. After the hearing, Crighton gave him a cigarette before taking him back to the gaol. A horde of cameramen were waiting for him outside the court. The *North China Herald* reported that at the hearing, mention had been made of "two undisclosed counts which were expected to be of a sensational nature." And indeed they were. Tittlebaum was most likely not even "Sam Titlebaum." He had tricked a friend, Mr Eric Shekury, into placing his fingerprints on the fingerprint card needed for the application form on the pretence that he could get Shekury the job. He had also concealed he had a seven inch scar on his body, apparently from a gunshot, and that one leg was shorter than the other. He was charged with

11 S.197b was added to the Act. For Lurton's appointment, see: *North China Herald*, August 27, 1941, p335.

two further counts of concealing his identity, to which he also pleaded not guilty.

Titlebaum was convicted on all counts by Lurton. Lurton did have to deal with one question. Was Titlebaum American? There was no evidence of who he was. Lurton could have relied upon the Ninth Circuit decision in the Husar case, that by virtue of his position as a Marshal, Titlebaum was subject to the jurisdiction of the court. However, Lurton just said simply that he was "satisfied that Titlebaum was an American citizen within the court's jurisdiction." Lurton then gave Tittlebaum a tongue lashing:

> "You are responsible for these things which are not in accordance to law and order which an American should uphold here, in China. We are not at Home, we are guests here by courtesy of Congress and the Chinese Treaties which are sacred. You have brought shame upon yourself and imposed on the dignity of your country, betrayed men who have recommended you and heaped humiliation on yourself."

He sentenced Titlebaum to two years imprisonment on all of the embezzlement counts and one of the false identity counts and five years on one of the false identity counts, all to be served concurrently at McNeil Island.

A lucky embezzler

One British embezzler, Patrick MacKellar, was to be slightly luckier than Tittlebaum. The last appeal ever before the Full Court of the British Supreme Court for China was heard in August 1941. By this time, the threat of war in the Pacific loomed over Shanghai. America had imposed sanctions on Japan over its occupation of China and incursions into Indochina. Local newspapers were full of articles about the breakdown in relations between the US and Japan. By mid-1941, the British Prime Minister, Winston Churchill, announced that if Japan went to war against the United States, then Britain would join the war "within an hour."[12]

MacKellar had worked for American Express since 1935, starting out as a stenographer. He had been promoted to be a travel clerk in 1937 and was a trusted employee. However, by 1940 he was suspected of embezzlement for pocketing some of the money clients had paid to him for travel bookings. His supervisor, Mr Riggs, had confronted him and MacKellar had confessed immediately saying: "What is there to say? The whole thing has been preying on my mind and the fear of exposure has kept me from sleeping for weeks." MacKellar was tried before Grant Jones and a jury of five in late December 1940. John McNeill prosecuted and Hugh Reeks defended. It was not the first time that MacKellar had been inside the Supreme Court court room; nor for him to see John McNeill prosecute a case. MacKellar had been a member of the jury in the Eckford murder prosecution. This time, however, it was MacKellar who was being judged by his peers.[13]

The only real defence MacKellar could offer was that it was a conspiracy amongst the other employees to set him up. The jury took an hour to return a verdict of guilty. Grant Jones sentenced him to five years hard labour saying in true Grant Jones fashion: "Embezzlement is a particularly despicable crime for it involves the betrayal of a fiduciary relationship," and adding "there may have been temptations in the conduct of the American Express Company but temptation is no excuse."

MacKellar appealed against his conviction and the sen-

12 "An Attempt to Intimidate Japan Seen", *North China Herald*, November, 19, 1941, p272.

13 *R v MacKellar*, *North China Herald*, January 1, 1941 p25 and January 8, 1941, p63 (trial); August 13, 1941, p306 (appeal). The English appeal case cited by the judges to reduce the sentence is *Hervey v Goodwin* 27 C.A.R. 146. The members of the jury were T. Brennen, W.T. Cromby, E. Noakes, S.A. Judah and F.C. Mallett.

tence of five years. However, before the Full Court he only maintained his appeal against conviction. The appeal was heard by Chief Justice Atholl MacGregor of Hong Kong, Mossop and Grant Jones in August 1941. In their decision, the Full Court quickly disposed of the appeal against conviction holding that the conviction was safe. But in an extremely rare move, the court decided to review MacKellar's sentence even though he had not provided any grounds for doing so. British appellate courts normally do not do this. If a prisoner has chosen not to appeal against sentence, that is their choice. The court will not interfere. However, citing a recent case where the English Court of Appeal had allowed an appeal against two out of four convictions and then reduced the total sentence imposed, the judges held they did have the power to review the sentence. They said that it was unusual to send a first offender to jail and reduced MacKellar's sentence to 18 months.

Atholl MacGregor, CJ of Hong Kong, presided over the last appeal hearing in Shanghai.

Grant Jones did not write a separate opinion or dissent from this despite having been the sentencing judge. The only explanation for this unheard-of generosity must be that the judges could clearly see that war was coming, Shanghai would be occupied by the Japanese, and they did not want to leave MacKellar in prison under Japanese occupation.

MacGregor wrote the last-ever entry in the Judge's Note Book for appeal cases which read:

"Appeal dismissed, conviction on each charge confirmed, sentence reduced to one of 18 months imprisonment with hard labour in each charge, to run concurrently and from date of conviction.

[Signed]
ADA MacGregor CJ
5.8.41"[14]

Out with a bang

It was clear to everyone that war was coming soon, it was just a question of when. The weather in October 1941 was as absolutely glorious as Shanghai weather can be in autumn, so much so that Sapajou drew a cartoon headlined "The Golden Autumn." The cartoon lamented that all the wonders of autumn trips to the mountains or lakes could not be enjoyed because the city was surrounded by barbed wire.[15]

In mid-November 1941, President Roosevelt ordered all remaining US Marines, 750 in Shanghai, 165 in Peiping and 55 in Tientsin to leave China. Roosevelt could see war was coming and stated the reason for the order was because the garrison "offered protection to comparatively few Americans." Seeking to avoid war, the Japanese had arranged for a special envoy, Saburo Kusuru, to fly to Washington for talks.[16] Due to this, American lawyer, Norwood Allman, arranged a business trip to Hong Kong saying he was "lulled into a temporary sense of security by the knowledge that Japan's special peace ambassador, Kusuru, was already on route to Washington." He thought that he would have time to get back to Shanghai before war started.[17]

14 FO 1092/337 "Hong Kong Judge" Full court Note Book 9th Dec 1933 to [blank]; UK National Archives, p54-63. In this note book were notes of 19 cases on appeal from 1933 to 1941.

15 Sapajou Cartoon: North China Daily News, October 10, 1941.

16 "President Roosevelt Orders All Marines to Leave China", *North China Herald*, November 19, 1941, p274.

17 N. Allman, "*Shanghai Lawyer*", p260.

The Golden Autumn

Mossop, on December 1, 1941, seeing that war with Japan was approaching fast cabled the British Ambassador at Chungking saying that in the event of war, he and Grant Jones would both be "incapacitated" and that an Assistant Judge should be appointed to fill their place.[18]

The courts kept on functioning until the last. The last full reports of cases before the British and American courts in China were carried in the *North China Herald* of Wednes-

18 FO369/2719 Mossop, Report Relating to His Britannic Majesty's Supreme Court in Japanese Occupied China, dated September 24, 1942.

US-Japan tensions mount in November 1941

day, December 3, 1941. The largest case was a probate action over Liza Hardoon's estate. She had died during the previous year and, not surprisingly, a number of her and her husband's relatives were again fighting over her fortune. Mossop adjourned the case and it was never to be heard again in a British Court.[19] Grant Jones heard a case where a Russian, Mr Kobeneff sued the Cathay Laundry for losing a coat. The laundry relied on a limitation of liability clause. Kobeneff said he could not read English so the laundry could not rely on the clause. Grant Jones found for the laundry.[20] Grant Jones, true to form, dismissed a judgment summons brought by Kagar Singh against Basant Singh because Kagar could not prove that Basant had the means to pay.[21] He also made a decree absolute for a divorce between Mr and Mrs Smoleff.[22] In the United States Court, Helmick, who had returned from leave a few weeks before, granted Mr and Mrs Condon a *decree nisi* for their divorce.[23] He also granted Mrs Sadie Wilholt a divorce *decree nisi* by default against her husband, Mr Harry Wilholt.[24]

The Judges' notebooks record one of the very last criminal cases in the British Supreme Court as the prosecution of Charles Percival Archer, a former member of the Shanghai Municipal Police, for false pretences. Archer was accused of passing bad cheques in a number of shops in August 1941. He had then left Shanghai but had been arrested when he arrived back in town on a steamer from Singapore in November. He was convicted on December 2, 1941 and sentenced to six months imprisonment.[25]

Norwood Allman had been wrong that he would have time to get back to Shanghai. Mossop had been right that he and Grant Jones may soon be incapacitated. On Monday, December 8, 1941 (Japan and China time), Japan declared war on

19 *Probate Proceedings in the Matter of the Will of the late Mrs Liza Hardoon, North China Herald*, December 3, 1941.

20 *J Kobeneff v Cathay Laundry Ltd, North China Herald*, December 3, 1941, p363.

21 *Kagar Singh v Basant Singh, North China Herald*, December 3, 1941, p363.

22 *Smoleff v Smoleff, North China Herald*, December 3, 1941, p363.

23 *T.C. Condon v S.N. Condon, North China Herald*, December 3, 1941, p363.

24 *Mrs S. M. Wilholt v H Wilholt, North China Herald*, December 3, 1941, p363.

25 *R v Archer*, Judge's Notebook; *R v Archer, North China Herald*, November 19, 1941, p291 for committal proceedings.

Britain and the United States. By this time, Britain and America had only two navy ships in Shanghai. The HMS *Peterel,* a former Yangtze River gunboat, was moored off the Bund near the consulate and was being used as a communication station. Its larger guns had been removed and it only had machine guns on board. The USS *Wake,* also a Yangtze River gunboat, was tied up at a pier. The ship was also being kept in Shanghai to also act as a communications station. Most of its crew had been ordered to the Philippines 10 days before and it had only a skeleton crew of 14.

In the early morning of December 8, a Japanese navy party from the Japanese battleship HIJMS *Idzumo* boarded the HMS *Peterel* under a flag of truce and demanded its surrender. Her commander, Lieutenant Polkinghorn, even though completely outgunned, in the best British tradition of not going down without a fight, refused and ordered the party to "get off my bloody ship." Having boarded under a flag of truce, in accordance with the rules of war, the party left. Approximately 15 minutes later, the *Idzumo* opened fire with its powerful guns assisted by artillery from the Bund. The *Peterel* returned fire with its Lewis machine guns. After a short fight, the *Peterel* was sunk with the loss of six sailors. Many other sailors were saved by Chinese sampans that came to the rescue.[26]

The USS *Wake* had been rigged with explosives to be scuttled in the event of war but was captured without a fight. The Japanese navy party that went on board to demand surrender found that the Captain was onshore and the ship surrendered. While in the circumstances, discretion was probably the better part of valour, one has to admire Polkinghorn's British pluck. The USS *Wake* became the only United States warship captured during the entire war.[27]

---

26 G. Leck Gregory, *Captives of Empire.*

27 Dictionary of American Naval Fighting Ships: http://www.history.navy.mil/danfs/w1/wake.htm and http://www.combinedfleet.com/tatara_t.htm. She was given by the Japanese to the puppet Chinese government and recaptured by the Americans at the end of the war. She was then given to the Nationalist government and subsequently

With this warning of the commencement of hostilities, the staff at the British Consulate and Supreme Court commenced destruction of confidential materials. At 10 o'clock that morning, the British Consulate received a phone call from the Japanese Navy stating that the operations of the Consulate and Court were to be suspended, and at 11 o'clock in the morning the premises were occupied.[28]

Mossop, in a report to the Secretary of State for Foreign Affairs detailing the Japanese take over the court, wrote:

> "The exercise of His Britannic Majesty's Supreme Court for China of its jurisdiction under the China Orders in Council was effectively interrupted, in that area of China falling under Japanese occupation, at 11am on December 8, 1941. At that hour armed forces of the Imperial Japanese Navy, accompanied by members of the Japanese Consular Service, entered and took possession of the Consular Compound and premises of the Court at Shanghai, posted sentries, cut-off all telephones, and sealed up all safes, cupboards and rooms."

The US Consul in Shanghai, Mr Edwin Stanton, reported to the State Department:

> "I have received a formal communication dated today (Dec 8) from the Japanese Consul General reading as follows: 'I have the honour to inform you that I have been instructed by His Imperial Japanese Majesty's Government to request you that the function of the American Consulate General at Shanghai will be henceforth suspended and that the office of the American

captured by the Communists who finally decommissioned her in the 1960s.

28 Details of occupation of the British Consulate are from Mossop, Report Relating to His Britannic Majesty's Supreme Court in Japanese Occupied China, dated September 24, 1942, FO369/2719 for the US Consulate, see: "US Officials kept in Hotel", *New York Times*, December 9, 1941.

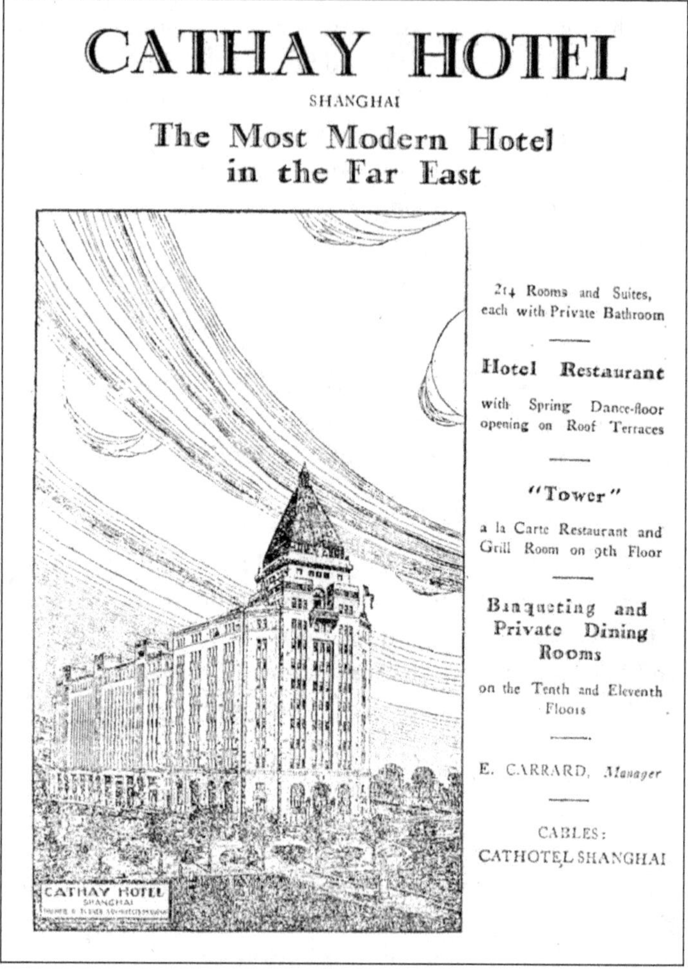

The Cathay Hotel (now the Peace Hotel). One of Shanghai's luxury hotels where Judge Mossop and others were interned.

Consulate General be closed as from today. All the officers of the American Consulate General will be treated in accordance with international law and the principle of reciprocity.'"

Stanton said that the US Consulate General was closed up at 1pm and sealed by the Japanese authorities.

The judges and the other staff of the courts were interned at the Cathay Hotel (for the British), the Metropole Hotel (for the Americans) or their homes. Both hotels were top hotels in the city at the time and internship in them cannot have been too much of a hardship.

Following negotiations with the Japanese, an exchange of consular officials was agreed. In the case of Britain, it was easier to secure the agreement for return of the judges and court staff because they were Foreign Office employees and, hence, entitled to diplomatic protection. The US Court had been under the Justice Department since 1934, so technically they were not diplomats. The US in their negotiations therefore specifically identified the officials of the US Court as being part of the transfer agreement. In the end, the Americans were able to reach an agreement with Japan that all their nationals interned in Hong Kong and a large number of their nationals in Japan and China could be repatriated.

The British officials were taken aboard a Japanese boat, *Kamakura Maru*, to Lorenco Marques (now Maputo) in Mozambique, then a Portuguese colony and neutral territory. They travelled from there to Cape Town in South Africa, and then on to England aboard the P&O ship, the SS *Narkunda*.[29]

The Americans were also evacuated to Lorenco Marques where they were transferred to a Swedish ship, the *Gripsholm*. The *Gripsholm* arrived in New York in late August 1942 with over 1,500 diplomatic and consular staff from China and Japan. Judge Helmick took charge of keeping morale up. Just before the ship arrived in New York, he organized a party for all those who had been interned in China and somehow managed to collect baseball caps and jockstraps all adorned with the Chinese characters for the prisons that they had been

29 *The Times*, September 2, 1942 re sailing on the *Kamakura Maru*; Mossop's report re sailing on the SS *Narkunda*.

interned in.[30]

In April 1942, the British court and its premises were passed to the control of the Swiss Consul-General at Shanghai. On May 5, 1942, the Court seals (including an old seal for the Supreme Court for China and Corea) were handed by Registrar Haines to the Swiss Consulate General.

Mossop reported that on December 8, 1941, eight civil cases, 26 divorce cases and 24 probate cases were pending in the British Supreme Court. There were no criminal cases pending. One civil case was pending in Canton and two were pending in Tientsin. In addition, there were eight prisoners in Ward Road Gaol at the outbreak of hostilities. They were:

Aser Khan (Indian male) – Manslaughter
Chainchal Singh (Indian male) – Buggery
Dalip Singh (Indian male) – Murder
Bishan Singh (Indian male) – Murder
Patrick John MacKellar (European male) - Embezzlement
Charles Anthony Cameron (Eurasian male) – Robbery with violence
Stanley Grant Skinner (European male) – Forgery
Charles Percival Archer (European male) – False pretences

All of these prisoners, other than Dalip Singh and Bishan Singh who had been convicted of murder, received "Get Out of Jail" cards from Mossop. Mossop had obtained advance permission from the British Ambassador to cut their sentences if hostilities broke out. On the morning of December 8, 1941, Mossop signed orders to allow them to be freed and they were released some days later. While this got them out

30 "Gripsholm brings 1,500 from the Orient", *New York Times*, August 26, 1942; N. Allman, *Shanghai Lawyer*, p20. Allman writes of taking the Gripsholm from Lorenco Marques. He had arrived from Hong Kong on board the *Asama*. His wife had arrived from Shanghai on the Italian ship, the *Conte Verde*. Re Helmick: J. Sherwood, *Fond Memories of a Young Man in Old China*, p276. Sherwood also recounts the strict interrogation and searches given to all non-diplomats who returned on the ship.

of jail, whether that made them free, in Japanese-occupied Shanghai, is another question.

In accordance with Mossop's recommendation, the Vice-Consul in Kunming, Yunnan, which remained outside Japanese control throughout the war, was appointed an Acting Assistant Judge of the Court.[31] There appears to have been little work for the court in Yunnan - any civil cases that were brought were settled quickly. Attempts were made to recruit a Registrar, and a Mr Wilson formerly Registrar of the High Court of Tanganyika was interviewed by the Foreign Office to go out to Yunnan. He was said to be so patriotic "as to suggest that he might be sent to Malta or some other place where he would be bombed."[32]

Wilson was not to get a chance to be bombed; the attempts to recruit a Registrar were abandoned when negotiations with the Japanese moved forward to allow the release of the court staff so that, if necessary, Registrar Haines could be sent to Kunming.[33] Mr Beckett wrote to Wilson to give him the bad news, saying: "After we saw you on 12 May, we were congratulating ourselves on finding someone we thought would be just right for that job in China, and then another development occurred which I need not put down here, and the result is that we shall not want to send anyone at all."[34]

The British Embassy in Kunming later telegraphed the Foreign Office that Haines would not be needed because no legal cases had come before the Court since the outbreak of the Pacific War and "there would be no work for him to do other than that of junior Vice Consul of Yunnanfu." For legal matters, the Government of Burma had offered to help if necessary.

31 FO 369/2719 Note from the Foreign Office to Mossop thanking him for his report dated November 20, 1942.

32 FO369/2719 Letter from Beckett of Foreign Office to Duncan of Colonial Office, March 5, 1942.

33 FO369/2719 Telegram from Foreign Office to Chungking, May 15, 1942 and reply May 22, 1942.

34 FO 369/2719 Letter to Wilson from Beckett dated May 27, 1942.

Casement wants out

The commencement of the Pacific War did not bring a complete end to cases before the American courts. Eugene Casement, now imprisoned on McNeil Island, filed a writ of *habeas corpus* against the Warden of McNeil Island, Mr Squier.[35] His sole appeal ground was that he had been denied a jury trial. This was rejected at first instance and then on appeal by the US Ninth Circuit relying on the Supreme Court decision in the Ross case. District Judge Black in his first instance decision added, in the understated tone of many judicial opinions, a very practical reason why a new trial should not be ordered:

> "By reason of recent and present historical events involving Shanghai, the witnesses necessary to another trial for this petitioner could undoubtedly never in the future be presented before any court."

Extraterritoriality was not, however, dead yet. Agreements still needed to be reached to bring it to an end.

35 *Casement v. Squier Warden*, 46 F. Supp. 296 (First Instance) and 138 F.2d 909 (9th Cir. 1943) (appeal). Appellate decision per Garrecht, Stephens and Healy, Circuit Judges, November 5, 1943. Casement did not serve his entire natural life in McNeil Island. He was released at some point and died in Saronville, Nebraska in 2002. (Record for Gerald E Casement at www.death-record.com).

Part Thirteen

The End
(1942 to 1943)

Chapter 60

The End of Extraterritoriality

With the war raging against Japan in Asia and Germany in Europe and Africa, America wanted as many friends as it could get. With most of China occupied by the Japanese, agreeing with the Chinese to end extraterritoriality was a good way to keep the Chinese government on side without creating any immediate practical difficulties.

On September 1, 1942 the United States Secretary of State, Cordell Hull, wrote to the British Foreign Secretary, Anthony Eden, saying that the US State Department had been studying the relinquishment of extraterritorial rights in China and it:

> "has been obvious from speeches by and letters received from interested persons and also from editorial comment that popular sentiment in favor of action toward abolishing extra-territoriality is fairly widespread, even though there has been no strong concerted pressure upon this Government to take action."[1]

Nevertheless, Hull considered that it was an opportune time to raise the question with the Chinese government with the view of reaching the most favourable agreement possible. He therefore suggested a confidential approach by the Americans and the British to the Chinese government offering to bring to an end extraterritoriality.

1 War Cabinet Memo, WP (42) 404, September 8, 1942 "Extraterritoriality in China."

The British Cabinet considered this and concluded that:

> "while the present time is not altogether opportune to raise this question with the Chinese Government, it is doubtful whether any much more favourable occasion is likely to occur in the near future, and they see considerable advantage in acting while the initiative in the matter still rests with the Powers possessing extra-territorial rights."

Cabinet agreed with the proposal to approach the Chinese with the caveat that some agreement should be reached regarding Shanghai. They appreciated that the Chinese government would demand the return of Shanghai, but suggested that a special status be granted to Shanghai "to enable the development of the port to continue with the co-operation of foreign commercial interests."

Hull later wrote that he pushed the British to give up all rights saying:

> "I stated that what we had in mind was the complete wiping out of all rights of a special character. Any hold-over from the existing anomalies would be a further problem and the cause of continuing friction. Britain agreed."[2]

On October 9, 1942, one day before the Chinese National Day, the British and American governments approached the Chinese ambassadors in London and Washington to let them know that they were willing to begin negotiations to end extraterritoriality. These went on over the next few months.

The British and Americans negotiated the treaties in tandem and attempted to keep the terms (and Chinese ver-

2 W. Fishel, *The End of Extraterritoriality in China,* p209.

sions) of the treaties as consistent as possible, which the British described as seeking to make the "signing of the treaties an Anglo-American-Chinese act of political solidarity." The basic terms of the treaties had been agreed by the end of December and the original plan had been to sign the treaties on January 1, 1943. However, the need to finalize translations and prepare formal versions for signature pushed the date back.

The Anglo-Chinese treaty was almost not signed when the Chinese insisted that the treaty also deal with the return of the New Territories in Hong Kong. The British refused this because the question did not fall under the "question of abrogation of extraterritoriality." The British said that it could be raised for discussion when "victory is won." The Chinese backed down.[3]

As the treaty negotiations were being finalized, in December 1942, the Foreign Office decided to terminate the employment of all the established staff of the British Supreme Court when the treaty came into force, namely: Mossop, Judge; Grant Jones, Assistant Judge; Haines, Registrar; Morris, Chief Clerk; Abbey, Judge's Clerk; and McGeown, Marshal.[4]

John McNeill, the Crown Advocate, was given notice on December 3, 1942 by a letter signed by the British Foreign Minister, Anthony Eden. Eden added in the final paragraph of the letter:

> "The termination of your appointment is solely due to the fact that, as a result of negotiations with the Chinese Government, it is expected that His Britannic Majesty's Supreme Court for China will cease to exist."[5]

---

3 Foreign Relations of the United States, 1942, p414; note from the Charge in the United Kingdom (Matthews) to the Secretary of State, December 29, 1942.

4 FO369/2719 Letter from Foreign Office to Treasury dated December 23, 1941.

5 FO 369/2719 (ref K 12500/1809/210).

There were some discussions with McNeill about him acting as a legal adviser to the Embassy in Nanking after the war. On March 1, 1943, McNeill wrote to the Foreign Office saying that he had not received his letter of termination that he had been told was sent in December 1942. In any event, he said he had "decided to accept an excellent offer from a big industrial concern and would not be available after the war."[6]

The formal end to Extraterritoriality in China

On January 11, 1943, China signed treaties for Relinquishment of Extra-Territorial Rights in China with both Great Britain and the United States. The British treaty was signed in Chungking (Chongqing) between the British Ambassador Sir Horace Seymour and Dr T.V. Soong, the Chinese Foreign Minister. The American treaty was signed in Washington by Dr Tao-ming Wei, the Chinese ambassador, and Cordell Hull.

To celebrate the signing of the treaties, the Chinese Government proclaimed January 11 as "Justice Day" and February 5 to 7, 1943 as a three day national holiday. The Chinese Foreign Ministry later claimed that "throughout the country people could be heard singing the 'Song in Celebration of the New Equal Treaties.'" The song went (in translation):

"50 years of revolutionary bloodshed,
Five and half years of fighting and sacrifice,
Struggle to break the chains,
Bring back the Chinese soul,
Bury the burden of history,
Launch a national renaissance,
Justice has been won,
Our divine land has seen the light......"[7]

6 FO369/2719 Note from McNeill to Beckett dated March 1, 1943.

7 http://www.huanghuagang.org/hhgMagazine/issue01/page014_FeiChuTiaoYue.html, reproducing National Government Capital News Chongqing History, published

A set of stamps were issued in 1945 to commemorate the treaties.[8]

Both treaties contained essentially the same terms. Article 1 of the US treaty and Article 2 of the British treaty both provided that all of those provisions or treaties or agreements in force between Britain or America and China which authorized Britain/America or their representatives to exercise jurisdiction over nationals or companies of Britain or America were abrogated. Then, most importantly, bringing an end to almost 100 years of British and American extraterritorial rights in China, the treaties provided that the nationals and companies of Britain or the United States:

> "shall be subject in the territory of the Republic of China to the jurisdiction of the Government of the Republic of China, in accordance with the principles of international law and practice."

With regard to cases that had already been decided, in an annex to the British Treaty, it was agreed that all decisions made and judgments given by the British courts would be treated as binding and "shall when necessary be enforced by the Chinese authorities."[9] With regard to pending cases, of which given the state of war and the Japanese occupation of large parts of China, there were very few, Article 1(f) of the Annex to the Treaty provided that if the plaintiff or petitioner elected to do so, the case would be transferred to the appropriate Chinese court to dispose of "as expeditiously as possible." In handling the cases, the Chinese courts were required as far as practicable to apply "the law the court of His Majesty

by the Southwest Normal University Publishing Company.

8 "A Century of Resilient Tradition: Exhibition of Republic of China's Diplomatic Archives", National Palace Museum, p156. February 5, 1943 was Chinese New Year's Day.

9 The Annex was declared to be an integral part of the treaty by an exchange of notes between the Sir Horace Seymour, the British Ambassador in Chungking and Dr Tse Vung Soong, the Chinese Foreign Minister.

would have applied", that is, in most cases, English law.[10]

An almost identical provision was agreed in the US treaty, save, of course, that the Chinese courts would apply American law.

The very last case

Fittingly, perhaps, given it was the military who brought the courts to life, the very last trial in a British or American extraterritorial court in China was before a court where the judge, prosecutor and defence attorney were all in active military service. Three days after the signing of the US-China treaty on 14 January 1943, in Kunming, the United States Court for China heard its very last case. The treaty had not yet been ratified, so extraterritorial rights were still in place.

A year and a half before, on August 16, 1941, Boatner Carney had shot and killed another American, Sgt W.R. Reichmann during a poker game. Carney was an American Aviation Instructor with the Chinese Air Force, or as they were usually referred to, a Flying Tiger. The Flying Tigers was a group of former US military pilots who had come to assist China in its war with Japan, under the command of General Claire Chennault. As a Flying Tiger, Carney was not part of the US military and could not be tried by a military court. The US Consular Court in Kunming held a preliminary hearing and on August 31, 1942 committed Carney to trial before the United States Court for China.

This created a difficulty. There was no United States Court for China to try Carney in. Helmick had only just arrived back in the US following his internment and would have no inclination to immediately turn around to try a case in Kunming. The Department of Justice and the Judge Advocate General agreed to appoint two military officers to be judge and prosecutor for the case. Major Bertrand E Johnson with the Judge

10 English Courts do have the power to try cases under the law of another country, if that is what the parties have agreed.

Advocate's department of the US Army Air Corps, then based in India, was appointed a special judge to try the case. Johnson had been a judge in Tulsa, Oklahoma, before joining the military. Captain Edward Kessler, an Air Corps supply officer, prosecuted. Lieutenant Lincoln C Brownell defended. The case was heard at the US Consulate General in Kunming with the US Consul, Raymond P Ludden, in attendance.[11]

Despite the judge and prosecutor and defence attorney being military officers, the case was tried as a civil case and all the proper forms were observed. The Vice-Consul in Kunming, Alfred T. Wellborn acted as Clerk of the Court and Stanley A McGeary, a clerk of the consulate, acted as Marshal. Mrs L.D. Taylor, a civilian employee of the US Army, acted as the court recorder. All present were aware of the historic nature of the hearing and posed for a formal photograph, Johnson, Kessler and Brownell all in their uniforms, on the balcony of the consulate.

Carney pleaded not guilty on the basis of temporary insanity. Witnesses said that during a friendly poker game, Carney, who had been drinking, waved a pistol and said: "I am taking over." The gun discharged killing Reichman. Carney exercised his right to silence. Johnson convicted Carney and sentenced him to two years imprisonment and fined him $10,000. An application for a new trial was made which Johnson rejected. Carney returned to the United States to be imprisoned. On the special request of General Chennault, the head of the Flying Tigers, Carney was pardoned by President Roosevelt in June 1943.

There appears to be no surviving transcript of the final hearing. However, almost certainly Johnson sitting as the

---

11 Foreign Relations of the United States, 1942, p287, footnote. Scully, E, Bargaining with the State From Afar, p193 and footnote 124; *The Judge Advocate Journal*, Summer 1945, p47; Oyen, M, Allies, Enemies and Aliens: Migration and U.S.-Chinese Relations, 1940–1965, p 65, footnote 10; *Miami Daily New Record*, January 18, 1943, p2 (re conviction); *Daily Herald*, January 18, 1943 (re trial); *Daily Herald*, June 7, 1943, p3 (re pardon); *American Foreign Service Journal*, Vol 20, p528 (1943), brief report and formal photograph.

last special judge of the United States Court for China would have noted the end of extraterritoriality and that the hearing was the last-ever sitting of the Court.

No formal steps were taken to close the US Court for China, presumably because under American law the treaty ending extraterritoriality, once ratified on May 20, 1943, was self-executing. The act creating the United States Court for China was repealed in 1948.[12]

Formal closing of the British Supreme Court for China

The British did take steps to formally close the British Supreme Court for China. On March 22, 1943, an Order in Council, which came into effect on May 20, 1943, was issued. The Order repealed 20 other Orders in Council; ordered that companies that had not already moved their registered offices from China were now deemed to be registered in Hong Kong; and, for any divorces where a *decree nisi* had been granted, deemed that a *decree absolute* had been granted. The records of the Supreme Court were ordered to be kept in China for at least 10 years so that Chinese courts could take over pending cases or refer to judgments that had been delivered.[13]

Most importantly, and formally closing the British Supreme Court for China, S.3(1) provided:

> "All courts established under the principal Order shall be closed on the date of the coming into force of this Order and the appointment of the Judge, Assistant Judge, Acting Judge and all officers of the said courts shall terminate on the same date."

Unlike the British Court for Japan, or even the United

12 The act of June 30, 1906 (34 Stat. 814), which created the United States Court for China, was repealed by act of June 25, 1948 (62 Stat. 995).

13 China Order in Council, 1943, *London Gazette*, 25 May 1943, p2331. Many of the records have survived to this day and are now in the National Archives in London.

States Court for China, there was no formal final hearing in the British Supreme Court for China.

In honour of all those who served in or appeared before the British Supreme Court for China and Japan, it is appropriate to bring closure as it would have happened if the war had not intervened:

> "Know all men, this court stands adjourned. God save the King."

Chapter 61

Summing Up

Ladies and Gentleman of the jury, you have now heard the evidence on the case of extraterritoriality as practiced in China, Japan and Korea by the British and Americans. What is the verdict of history?

Was it Gunboat Justice? Or, was it a necessary evil?

Each one of us will have a different view.

Clearly, extraterritoriality is not a system that any country would willingly accept unless forced to by military or economic pressure.

Its original purpose was to allow foreigner to judge foreigner, and for the whole time extraterritoriality was practiced it served this purpose. For the majority of cases before all extraterritorial courts, this caused no problems when the parties were all nationals of the court concerned. Contractual disputes were resolved; tort claims were decided; divorces were granted and criminal were punished. The courts functioned as they would in their home countries. Would Edith Carew have been investigated as thoroughly and prosecuted if she had committed her crime three years later under Japanese jurisdiction?

Problems arose, however, when parties of different nationalities were involved, particularly when nationals of the host country had suffered at the hands of foreigners. Then, genuine problems arose. Chinese, Japanese and Koreans had to bring cases in foreign courts in foreign languages. For criminal cases, the prosecutors were also foreigners. They clearly lacked zeal in some cases and, in the case, of the British courts, English juries would not convict or only convict on lesser offences.

These shortcomings were recognized and after long struggles by both countries, ultimately, extraterritoriality was brought to an end, first in Japan and then in China, to much celebration. In Korea, there was nothing to celebrate, as extraterritoriality ended with Japan's annexation of the country.

What, however, was the result of extraterritoriality?

Strangely, for the two main countries on which it was imposed, it produced completely different results. For Japan, extraterritoriality was an important impetus to legal, economic and political reforms that created a country that during World War II was able to occupy most of East Asia. While World War II ended in defeat, the structure of modern Japan as a rich democratic outward-looking country owes much to the reforms that were carried out in the late 19th century.

For China, extraterritoriality was an unmitigated disaster. It weakened the Manchu rule at the end of the Qing Dynasty, but did not bring it to an end. Indeed, towards the end, foreigners kept the Qing Dynasty alive because it suited their purposes. Extraterritoriality did eventually lead to the development of a modern legal system by the Nationalist Party. However, this was abolished in Mainland China when the Communists took over.

The legacy of extraterritoriality in Korea and Taiwan is more complex. Korea inherited a Japanese-based legal system at the end of the war. After decades of military dictatorship, this system has now contributed strongly to Korea's economic growth. The same can also be said of Taiwan, to which the Nationalist Party brought its modern legal system after the war.

Some will view extraterritoriality as having been a good thing, although in these days of general anti-Imperialism, their numbers will be small. Others, such as the Chinese Communists and the Chinese Nationalists consider it an evil system that oppressed their country. The Japanese view is more nuanced, no doubt because Japan suffered from yet also imposed extraterritoriality on others. For them, it was a necessary evil brought about by their undeveloped legal system. However, once they had developed their modern system, which remains in place to this day, had to be abolished.

For myself, I find it very hard to say. I have called this book Gunboat Justice because that is what extraterritoriality was: a system of justice imposed at the point of gunboat barrels.

Nevertheless, there were good things about the system – purely foreign cases were dealt with better than they would have been if tried in local Chinese or Japanese court. This led to many of the treaty ports, including Shanghai, Tianjin, Yokohama, and Kobe becoming and remaining to this day as major trading cities. There were bad things about the system. There were cases of injustice brought about by judges or juries favouring their own. But, no legal system is free from injustice. The judges and administrators of the British and American courts were as far as can be told good men who strove to be fair. They were, of course, men of their time and believed in the use of gunboat diplomacy to enforce treaty rights – many of them personally called in gunboats at different times.

The instability of the Chinese governments following the Republican Revolution in 1911 extended the life of extraterritoriality in China longer than it should have perhaps lasted. Extraterritoriality contributed, in no small part, to this instability. The fact that foreigners could rely on their own courts and authorities to protect them meant there was no strong pressure to ensure there was a stable government in China. A weak government suited them. It is this era that now forms the cornerstone of how many Chinese, and particularly the Communist Party, see the world. Foreigners – to this day - are seen as trying to split and weaken China. Mao threw all foreigners out in the 1950s for this reason. Even following Deng Xiaoping's reform and opening, China tightly guards it sovereignty. Almost all foreign investment must be through locally incorporated companies. Chinese courts do not enforce judgments of foreign courts. Anti-foreign and, in particular, anti-Japanese rhetoric is regularly spouted by senior leaders. China as it grows stronger shows no compunction about using gunboat diplomacy against its neighbours.

On Tiananmen Square, there are two slogans written on Tiananmen Gate on either side of the portrait of Chairman Mao. Most foreigners know one slogan reads "Long Live Chairman Mao." Most do not know that the other is "Unity is Strength." While 21st century Chinese leaders pay lip-service to the first slogan; it is the second slogan that forms the bed-rock of Chinese thinking – only a strong unified government can control and protect China from foreign encroachments - and explains why despite its many shortcomings, one party rule has survived so long in China.

No matter what your view of extraterritoriality, the one thing of which there can be no doubt is that it changed and continues to influence the course of history in East Asia.

Sapajou on Sino-Japanese relations in 1937. As valid today as it was then?

POSTSCRIPT
Life After Death

WORLD WAR II CAME to an end with the nuclear bombing of Hiroshima and Nagasaki, ending Japanese adventurism for the rest of the 20th century. The Nationalists re-occupied most of China, but following four years of civil war with the Communists, they were expelled to Taiwan.

Set out below is information on what happened to some of the characters, one ship and a building in our story.

Norwood Allman

Allman was interned by the Japanese in Hong Kong in the same camp as Gwen Priestwood and Atholl MacGregor. He was repatriated in June 1942. He published the book *Shanghai Lawyer* in 1943 describing his time as a Mixed Court assessor and lawyer in China. He joined the OSS during World War II and later worked with the CIA. He returned to China after the war and practiced law until 1950. He died in 1987.[1]

Archibald Clark Kerr

Clark Kerr went on to become the British Ambassador in Moscow during the war. He became famous for sending a letter (which can be found on the internet) to Lord Pembroke, the Foreign Secretary, sharing with Pembroke "a tiny flash that has illuminated my sombre life" and telling him that a new Turkish diplomat in Moscow was called "Mustapha Kunt."

1 *New York Times*, March 2, 1987.

In 1946 he became the Baron of Inverchapel. He died in 1951.[2]

Stirling Fessenden

Fessenden, who had stepped down as Secretary-General of the SMC in 1939 due to failing eyesight, remained in Shanghai. He was interned with Russian refugees during the war. He was offered a passage to America in September 1943 but declined due to his ill health. He died in Shanghai on 20 September 1943.[3]

Cornell Franklin

Franklin was interned by the Japanese in early 1942. He was repatriated on the MS Gripsholm in 1943. He returned to Shanghai after the war and established a legal practice with R.T. Bryan. Franklin stayed on after the Chinese Communist Revolution and was granted an exit visa in 1951. Franklin died in February 1959, in Charlottesville, Virginia. William Faulkner, the new husband of his ex-wife, Estelle - who he had divorced in 1930, won the Nobel Prize for Literature in 1949.[4]

Penrhyn Grant Jones

After returning to England, Grant Jones retired to Ticehurst in Sussex. He died on June 15, 1945. His wife, Silvia, married Mr D.M. Stewart later that year.[5]

Cyril Haines

Haines remained in Foreign Office Service for many years. He served as Head of the Claims Department in the Foreign

2 See D. Gillies, *Radical Diplomat: The Life of Sir Archibald Clark Kerr, Lord Inverchapel, 1882-1951* for full biography.

3 *Time*, January 24, 1944 and John B Powell, "*My Twenty-Five Years in China*", p327

4 *Lowell Sun*, Nov 5, 1943, p9; *The China Weekly Review*, Nov 9, 1946, p301; Indiana *Evening Gazette*, Dec 12, 1951, p15; and *Niagara Falls Gazette*, Feb 25, 1959, p20.

5 *The Times* July 19, 1945 (obituary); Deaths registered in July, August and September 1945; *The Times*, January 7, 1946, p7 (Wife's remarriage).

Office and Judge of HM Court in the Persian Gulf. He was awarded a CBE in 1953 and knighted (KBE) in 1962. In that year, he became Chairman of the South West London Rent Tribunal, quite a change from hearing committal proceedings against policemen accused of throwing a beggar in the river or acting as coroner for an ex-policeman killed by Japanese soldiers.[6]

Bertrand Johnson

Johnson became a colonel during the war and remained with the Judge Advocate General's Department after the war. He later transferred to the United States Air Force and served in Japan. He retired at the rank of Brigadier General and died on October 16, 1983.[7]

Lawrence Kentwell

Lawrence Kentwell remained bitter and twisted towards the British government. He continued to bombard them with letters complaining of his treatment and the loss of Chinese sovereignty. In the 1940s, he was appointed to the Chinese Legislative Yuan of the Japanese-backed Reorganised Government of China. In 1942, he returned to Shanghai and practiced as a lawyer during the war. After the war, he was prosecuted by a Chinese court for treason. He represented himself, with the same results as when he represented himself in the British courts. Bizarrely, he claimed he was not a Chinese citizen. He was convicted and sentenced to seven years in prison, but this was reduced to two and half years following an appeal. He was released on bail after suffering a paralytic stroke in January 1947. No one appears to know what happened to him after this.

The sins of the father were not visited on the son. His son, Lawrence Holt-Kentwell, to his father's "great sorrow," but

6 Who's Who 1967 entry for Haines.

7 US Air Force Biography. http://www.af.mil/information/bios/bio.asp?bioID=5953.

with prayers for his safety, served as an officer in the British Army in World War II. He later joined the Colonial Service serving in Uganda and Hong Kong. In Hong Kong, he served on the Legislative Council and was awarded an MBE. He died in 2012.[8]

Milton Helmick

Helmick returned to China in 1944 to study the new Chinese legal system to prepare for dealing with the system after the defeat of Japan. He then worked for the Standard Vacuum Oil Company in Shanghai from 1945 to 1951.

In 1953, he was appointed Judge of the United States Consular Court for Casablanca and Tangiers where he tried one of the few cases of piracy against an American citizen in the 20th century. He retired in January 1954 and died in San Francisco in October 1954.[9]

Nelson Lurton

Nelson Lurton returned to the United States on the *Gripsholm* and served on the Missouri State Workman's Compensation Commission until 1956 when he died.[10]

Atholl MacGregor

MacGregor was interned by the Japanese in the Stanley prisoner of war camp in Hong Kong. While in the camp, he and other Hong Kong judges continued to hear cases. MacGregor even granted a number of divorces. He survived the internship but contracted beri beri and died on board the boat tak-

8 B Wasserstein, Secret War in Shanghai, pp192-194 and 282-284; *The China Weekly Review*, Aug 3, 1946, p233; *South China Morning Post & the Hongkong Telegraph*, Jul 10, 1947, p4. Correspondence with the Kentwell family. Detail of Lawrence Holt-Kentwell, *Oxford Times*, September 6, 2012 (Obituary); Official Report of Hong Kong Legislative Council Proceedings, July 8,1970.

9 *New York Times*, November 25, 1944; *Albaquerque Journal*, November 3, 1954, p3; *Singapore Free Press*, December 22, 1952, p1.

10 Genealogy.com page for Nelson E Lurton. http://familytreemaker.genealogy.com/users/r/u/h/Steven-R-Ruhl-IL/WEBSITE-0001/UHP-0928.html.

ing him home to England. He was buried at sea.[11]

John McNeill

McNeill, who had become Custodian of Enemy Property in China as Crown Advocate, remained in that position after the court ceased to exist. A special Order in Council was passed on January 20, 1944 to continue to allow him to deal with the property despite the fact he no longer held the post of Crown Advocate.

After the war, rather than working for a big industrial concern as he had suggested in correspondence with the Foreign Office, he went to the bar in Hong Kong. He became a King's Counsel (K.C.) in Hong Kong in 1950 (and a Queen's Counsel (Q.C.) when Queen Elizabeth became Queen in 1952). He was Chairman of the Hong Kong Bar Association in 1955, 1956 and 1958. He was described by one barrister who later became a Justice of the Hong Kong Court of Appeal, the late Benjamin Liu, as the best advocate in Hong Kong at the time. McNeill retired to Scotland in 1960.

His daughter Jane McNeill became a model and in 1953 at the age of 22, married the Earl of Dalkeith who was later to become the Duke of Buccleuch, making her the Duchess of Buccleuch. The Queen attended her wedding, arriving by a special train so as to avoid possible assassination attempts by Scottish Nationalists. A reception attended by 1,800 people, including Princess Margaret, was held in London following the wedding in Edinburgh. Jane died in April 2011.[12]

Allan Mossop

Mossop returned to China and from 1945 until his retirement

11 G Emerson, *Hong Kong internment, 1942 to 1945: life in the Japanese civilian camp at Stanley*, pp25-26; Steve Tsang, *A Modern History of Hong Kong*, p138.

12 Trading with the Enemy (China Custodian) Order in Council, 1944, *London Gazette*, 3 March 1944, p1063; *Sunday Herald*, January 11, 1953, p19; Discussion with Benjamin Liu in October 2013; *Times*, May 5, 2011, P61; *New Scotsman*, April 28, 2011, Obituaries of Jane, Dowager Duchess of Buccleuch. Thanks to Dr Gerry McCoy QC SC for bringing this to my attention.

in 1946, he was Counsellor (Legal) to the British Embassy in China and, amongst other things, advised on issues arising from the liquidation of foreign assets in the Shanghai International Settlement.

Mossop's first wife (who he had married in 1920) died in 1949. In 1950, Mossop re-married to Jean Maud Bennett, M.B.E., widow of Lieutenant-Commander William Alexander Elliot. He died in June 1965 in Cape Town, South Africa.[13]

Gwen Priestwood

Gwen Priestwood was interned in Hong Kong at the Stanley prisoner of war camp with Atholl MacGregor and Norwood Allman. She managed to escape after about three weeks there and made her way to Chungking. She wrote a book of her experiences, *Through Japanese Barbed Wire*, and went on lecture tours in America in 1943 and England in 1944. She and Victor divorced during the war and she moved to Canada. She died in 2000.[14]

Victor Priestwood

Victor served in the RAF during the war. He appears to have re-married in 1944. He died in 1954 in Surrey, England.[15]

Leighton Shields

Leighton Shields returned to the United States on the *Gripsholm*. Upon his return he was made a special assistant to the US Attorney General in the Boston office. He died in Massachusetts on April 27, 1957.[16]

---

13 Problems with the Liquidation of Assets in the Former International Settlement at Shanghai and the Diplomatic Quarter at Peiping, p1409; Foreign Relations, 1947, Volume VII; Obituary, The Times, June 19, 1965, p10.

14 *North Devon Herald*, April 20, 1944; email correspondence with Gwen's nephew, Richard Wheeler.

15 *London Gazette*, 28 March 1941; Deaths registered in July, August and September 1954.

16 United States Congressional Serial Set, Vol 7, 1958, p191; Harvard Alumni Bulletin, No.59, 1956.

SS Narkunda

The *SS Narkunda* which brought Mossop, Grant Jones and others from the British Supreme Court back to England was sunk off the coast of North Africa in November 1942 while it was being used as an auxiliary troop transport.[17]

The British Consulate and Supreme Court Building

The Consulate and court buildings were left empty during the Japanese occupation. The British returned to the Consulate buildings in 1945 after the war ended. By this time, extraterritoriality had come to an end in China. Presumably the courtrooms, which were no longer necessary, were converted into offices. Allan Mossop suggested the library books be donated to Hong Kong or Singapore. Some of the books do appear to have ended up in the Hong Kong University Library.[18]

After the 1949 revolution, the British continued to maintain a *de facto* presence in Shanghai without any specific agreement with the new Communist government, which took no steps to expel them. An oral agreement was reached at the 1954 Geneva Conference that the British could maintain a Consulate in Shanghai. It seems the Chinese were hoping to be allowed to open a diplomatic office on similar terms somewhere else such as Singapore, or outside London. In 1967, during the Cultural Revolution the British were expelled from Shanghai. The premises of the consulate were occupied by the Shanghai Revolutionary Committee on September 9, 1967. The Shanghai *Wenhuibao* reported on September 13, 1967 that a rally had been held in the Compound and that the "requisitioning was a great victory in the struggle against revisionism and imperialism, for the cultural revolution and the prestige of China." The British protested the violation of diplomatic premises, but did not complain about the seizure of their property. An investigation had revealed that the British Government did

17 SS *Narkunda*, http://www.wrecksite.eu/wreck.aspx?96586.

18 FO 3711/1261 Letter from Mossop to L.H Lamb of the British Embassy in Nanking.

not own the land. They had leased the land for the Consulate in 1848 and, it seems, never paid any rent. This meant they did not have a particularly strong argument that the buildings belonged to the British Government. If they did make a claim for the buildings to be returned, there was a strong concern that the Chinese might claim back rent. The Chinese government, in any event, considered that all land belonged to the people.[19]

For a period from sometime in the 1970s to 1984 the buildings were used as a "Friendship Store," a store where foreigners could go to purchase imported items for foreign currency as well as tourist products. The main building was then used as an office for the Shanghai City Government's "No.2 Office." The Consul-General's house to the north was used as the Shanghai Branch of the China International Travel Service and the house for the Assistant Judges to the south was used by the Shanghai City Foreign Services Company.[20] At some point, the front verandah area on the second floor of the courthouse was enclosed by walls in a very poor renovation.

The records of the Supreme Court as well as certain records of the United States, including those of the US Court for China and some records from the Philippines, that the British had agreed to keep safe when the Americans were expelled from China in 1949 were left behind in the Consulate. The British records were returned by the Chinese Government in 1984. There is no record of what happened to the US documents.[21]

After the Shanghai government institutions moved out

19 FO 676/558 which was closed until 2001, details the history of the Consulate after the Revolution up to its seizure. The quote from the *Wenhuibao* is from the file. The file also records the very poor treatment given to the Consul's wife, Mrs Hewitt, and children when leaving Shanghai in May 1967.

20 Shanghai History Guide Map (Shanghai Rekishi Gaido Mappu), Makoto Kinouchi 1999, Taishukan Shoten, p3.

21 British Supreme Court Records: The National Archives Note regarding the records (FO 656); US Court Records: "Records of the United States Court for China", The American Journal of Legal History, Vol 1, p234. Some records are in the US National Archives.

in the 1990s, the buildings remained unused and in a very dilapidated condition until the mid-2000s when a re-construction project of the Consulate and surrounding area was commenced. The Assistant Judge's house was torn down, but the Supreme Court, Consulate Building and Consul General's house have been renovated. The Peninsula Hotel was built next to the southeast of the Consulate building. The lobby bar sits almost exactly where the Assistant Judge's house was. Yuanmingyuan Road has been completely restored and the area is now called "Rock Bund."

The Supreme Court Building and Consulate Building has now been renamed No.1 Waitanyuan. It is managed by the Peninsula Hotel and mainly used as a state guest house. The rooms inside the old Consulate and Supreme Court Buildings have been converted into dining areas, a bar, a cigar room and meeting rooms. The courtyard between the Supreme Court Building and the Consulate Building has been converted into an atrium with a seating area. The main Supreme Court Room has become a large function room. Both the smaller civil court and the police court have been converted into kitchens. The Consul-General's house is now a high-end boutique selling Patek Philippe watches.[22]

Following the renovations, Chinese President Hu Jintao and Vladimir Putin, who was at the time Russian Prime Minster, held a meeting exactly where the dais of the Supreme Court had been located. One wonders if they felt the ghosts of British Chief Justices past listening to their conversation.

The Court building can be seen from Yuanmingyuan Road. As I completed an early draft of this book, I spent a late afternoon and evening on the balcony of Otto E Mezzo Bombana which directly overlooks the old Supreme Court building.

As I watched the sunset, the many fabulous scenes that had played out in the court came to life in my head. As I left,

22 Photographs of the renovated buildings from "Park 33 by Kokai Designs." See: http://www.architecturelist.com/2011/01/10/park33-by-kokaistudios/.

I imagined all of the judges of the court waving farewell from the balcony.

A NOTE ON THE WRITING OF THIS BOOK

On a beautiful day in mid-April 2011, I had a meeting at the Customs House on the Bund in Shanghai. Having arrived early, I had about 30 minutes to kill, so I went next door to one of the most beautiful buildings on the Bund, the former headquarters of the Hongkong and Shanghai Banking Corporation, now the Pudong Development Bank. As you enter and look up, there is a high dome. Tile reliefs have been fitted showing the various cities where HSBC had its main branches at the time the building opened in 1923. The cities, in addition to Hong Kong and Shanghai, were Tokyo, New York, London, Paris, Calcutta and Bangkok. Each is beautifully pictured on the ceiling. Further inside is a traditional English banking hall with high ceilings, a long wood panelled transaction counter and extremely comfortable benches for waiting customers. The whole bank, now a branch of the Shanghai Pudong Development Bank, is extraordinarily well preserved and always worth visiting.

On the right had side of the main entrance is a plaque commemorating the opening of the building. Despite having visited the building numerous times, I only saw this plaque for the first time on this beautiful Spring day.

The plaque reads:

THIS BUILDING
WAS OPENED BY
HIS EXCELLENCY
SIR RONALD MACLEAY K.C.M.G
H.B.M. MINISTER TO CHINA
ON THE 23RD OF JUNE 1923
IN THE PRESENCE OF

H.E. ADMIRAL SIR ARTHUR LEVSON K.C.M.G
COMMANDER-IN-CHIEF, CHINA STATION.
SIR WILLIAM REES DAVIES
CHIEF JUSTICE OF HONG KONG.
LIEUT. OSBORNE WOOD
US ARMY A.D.C. REPRESENTING THE GOVERNOR
GENERAL OF THE PHILIPPINE ISLANDS.
SIR SKINNER TURNER
JUDGE, H.B.M SUPREME COURT FOR CHINA.
SIR ERNEST WILTON K.C.M.G
CHIEF INSPECTOR SALT REVENUE
CHINESE GOVERNMENT.
H.H. FOX, C.M.G
H.B.M. COMMERCIAL COUNSELLOR.
SIDNEY BARTON C.M.G.
H.B.M CONSUL-GENERAL, SHANGHAI.
HON MR C McI. MESSER O.B.E.
COLONIAL TREASURER, HONG KONG.
L.A. LYALL
COMMISSIONER OF CUSTOMS, SHANGHAI
JOHN PRENTICE
CHAIRMAN OF DIRECTORS,
SHANGHAI DOCK COY LTD.
A.O. LANG, CHAIRMAN OF DIRECTORS.
D.G.M BERNARD, VICE-CHAIRMAN.
A.G. STEPHEN, CHIEF MANAGER.
G.H. STITT, MANAGER SHANGHAI.

G.L. WILSON, P.A.S.I

ARCHITECT

The plaque gives some clue to just how powerful Britain was in China at the time and, I should add, why China calls the century covered by this book the Century of Humiliation.

The British Minister was in charge of all British interests in China. The Royal Navy China Station based in Hong Kong and Weihaiwei had more ships in its fleet than the navies of most other countries. British subjects ran the Chinese Customs service, the government's principal source of revenue, and collected its salt revenue.

What piqued my interest, however, was the reference to H.B.M's Supreme Court for China and its Judge, Sir Skinner Turner. I had studied Chinese and Japanese history at university. I had spent 20 years in Mainland China and Hong Kong. I had studied law in Shanghai and Hong Kong. I had been a Hong Kong solicitor for 15 years. I had practiced as a lawyer for 11 years in Shanghai. Despite this, I had never heard of His Britannic Majesty's Supreme Court for China; nor of Sir Skinner Turner.

I was intrigued.

I then strolled leisurely along the Bund heading north. I came to the former British Consulate, recently restored. On such a day, the building looked beautiful set back in large gardens with lush green foliage. As I was to discover later, this beautiful scene had, in fact, been the home of the British Supreme Court for China. A little bit further up the Bund and across the Garden Bridge were the Astor House Hotel and the Russian Consulate.

That day, I met my wife for a very pleasant lunch at M on the Bund (thanks Michelle, Bruno and Matthew). We sat on the terrace overlooking the Bund and the grand colonial buildings of the concession area. My wife is a Shanghai history buff. I asked her if she had heard of the British Supreme Court for China. She had not.

When I returned home, I began my research. I turned first to Wikipedia. To my surprise there was no entry for the Supreme Court for China and Japan, just some brief mentions in entries for Havilland de Sausmarez and Charles Wycliffe Goodwin that they had been judges of the Supreme Court for China, or in Goodwin's case, the Supreme Court for China and Japan. A history of Tobermore in Ireland mentioned that a Hiram Shaw Wilkinson had also been a judge of the Supreme Court for China and Corea.

I dug further.

For some judges, there was a wealth of information that could be found. Edmund Hornby, for example, had written an autobiography that his daughter, Constance Drummond, published posthumously and many articles were written about him when he was alive. Charles Goodwin was a famous Egyptologist so there were a number of books about him that provided an insight into his life. Nicholas Hannen was obviously well liked and, on his untimely death just before he left office, numerous obituaries were published. Gilbert King was featured in numerous newspaper articles and was clearly a well-liked man about town.

Some of the other judges led much quieter lives and very little was written about them. George French was, from start to finish, almost a mystery. It was difficult to find any information about him, even though he died in office. The obituaries I found were very short. At first, I suspected the reason for this paucity of information was that he was not popular. It turned out the reason was more that he was well-respected but, as one newspaper reported, he was not suited to the Oriental climate and was ill most of the time he was in Shanghai. He was also a very careful judge who was slow to issue decisions. This reduced his popularity, particularly with the *North China Herald*, leading to very little being written about him. He was one of two full-time judges of the court buried in Asia and his is the only one grave that remains.

I originally intended to write only about the British Courts, but realised soon that the story could be best told by combining the stories of the British and American courts. For the United States Court for China, more information was available. There was a short Wikipedia entry. Eileen Scully has written an excellent book on its history. Still, there were many more stories to tell, and I have focused on these.

Having lived in Shanghai for 13 years, I have, over the years, visited many of the places mentioned in the book. It took me some time to work out that where the Supreme Court had been located and it was only after finding an old photo that I realized the former British Consulate Building was made up of two buildings, the Consulate and the court, not one.

In China, I visited the old Summer Palace in Beijing that was burnt by the British and French in 1860; the Chinese National Museum on Tiananmen Square; the National Museum in Taipei; the Opium War Museum in Humen, Guangdong Province and the Dagu Fort Museum in Tanggu, Tianjin. The latter two museums have very good displays on the opium wars. I also visited Shamian Island in Guangzhou, which has been restored and has an interesting little museum on its history.

In Japan, I also travelled to Shimonoseki to see where the Treaty of Shimonoseki was signed and to Kagoshima, the city bombarded by the British in 1863 to assert their treaty rights. I also visited the Japanese Maritime Self Defence Force Museum in Sasebo and the Mikasa museum in Yokosuka. Both have very good displays on the development of Japanese naval power and the war with Russia. The Dutch Factories in Dejima Island have also been faithfully restored and provide a good feeling for what life was like in the factories.

In St Petersburg, I was able to board the *Aurora,* one of only three Russian ships from the Russian fleet to survive the Russo-Japan war of 1905. It is still in active service but is now used as a museum.

The histories of China and Japan and the law are my favourite topics. This was, therefore, a very enjoyable book for me to research and write. I hope you have enjoyed it as well.

Acknowledgements

Firstly, thank you to Graham Earnshaw of Earnshaw Books for commissioning and editing this book and Sir Robin Jacob for writing the foreword.

The research on this book has taken me to the archives of the Shanghai Library in Xujiahui, formerly the Catholic Church Library; the British National Archives in Kew Gardens, London, which also now houses part of the Foreign and Commonwealth Office Library to dig through the old foreign office and court files; the Public Records Office of Northern Ireland; the Yokohama Archives of History housed in the grounds of the former British Consulate and location of the Court for Japan which has a comprehensive collection of materials from Japan of the concession era; the Kobe City Archives; the Kobe Museum of History; the Nagasaki Museum of History; the Kobe Foreigners' Cemetery high above Kobe to visit the grave of George French; and the Yokohama Foreigners' Cemetery. Thank you to the staff of all these organisations for your assistance and particularly to Mr Fujii of the Kobe Foreigners' Cemetery who helped with the special arrangements to see George French's grave.

I have also received assistance in my research from a number of relatives of judges and lawyers.

Thank you to Pippa Pettifer (nee Hannen), the great great granddaughter of Nicholas Hannen, and her husband Tom for the hospitality in welcoming to their home in Devon and making available the Hannen family albums that they had stored in a trunk in their garage. The photos of the Hannen family and Sir Nicholas Hannen's funeral in Shanghai are all courtesy of Pippa and Tom. Thank you to Peter Delaney of the Wargrave Historical Association for putting me in touch with Pippa. Pippa also put me in touch with Sarah Collins who holds the Hannen family archive. I am grateful to her for some interesting background information on Sir Nicholas Hannen.

Thanks also to Hugo Read, the great grandson of John Carey Hall and Agnes Goodwin (and therefore the great great grandson Charles Goodwin) who was kind enough to allow me to reproduce the photo of Agnes in this book and provide other information on the family; and to John and Michael Turner for information on and the photograph of Sir Skinner Turner; as well as to Judy Bekker and Marion Naude, nieces of Sir Allan Mossop for taking the time to provide me with information on his life. Thank you also to Miles Mossop for putting me in touch with them.

Richard Wheeler, Gwen Priestwood's nephew, provided me with a photo of Victor Priestwood and also some more information about their relationship for which I am grateful. Thanks also to Nicholas Holt-Kentwell, Ann Curtis (nee Holt-Kentwell) and John Hudson for information on Lawrence Kentwell. Thanks to Ann, in particular, for the picture that is reproduced in this book.

John and Robert Piper, who were my neighbours in Australia for many years, provided information on their grandfather/father and a picture of Kenneth Piper and his wife for which I am grateful. Edward Schneider, Carl Ingenohl's great-grandson, kindly provided a photo of Ingenohl and a poster advertising his classic cigars.

Simon Drakeford, who has written a book on the history of rugby in Shanghai "It's A Rough Game But Good Sport", generously provided many useful photos, drawings and information.

Thank you to Hugh Davies of the China Association for allowing me access to photographs of the China Association dinners and allowing the reproduction of a number of pictures in this book.

Thank you, also, to Professor Yasuo Katayama for providing many useful photographs from historical records in Shanghai.

Peter Moll in the British Virgin Islands also very helpfully unearthed some interesting information on George French and his family. Lynn Josse of the Chatillon-DeMenil House Foundation, kindly provided the photo of Henry De Menil. Tom Duke also helpfully put me in touch with some contacts in Korea and introduce me to Sir Robin Jacob. I thank all three of them.

Robert Bickers, Paul French, Ian Ruxton and Meena Vathyam provided much needed encouragement and useful information. Robert unearthed the photo of John Douglas, a picture that had been eluding me. Thank you to all four. The University of Cape Town Library was also of assistance in providing me with copies of the Mossop Law Reports, clippings kept by Allan Mossop's wife of cases he heard. Dr Maureen Watry of the Sydney Jones Library at the University of Liverpool kindly helped me locate and gave permission for the use of the portrait of Sir Richard Rennie that is reproduced in this book. The staff of the Hong Kong University Library were also of great assistance in allowing me access to their Special Collection.

Thanks to Joan Philipson of Historical Research Associates in Belfast helped me to research the Wilkinson Archives in the Public Records Office there.

Andrew Mussel of Gray's Inn provided me with useful information about Harold and Gilbert King which Hannah Baker of the Middle Temple confirmed.

Elizabeth Ennion Smith of St Catherine's College Cambridge provided useful information about Charles Goodwin.

Thank your also to my former colleague, Matthew Nash, for putting me in touch with Rob Cheng and Cecilia Lui of the

Peninsula Group to arrange a tour of the old British Consulate and Supreme Court Building. Thank you to Rob, Cecilia and Flora Wang for arranging a marvellous tour of the entire building.

A number of friends have also provided useful assistance. Rieko Michishita helped me find some cases at the Yokohama Archives of History; John Hoyle read and provided useful comments on an early draft. Jon Glusman let me bore him to death in good humour. Henry Wheare helped me with the translation from Latin of the epitaph to Charles Goodwin. Benjamin Schwall attempted to find more about Boatner Carney at the National Library in Taipei. Udi Shiloah accompanied on a visit to Shamian Island. Paul Lau helped track down the photo of Lindsey Smith. Thank you to all.

Thank you also to Jacqueline Chan and Maddie Parker who took on the huge task of proofreading early drafts of this book and provided useful suggestions. Thank you also to Jacqueline, Frances Cheng, Lillian Chau and Cathy Chen for proofreading the page proofs.

In my chambers, a number of barristers have been very supportive. Phillip Ross (who was also my pupilmaster) James Thomson, Dr Nisha Mohamed and Katy Chung all gave me great encouragement. Dr Gerard McCoy QC SC and Dr PY Lo both passed useful information and documents to me. Gerard McCoy also provide useful comments on a draft. Daniel Hui was a very good sounding board for ideas. Thanks to all other members for their encouragement.

Thanks to my parents and my big sister, Tanya, for encouraging me to study in both Japan and China. I am grateful to all my teachers and lecturers at Nagata Senior High, the Australian National University, Fudan University and City University of Hong Kong over the years who taught me much over the years about China, Japan and the law.

Thanks also to my wife, Tomoko, and children, Leila, Kai, Ray and India for their support while I wrote this book.

Thanks to my brother Russell and his wife Michelle and sons Jarrett and Blake for accommodating me on the various occasions I visited London to conduct research in the National Archives in London.

My sister Nicola also was kind enough to visit the National Library in Australia on a number of occasions to find materials I was not able to locate elsewhere. My daughter Leila also carried out some research for me. A special thank you to both of them.

My father, mother and sister, Nicola, all reviewed drafts in detail and provided many useful comments.

Many others have assisted in the writing of this book and I apologise for any omissions.

I have dedicated the book to my late grandfather, Russell Skerman, who was a barrister in North Queensland, and for nine years the Northern Judge of the Queensland Supreme Court based in Townsville before he moved to Brisbane for three years before his retirement. Grandpa instilled in me his love of the law and was a true gentleman. As Northern Judge he was the sole Supreme Court judge trying all criminal and civil cases in North Queensland, an area four or five times the size of Great Britain. I like to think that the judges of the Supreme Court for China and Japan who tried cases over a huge area were much like him.

Further Reading
And Places of Interest

Many books have been cited in the footnotes to this book. For those interested in finding out more on extraterritoriality in China and Japan, here is a select list of the most interesting or useful books.

General histories

Robert Bickers, *The Scramble for China and Stuck in Shanghai,* tell the stories of the Imperial Maritime Customs and what life was like in Shanghai and for those who served in Europe during WWI.

Par Cassel, *Grounds for Judgment,* deals with extraterritoriality in both China and Japan.

Richard Chang, *Justice of Western Consular Courts in Nineteenth Century Japan* deals with some of the major cases that came before the British Court for Japan.

P.D. Coates, *The China Consuls,* is a comprehensive history of the British China Consular Service, including those consular officers who became judges.

Christopher Roberts, *The British Courts and Extraterritoriality in Japan 1859-1899,* provides a comprehensive history of the British courts in Japan and touches on the courts in China.

Eileen Scully, *Bargaining with the State from Afar,* is a very good history of the United States Court for China.

Carol Tan, *British Rule in China: Law and Justice in Weihaiwei 1898 to 1930* tells the history of British justice in Weihaiwei.

Personal histories

Norwood Allman, *Shanghai Lawyer,* is a first hand account of being a consular officer, Mixed Court Assessor and lawyer in China in the twentieth century.

Robert Bickers, *Empire Made Me,* tells the story of the Richard Maurice Tinkler and the Shanghai Municipal Police.

Paul French, *Midnight in Peking,* tells the story of the consular investigation into the death of Pamela Werner.

Sir Edmund Hornby, *An Autobiography,* is a rollicking story of Hornby's life including long sections on China and Japan.

Ernest Peters, *Shanghai Policeman,* tells the story of Peters' life as a policeman in Shanghai and his trial for the murder of Mau.

Ernest Satow, *A Diplomat in Japan,* tells the story of the early British consular service in Japan.

Case law database

Macquarie University in Australia on its Colonial Cases database has uploaded transcripts of judge's notes and case reports. The web address in early 2015 was: http://www.law.mq.edu.au/research/colonial_case_law/colonial_cases/less_developed/china_and_japan/

Places of Interest

There are many museums and other places of interest where

parts of the history recounted in this book can be seen. Some of the more interesting places or museums are listed below.

China

Beijing

The National Museum on Tiananmen Square has a wing dedicated to the Century of Humiliation called the "Road to Renaissance."

The ruins of the Summer Palace can be seen to the north of Peking University.

Shanghai

The area around the Bund remains fairly much as it was in the 1930s. Many buildings and places mentioned in this book can still be seen, including, the old British Consulate and Supreme Court building, the former United States consulate, the Shanghai Club, the former American Club and the Central Police Station.

The Shanghai History Museum in the base of the Pearl Tower also has a good display of items from the period including a mock up of the Mixed Court.

Guangzhou (Canton)

Shamian Island (Shameen Island) remains pretty much as it was in the 1930s. A stroll around the streets gives a feeling for what life would have been like there.

Tianjin

The streets of downtown Tianjin remain much as they were in the 1930s. The most interesting aspect is that because there were numerous foreign concessions the architecture changes as you move from one former concession to the next. It is like visiting Europe in a day.

The Dagu Forts Ruins Museum has an excellent history of the battles in the Second Opium War and Boxer Rebellion.

The remnants of one fort remains and you can look over the entrance to the Hai River and imagine the battles.

Humen

Humen has two museums showing the history of the Opium Wars, the Lin Zexu Memorial Museum and the Naval Battle Museum.

Tamsui, Taiwan

The old British Consulate in Tamsui is now a museum and has a very good display on the history of the consular service. The rooms that were used as a court and a prison can be seen.

Hong Kong

The Coastal Defence Museum and Museum of Maritime History have good displays on British naval power. The old Supreme Court is still located on Statue Square and is being converted into the Court of Final Appeal.

Japan

Yokohama

The Yokohama Archives of History in the grounds of the former British Consulate has a good display on the opening of Yokohama to trade. There is also a library where old newspapers can be looked at.

The Yokohama Bund has been retained and the Bluff can be visited, but all old buildings were destroyed in the 1923 earthquake. The Yokohama Foreigners' Cemetery on the Bluff has a number of graves of people mentioned in this book.

Outside Yokohama in Yokosuka, the former Japanese battleship the Mikasa has been turned into a museum with a good display on the Russo-Japanese War.

Kobe

The Kobe History Museum has a good display on the opening of Kobe. The old concession area has effectively disappeared but in the hills behind Kobe the Ijinkan area retains many of the houses originally built by foreigners' there.

The graves of George French and John James Enslie are in the Kobe Foreigners' Cemetery in Futatabi.

Shimonoseki

Sino-Japanese Peace Treaty Memorial Hall overlooking the Kanmon Straits in Shimonoseki displays the table where the Treaty of Shimonoseki was negotiated and has other interesting memorabilia.

Nagasaki

Dejima Island has been restored as an outdoor museum to provide a good insight into the life in the old Dutch Factory. Many old buildings remain in what was the old foreign settlement.

Sasebo

The Naval Self Defence Museum has very good history of the development of the Japanese Navy and battles up to World War II.

Kagoshima

The Reimeikan Prefectural Museum has an interesting display on the bombardment of Kagoshima.

Hakodate

The former British Consulate in Hakodate now serves as a museum on the old consular system.

Russia

The *Aurora* which survived the battle of Tsushima is docked in downtown St Petersburg and has a very interesting display on the battle.

British Courts in China and Japan

Table of Appointments

The following pages set out in tabular form appointments to the British courts in China and Japan.

Substantive appointments are shown in bold type. Acting appointments are in normal type.

Only substantial acting appointments as Crown Advocate are shown. A number of other lawyers acted as Crown Advocate on short term or case by case bases.

Name	SCCJ – Chief Judge/ Chief Justice	Court for Japan - Judge	SCCJ Judge/ Asst Judge	High Court for Weihaiwei – Judge
Edmund G Hornby	**1865-1876**			
Charles W Goodwin	1871-1873 1876-1878+		**1865-1878+**	
John Fraser				
George French	**1877-1881**			
Robert A Mowat	1876-1878* 1881, 1888 1891	**1891-1897**	**1878-1891**	
Richard T Rennie	**1881-1891**	**1879-1881**		
Nicholas J Hannen	**1891-1900** 1881-1883	**1881-1891**	1871-1874+	
Alexander Myburgh				
Hiram S Wilkinson	**1900-1905**	**1897-1900** 1894-1895	1879-1880	
Russell Robertson		1881-1883		
George Jamieson	1892 1894-1896	1888-1889	**1891-1897** 1886-1888	
John Carey Hall		1888	1888-1889	
Robert W Mansfield			1891, 1897	
W Vernon Drummond				
Hiram P Wilkinson	1898		1898	**1916-1925** 1915
Frederick SA Bourne	1902-1903 1908-1909 1911, 1914		**1898-1916**	**1903-1916**
Eustace H Burrows				
Harold F King			1902-1903	

Crown Advocate	Registrar/ Law Secretary	Call/ Admission	Comments
		Middle Temple	Previously Judge, Ottoman Empire Knighted, 1862
		Lincoln's Inn	+ Based in Japan 1874-1877 Father in law of JC Hall Died in office
	1865-1867 LS		Died in office
		Lincoln's Inn	Previously Chief Justice, Sierra Leone Arrived in Shanghai early 1878 Died in office
	1868-1878 LS **1879-1891** 1867-1868 LS	Inner Temple	China Consular Service, 1864 * As Deputy Chief Judge
		Inner Temple	Knighted, 1882
1878-1881		Inner Temple	Also Consul-General, Shanghai 1891-1897 Knighted, 1895 Died in office + Based in Japan
1880-1882		Inner Temple	Practicing barrister Later became Chairman of Shanghai Municipal Council.
1882-1897	1877-1878+ LS 1879-1880	Middle Temple	Japan Consular Service, 1864 Knighted, 1903 +Based in Japan Father of HP Wilkinson
		Middle Temple	Japan Consular Service, 1860
	1891-1897 1869-1871 LS 1886-1888	Middle Temple	China Consular Service, 1864 Also Consul, Shanghai 1891-1897 CMG, 1897
	1888-1889	Middle Temple	Japan Consular Service, 1868 ISO, 1902, CMG, 1912 Son in law of C Goodwin
	1891, 1897		CMG, 1902 China Consular Service, 1870
1894		Lincoln's Inn	Practicing barrister
1897-1925 1894-1895 1896-1897		Inner Temple	Acting Asst Judge, Siam, 1903-1905 KC, 1928 (Northern Ireland) Son of HS Wilkinson
	1898	Lincoln's Inn	China Consular Service, 1876 CMG, 1909, Knighted, 1916
	1898- 1901	Solicitor	Resigned, 1901
	1901	Middle Temple	China Consular Service, 1891 Elder brother of GW King

Name	**SCCJ - Chief Judge/ Chief Justice**	**Court for Japan - Judge**	**SCCJ Judge/ Asst Judge**	**High Court for Weihaiwei - Judge**
John CE Douglas			1904-1905	1905
WC Platt				
Duncan McNeill				
Havilland de Sausmarez	**1905-1921**			
Arthur R Vincent			1908-1909	
Lindsey Smith			1909-1910	1909
Skinner Turner	**1921-1927** 1920-1921		**1916-1921**	
F Alan Robinson				
Peter Grain	**1927-1933** 1926		**1921-1927**	**1925-1930**
Gilbert W King			**1927-1931** 1917, 1925	1925, 1929
Idwal T Morris				
A J Martin				
Charles GO Anderson				
Cyril H Haines			1936-1937	
Penrhyn Grant Jones	1933-1934 1936-1937 1940-1941		**1931-1943**	1919
Allan G Mossop	**1933-1943**			
Victor Priestwood				
John McNeill				

Crown Advocate	Registrar/ Law Secretary	Call/ Admission	Comments
	1901-1908	Gray's Inn	Resigned to practice at bar in Shanghai Killed in Action in WWI (1915)
1900-1901 1903-1905		Lincoln's Inn	Practicing barrister
1901-1903		Inner Temple	Practicing barrister Father of John McNeill
		Inner Temple	Foreign Office Judicial Service Previously Judge, Ottoman Empire Knighted, 1905, Baronet, 1928
		Munster Bar	Foreign Office Judicial Service Later Irish Senator
		Middle Temple	Foreign Office Judicial Service Later Chief Justice of East Africa Knighted, 1914
		Inner Temple	Foreign Office Judicial Service Previously Judge, Siam Knighted, 1923
	1918-1919		Chief Clerk
		Middle Temple	Foreign Office Judicial Service Knighted,1928
	1908-1927	Gray's Inn Solicitor until 1912	Joined court as clerk in 1903 OBE, 1925 Younger brother of HF King
	1926 1927-1928 1929-1930 1934-1935 1938-1939	Solicitor	Chief Clerk
	1928-1929		
	1930	Middle Temple	Consulate staff member
	1930-1943	Middle Temple	Joined Foreign Office, 1920 MBE, 1930, CBE, 1953. KBE, 1962 Later Judge, HM Court Persian Gulf
		Inner Temple	China Consular Service, 1902 CBE, 1928
1925-1933 1921		Inner Temple	Knighted , 1937
1934-1939 1930, 1934		Inner Temple	Appointment terminated, 1939
1940-1942 1937, 1939		Inner Temple	KC, 1950 (Hong Kong) Son of Duncan McNeill

Judges and District Attorneys of The United States Court for China

Judges

Lebbeus R. Wilfley	(1906 to 1908)
Rufus H. Thayer	(1909 to 1913)
Charles S. Lobingier	(1914 to 1924)
Milton D. Purdy	(1924 to 1934)
Milton J. Helmick	(1934 to 1943)

Special Judges

Nelson Lurton	(1938 and 1941)
Bertrand Johnson	(1943)

District Attorneys

Arthur Bassett	(1906 to 1910)
Frank E Hinckley	(1910 to 1915)
Chauncey E Holcomb	(1915 to 1922)
Leonard Husar	(1922 to 1926)
George Sellett	(1926 to 1934)
Felthan Watson	(1934 to 1936)
Leighton Shields	(1936 to 1943)

Introduction to Vol I

Extraterritoriality – an Extraordinary System

In 1874, Sir Edmund Hornby, Chief Judge of the British Supreme Court for China and Japan, entered a court room in the northern Chinese seaport of Chefoo in the full red robes of a British criminal judge. All those in court rose and bowed to him. As he took his seat, behind him was the British coat of arms bearing the words "Dieu et Mon Droit" ("God and my Right"). Before him in the dock was Thomas Fawcett, a British foreman accused of killing a Chinese man. After a trial in which Chinese witnesses were brought to court in chains to give evidence, Fawcett was acquitted by the British jury. For the next three days and two nights, the local Chinese population besieged Hornby's house demanding proper justice. He wrote later: "Of course, I never tried another British subject accused of killing a Chinaman at an outlying port, unless there was a gun-boat at hand."

What was a British judge, bewigged and fully robed in red, doing trying a criminal case against a British subject in northern China? Why was there a British jury? Why the gunboat? The simple answer is: extraterritoriality.

In China, for almost a century, Britain, America and other foreign countries ran their own civil and criminal justice systems. These legal systems were, as far as possible, entirely separate from the Chinese system. They had their own courts, judges, lawyers and, even, prisons. In Japan, almost identical foreign legal systems to those in China also existed for just over forty years.

These justice systems were created as part of the forced opening of China and Japan in the 1840s and 1850s. Until then, for more than 200 years, both China and Japan had been closed to Westerners and in both countries, only limited foreign trade had been allowed at a single port far away from the capital.

Britain and America changed this. In 1842, following the two-year Opium War, a British Navy flotilla led by Captain Henry Pottinger forced China to sign - at the point of their gunboat barrels - the Treaty of Nanking which opened five ports to Western trade. In 1854, an American naval squadron, led by Commodore Matthew Perry, forced Japan – also at the point of their gunboat barrels – to open to Western trade and sign a Treaty of Amity and Commerce. Other Western countries were quick to follow Britain and America's lead and signed similar treaties with both countries.

The Chinese and Japanese, not surprisingly, hated the "unequal treaties" that had brought foreigners to their shores. They, however, had no choice but to accept them. The treaties allowed the treaty powers to base army and naval forces in China and Japan, and on numerous occasions, British, American and other treaty powers' gunboats and armies were brought in to enforce "treaty rights." Peking was attacked and the Summer Palace burnt to the ground by the British and French in 1860. Kagoshima in southern Japan was shelled and all but destroyed by the British in 1863. Shimonoseki was held to ransom by the British, American, French and Dutch navies in 1864. China fought and lost numerous wars with foreign powers in the late 19th century. Right up to the 1940s, foreign navy boats, exercising treaty rights, patrolled the coast of China and the Yangtze River to protect foreign interests. Foreign troops were stationed in Peking and all along the railway line between Peking and Tientsin.

China and Japan's reaction to their forced opening to the

West continues to this day to have a strong impact on how they both view and treat each other and the rest of the world. Each country faced an almost identical challenge, but the results were diametrically opposite. Japan was the big winner from the unequal treaties while China was the big loser. Neither country has forgotten this – and neither country will. Ever.

This history explains the deep enmity that exists to this day between the two countries and why the 21st century tensions between the newly-strong China and still-strong Japan are so dangerous. If pushed, neither side will back down to the other.

For Japan, its forced opening is, now, a matter for celebration. All over Japan can be found memorials to the arrival of the foreigners and their contribution to the development of Japan. Museums commemorating the foreign settlements and the foreigners who helped build them can be found in all treaty ports. In a country where land is scarce, and despite having fought the British and Americans in World War II, foreign cemeteries from the 19th century have been preserved and are well maintained. On the 150th anniversary of the British and Japanese Treaty of Amity and Commerce, the Japanese Foreign Minster, at the Foreign Office in London, launched a "Japan-UK 150" celebration.[1] In Yokohama, you can enjoy lunch at "Le Jardin de Perry" near where Matthew Perry landed.

For China, its forced opening and the 100 years that followed are now described as "the Century of Humiliation." Anti-foreign sentiment is taught in schools, fills China's history books and is on display in all its museums. Foreign cemeteries have all been destroyed. You could never imagine any Chinese Foreign Minister celebrating an anniversary of the

1 Speech by Mr Shintaro Ito, State Secretary for Foreign Affairs, at a Reception to celebrate 150 Years of Diplomatic Relations between the United Kingdom and Japan at the Foreign & Commonwealth Office, London, September 16, 2008.

Treaty of Nanking anywhere, let alone at the Foreign Office in London. There is no "Le Jardin de Pottinger" in modern-day Nanjing.[2]

How can two countries which faced almost identical challenges have travelled such different roads?

In Japan, the opening of the country led to a civil war between reformers and those who wanted to retain the old feudal government under the Shogunate. The reformers won. From the late 1860s, the basic policy of the Japanese government was "reform or die."

Japan launched headlong into a program of rapid and large scale Westernisation. The Shogunate and old feudal system was abolished; foreign laws were studied and adopted; and, democracy was steadily introduced. The results were amazing. Japan went through a period of massive industrialization and economic growth and year after year became, politically, economically and militarily stronger. In less than 40 years, by 1894, Japan was strong enough to be able to reach agreements with all foreign countries to abolish all the unequal treaties. The following year, it defeated China in war and imposed its own unequal treaty on China. It continued to go from strength to strength, defeating Russia, annexing Korea and, over time, taking over large parts of China. Ultimately, during World War II, Japan occupied almost half of Asia.

China, on the other hand, was at the time of its forced opening already ruled by foreigners, the Manchus from Manchuria in what is now northeast China. The basic policy of the Manchu-run Qing Dynasty can be summarized as "if we reform we will die." Any change in China's system of governance, they believed, would weaken Manchu rule. One large-scale revolt in the 1850s and 1860s, the Taiping Rebellion, did threaten the government (and the Foreign Settle-

2 There is a Pottinger Street in Hong Kong, but that is another story.

ment in Shanghai), but was put down. The Qing Dynasty futilely resisted reform, relying instead on "self-strengthening," modernization in certain limited areas. This response, which led to further wars with foreign powers which China almost invariably lost, allowed China's sovereignty to be chipped away by more and more unequal treaties.

The Republican Revolution in 1911 offered hope, but collapsed into civil war. Germany's defeat in World War I and the Russian Revolution brought the end of extraterritorial rights for Germans and Russians, but saw Japan take over most of Germany's interests in China. Unification under the militarily powerful Nationalists in 1927 offered even more hope; the European powers and America were willing to give up some rights. But by this time Japan was too strong for China to resist alone. By the time World War II started, Japan occupied more than half of China.

To this day, anti-foreign and particularly anti-Japanese propaganda is a fundamental part of the Chinese Communist Party's hold on power. Regular anti-Japanese protests are encouraged (and then, when they get too big, discouraged) by the government. In the 2010s, Sino-Japanese tensions have been upped by the Chinese by the use of military threats to assert China's claims over the Diaoyutai/Senkaku Islands. In March 2014, almost eighty years after World War II finished, the Secretary General of the Chinese Communist Party and President of China Xi Jinping said on a visit to Europe that the "war of aggression committed by Japanese militarism alone inflicted 35 million Chinese military and civilian casualties. These atrocities are still fresh in our memory."[3]

How Japan which until the mid-1840s had co-existed relatively peacefully with China has became China's sworn enemy is a story that for most Westerners has long been forgotten. But given modern-day tensions between the two countries,

3 "Japan's wartime atrocities 'still fresh in memory'", *South China Morning Post* March 30, 2014, p3.

it is well worth remembering. The story is not just Chinese Communist Party propaganda: China was treated appallingly by foreign powers, including Britain and to a lesser extent, the United States, for over 100 years. Japan's treatment of China, after it threw off the unequal treaties that had been imposed on it, was even worse.

Extraterritoriality - foreign justice in foreign lands - was a fundamental part of this humiliation. Extraterritoriality underpinned the foreign presence in China. It served day to day to remind Chinese they were not sovereign in their own land and the assertion of "treaty rights" often resulted in military force being used against China.

Extraterritoriality meant that the governments of China and, while the treaties were in force there, Japan had almost no power to control foreigners enjoying treaty rights. Foreigners were allowed to freely enter the treaty ports, they were not subject to local laws and, could not be punished by local authorities. The most local officials could do was to arrest foreigners and hand them over to their own consular authorities for trial. They could not even deport them. Any threat by the Chinese or Japanese to breach these rights resulted in the dispatch of gunboats to enforce them.

Extraterritoriality created a remarkable system. Each treaty power established courts staffed by consular officers to try cases against their nationals. At its peak, in Shanghai, there were at least 23 different courts operating in the city: 19 foreign courts, three Chinese courts, and a Court of Consuls for bringing cases against the foreign-run Municipal Council. Close to twenty courts operated in the main Japanese treaty port, Yokohama. The consular courts were an alphabet soup of jurisdictions including German, Italian, Austro-Hungarian, Russian, Belgian, Danish, Dutch, French, Hungarian, Spanish, Mexican, Chilean, Norwegian, Swedish, Russian and Spanish courts.

While they hated the unequal treaties that allowed for-

A scene from the Italian consular court in Shanghai in 1920s. Italian and British witness give evidence before an Italian judge and assessors.

eigners freely to enter and trade with their countries, Chinese and Japanese attitudes towards extraterritoriality, at least at the beginning, were equivocal. Despite later protestations and propaganda, neither China nor Japan were against extraterritoriality in the early years. Extraterritoriality had been demanded to protect treaty foreigners from the "barbaric" Chinese and Japanese legal systems which, to be fair to the foreign powers, did regularly torture parties before the courts. For both the Chinese and the Japanese, foreigners handling disputes between other foreigners seemed like a good idea.

Indeed, perhaps most telling of their early attitudes to extraterritoriality is that in the 1870s, China and Japan agreed to provide for mutual extraterritoriality for their citizens in each other's countries. In the 1880s, when foreign countries entered into unequal treaties with Korea, both China and Japan also imposed extraterritoriality on Korea.

The real problems with extraterritoriality came as more and more foreigners arrived in China and Japan and interacted with the locals. Particularly in China, foreigners in the form of missionaries, traders and officers of the foreign-run Imperial Maritime Customs spread across the country. Everywhere they went they mixed with local Chinese, creating friction that lead to disputes and, in the worst cases, to a number of killings. The Japanese managed, for the most part, to restrict foreigners to treaty ports but even in these ports, just as in China, disputes would arise with and crimes be committed against Japanese. Local Chinese and Japanese could only seek justice – in their own country - by going to a foreign court using a foreign language and applying foreign law. They often felt that justice was not done when foreigner judged foreigner. This could lead to violence. The first British Chief Judge, Sir Edmund Hornby, quoted above, had had to call in the gunboat in Chefoo because a mob had besieged his bungalow for three days, angry at the acquittal of the British foreman.

The problems were exacerbated by the fact that most

countries did not appoint trained lawyers to handle legal cases. Cases were instead handled by consuls, often with no legal training. For many countries, consuls were not even professional consular officers, but merely local merchants appointed to handle their country's interests. Cases could be, and often were, very poorly handled and decided.

In order to deal with some of the problems with consular courts, the British, by far the largest Western power in East Asia, were the first to establish a formal court system in China and Japan staffed by professional judges. In 1865, the British Supreme Court for China and Japan was established in Shanghai. It was run from the British Foreign Office in London. The British Court for Japan, under the Shanghai Supreme Court, was established in Yokohama 14 years later. America, as its economic and political interests grew in China, established the United States Court for China in 1906 in Shanghai. This was for most of its life run by the Department of State from Washington DC.

These three courts tried in China, Japan, and, for a period, Korea (or Corea as it was then known), cases of every type imaginable: murder, sedition, rape, contract disputes, divorces, mass fights on board merchant ships, assault, battery, theft, fraud, ship collisions, and even, patent, copyright and trade mark infringement cases.

The courts were in almost all respects fully functioning British and American courts. They were staffed by professional judges. Qualified lawyers appeared before the courts. British or American law was applied and British and American rules of evidence and procedure were used. In the case of the British courts, juries were empaneled for all major civil and criminal cases. British judges and barristers all wore the traditional wigs and gowns, even in the oppressive heat of summer. Case reports were published and full records kept. Every quote from a judge, lawyer or witness in this book is from a contemporaneous report or record.

The only major anomaly was that there were no juries in the American courts. The United States Supreme Court had, in 1891, ruled that the constitutional right to a jury did not apply in extraterritorial courts. This was challenged on a number of occasions with Americans making comparisons to the much-preferred practice in the British courts of trial by jury. Even American judges would from time to time lament not having a jury to assist them in trying cases.

The following chapters tell the story of these British and American judges, their courts, and the lawyers and the parties that appeared before them. The story is told in 13 parts in chronological order beginning from the treaties that established extraterritoriality and continuing through to the end of extraterritoriality in, first, Japan and then China.

At a much higher level, this book also tells the story of China and Japan's forced opening to the world and how extraterritoriality influenced and guided the development the legal and political systems of both countries, so much so that the history of extraterritoriality still has a strong impact on how both countries view the world today.

The men who came to the Far East as judges and lawyers of these court were all adventurers; being willing to travel far away from home to be a judge or practice law in what in the early days were primitive conditions. For the British all, perhaps bar one or two lawyers, were men of Empire. They all believed in extraterritoriality and the benefits it brought to British interests.

The British judges of the 19th century were truly remarkable. The founder of the court, Hornby, was a force of nature who by his own personal will established a fully functioning legal system. His assistant, Charles Goodwin, was a genius, a world famous Egyptologist and Bible scholar. Many other judges had come to China and Japan as British consular officers, committing themselves to spend their entire career in the Far East. They all learnt Chinese or Japanese and could read, write and speak their chosen language fluently. As consular officers they were required to conduct official business with the Chinese or Japanese in the local language. Others were barristers from England who had come to China at a young age seeking their fortunes; one, Nicholas Hannen, achieving the rare honour of becoming both Chief Justice and Consul-General in Shanghai.

The 20th century brought many more changes. Extraterritoriality had been abolished in Japan. The United States Court for China was established to oversee the US consular courts. China was starting to reform its government and legal system, spurring further changes. Shanghai had also grown to be a cosmopolitan city and was no longer the hardship posting it had once been considered to be. These developments brought a new type of judge and lawyer to the courts. For the most part, in both the British and American courts judges were brought in from outside China, not always successfully - the first two American judges were forced to resign. The American legal profession also improved, helped in no small part by the overzealous efforts of the first judge of the US Court to clean up the quality and standards of the bar.

Change also brought new challenges to the courts. They had to deal with two Chinese revolutions, civil war, warlords and rising Chinese (and, in the British courts, Indian) nationalism. World War I brought cases of sedition to both courts as well as tricky questions of how to deal with enemy nationals who lived side by side with Americans and British in China. The entire existence of the US Court was challenged by one American lawyer who launched a large-scale attack on the court in Washington DC. One half-Chinese British barrister denounced the British court for practicing "gunboat diplomacy."

The Japanese incursions into and ultimate occupation of most of China in the 1930s and World War II brought its own difficulties. There were numerous cases before the courts involving spies; murders of, and by, Japanese soldiers; *habeas corpus* applications for the release of Chinese prisoners wanted by the Japanese; and, even whether it was necessary to pay rent when Chinese and Japanese troops were fighting pitched battles outside your front door.

Milton Helmick the last judge of the United States Court for China, who served right up to the commencement of the Pacific War, described the job of an extraterritorial judge:

> "For ordinary every day judging he ought to have known … all about extraterritoriality, a little international law, a smattering of the laws of other countries, something of Chinese law, a great deal about China, a lot about international politics, considerable about diplomatic usages, a bit of anthropology and a modicum about bomb dodging."[4]

So, where did extraterritoriality come from?

4 M. Helmick, "United States Court for China", Far Eastern Survey, Vol. 14, No. 18 (Sep. 12, 1945), p252.

Index

Name

A

Admiralty, jurisdiction in (British) Vol 1: 138, 279, 282, 322-4

Alaska, law of, application in US Courts Vol 2: 85, 184, 192, 252

Alcock, Rutherford Vol 1: 39, 42, 46, 123, 125 Vol 2: 317

Allman, Norwood

- Attorney Vol 1: 102 Vol 2 : 56n, 247n
- Cases Vol 2: 353, 356 Vol 3: 19-20, 90, 92
- Internment and repatriation Vol 3: 172, 175, 180n, 199, 204
- Judges, comments on Vol 2: 117 (Thayer), 266-7 (Purdy), Vol 3: 80-81 (Helmick)
- Shunpao (Shenbao), owner of Vol 3: 138-9
- Student Interpreters, on Vol 1: 88

Amalgamation of British Judicial and Consular positions Vol 1: 189-91, 304-6, 379-81

American Oriental Banking Corporation Vol 3: 90-99, 97i

American-Chinese See: Nationals, dual

Anderson, Charles Graham Overbeck Vol 3: 36

Andrews, Lorrin Vol 2: 81, 86, 97-99, 104, 110-1

Aoki (Viscount) Vol 1: 287-9, 328, 392, 396, 398

Arthur, Chester Vol 1: 219

Appeals

- British Consular/Provincial Courts, from Vol 1: 46, 135-8, 207, 258, 274, 278
- British Court for Japan, from and to Vol 1: 138-9, 207, 322
- British Supreme Court for China, from:
  - Jurisdiction Vol 1: 61, 111, 135-8, 141, 205-6 Vol 2: 59-60, 342-5
  - Full Court (Civil) Vol 2: 345 Vol 3: 21-24

• Full Court (Criminal) Vol 2: 345 Vol 3: 70, 162, 169, 171
• Privy Council (Civil) Vol 1: 107, 275, 322-4 Vol 2: 156, 335-6 Vol 3: 66
• Privy Council (Criminal) Vol 1: 364
Chinese Qing Dynasty Courts Vol 1: 171-2
Chinese Special District Courts, from Vol 3: 30
Hong Kong Supreme Court, from and to Vol 1: 46-7 Vol 2: 26, 174-175, 179-181
Japanese courts Vol 1: 157-8, 395
Mixed British and Chinese court (ad hoc): Vol 1: 169-72
US Consular Courts, from Vol 1: 45 Vol 2: 76
US Court for China
• Jurisdiction: Vol 2: 76, 93-5
• Criminal: Vol 2: 85, 86, 93-5, 269, 360-1 Vol 3: 98, 169, 182
• Civil: Vol 2: 238, 242, 245-6 Vol 3: 19, 83-4
Weihaiwei, High Court of, from Vol 2: 26
Archer, Charles Vol 3: 175, 180

B

Backhouse, Edmund Vol 3: 127
Ballard, James Vol 2: 17
Bank of East Asia Vol 2: 316-20
Barrett, E.I.M. Vol 2: 149-51, 195, 306-9 Vol 3: 13
Barristers
Admission of non-nationals Vol 2: 229n3, 313
Disbarment Vol 2: 228-30, 293-4
Practice in partnerships Vol 1: 73-4 Vol 2: 152-6
Bassett, Arthur Vol 2: 79, 79i, 81-2, 83-5, 88-9, 97, 107-8, 115, 141-3
Beijing See: Peking
Bennertz & Co Vol 1: 370-9
Bentwich, Norman Vol 3: 151-3
Bertie, Francis Vol 1: 347, 367-8, 397-8
Betthell, Ernest Vol 2: 121-134, 145, 153
Biddle, United States v (Biddle Case) Vol 2: 84-5, 104, 113, 114, 184, 192 Vol 3: 83
Bilibid Prison, Vol 2: 185, 245

Blaine, James Vol 1: 224-6
Boxer Indemnity Vol 2: 15, 203, 209
Boxer Rebellion Vol 2: 3, 5, 9-10, 15, 20, 60, 171 Vol 3: 223
British Court for China Vol 1: 26
British Court for Japan
  Closing Vol 1: 396-400 Vol 2: 32
  Establishment Vol 1: 15, 177, 207, 210i, 211
  Jurisdiction Vol 1: 207, 223-7, 278, 321-3, 329, 396-397
  Premises Vol 1: 212
British Court for Siam Vol 2: 37-8, 42, 49, 145, 189
British Protected Persons Vol 1: 279-280 Vol 2: 175 Vol 3: 65-7
British Supreme Court for China and Japan
  Closing Vol 3: 177, 187, 188-90, 192-3
  Establishment Vol 1: 15, 47, 59-61, 71-2, 180
  Japan branch Vol 1: 131-3, 135-40
  Jurisdiction
    • Admiralty Vol 1: 138, 279, 282, 322-4
    • British Military Vol 1: 196-7 Vol 2: 173-5 Vol 3: 161
    • British Protected Persons Vol 1: 279-82 Vol 2: 173-5 Vol 3: 63-67
    • Capital cases Vol 1: 61
    • China, in Vol 1: 60-1 Vol 2: 123 Vol 3: 177, 192
    • Conflicts of Vol 1: 195-6, 223-7, 323-3 Vol 2: 159-60, 327-8, 334 Vol 3: 129
    • Consular/mixed courts, compared to Vol 1: 61, 169-171
    • Customs Service (Chinese), over British employees of Vol 1: 105-7, 237-9, 247-8
    • Foreign Jurisdiction Act Vol 1: 39n, 59
    • Japan, in Vol 1: 60-1, 135-40, 207, 329, 396-7
    • Korea, in Vol 1: 277-8 396-7 Vol 2: 123, 134
    • Nationals, dual Vol 2: 297 Vol 3: 29-30
    • Nationals, non-British Vol 1: 75 Vol 2: 199, 202-3
    • Shanghai Municipal Council Vol 3: 69-71
    • Treaties, under Vol 1: 26, 173-5
    • Weihaiwei Vol 2: 26 Vol 3: 33
  Name Changes:

- "China and Corea" Vol 1: 397
- "China" Vol 2: 134

Premises Vol 1: 111-7, 121-3, 126-8 Vol 3: 205-208

Bourne, Frederick SA

Acting Chief Justice/Judge, sitting as: Vol 1: 406-9, Vol 2: 9, 16-19, 102-114, 106i, 125-130, 131-4, 132i, 135-9, 158-60

Acting Chief Justice/Judge, other mentions: Vol 1: 403-4 Vol 2: 35, 116, 145, 182

Appointment as Judge: Vol 1: 386-7, 389

Assessor, Mixed Court: Vol 1: 389

Biography Vol 1: 28, 230, 386-9, 387i

Chief Justices, relationships with: Vol 1: 389, 409 Vol 2: 36-7, 53, 147

Judge/Asst Judge, sitting as: Vol 2: 164-5,

Judge/Asst Judge, other mentions: Vol 1: 128 Vol 2: 50-1, 78, 154,195, 220, 339, 462

Knighthood Vol 1: 188-9

Land Law, on Vol 2: 161-5, 277

Retirement Vol 2: 187-8

Weihaiwei, Judge of Vol 1: 27-29, 187-8

Bourne, Kenneth Vol 2: 189 Vol 3: 106, 106i

Boxer Rebellion Vol 2: 3, 5, 9-15, 20, 33-5, 60, 171, 209

Boxer Indemnity Vol 2: 15, 203, 209

Brown, J. Warner Vol 3: 92-99, 105

Bryan, R.T. Vol 3: 25, 31, 68, 68i, 78-9, 80, 200

Burrows, Eustace Vol 1: 389 Vol 2: 47n

C

Calhourn, John Vol 1: 22

Canton (Guangzhou)

Attacks on: Vol 1: 25, 28 Vol 3: 10 (considered)

Canton Factory Vol 1: 23-4, 26, 45

Cases in Vol 1: 46, 237-43, 263-8 Vol 2: 40-41, 173-6, 316-20 Vol 3: 29, 145, 180

Claims Commission Vol 1: 269-72

Land tenure: Vol 2: 161
Riots and protests in Vol 1: 264-6, 265i Vol 2: 317
Carew, Edith, Vol 1: 337, 344-365 Vol 2: 551
Carew, Walter Vol 1: 337, 344-365
Capital punishment See: Death Penalty
Casement, Gerald Vol 3: 163-5, 182
Chalaire Walter Vol 3: 83-84
Chapman William Vol 2: 349-51
Char, Nick Vol 2: 269, 272 Vol 3: 18-9, 24-28
Cheek Arbitration (Siam) Vol 1: 382-5
Chefoo Convention Vol 1: 172-175, 371 Vol 2: 137 Vol 3: 30
Chen (Shanghai Mixed Court Magistrate) Vol 1: 154-6, 155i
Chennault, Claire (General) Vol 3: 190-191
Chiang Kai-shek Vol 2: 300 Vol 3: 9, 13, 57, 139. 149
China Association Vol 1: 325, 370, 381 Vol 2: 63, 76 Vol 3: 62
China Eastern Railway Zone Vol 3: 127-9
China Gazette Vol 2: 12, 98-9, 104-5, 111
China League Vol 1: 381
Chishima Case Vol 1: 321-4, 372
Church Missionary Society Vol 1: 231-237, 232i
Civil War (China) Vol 2: 5, 171-3, 323
Civil War (Japan) Vol 1: 10, 36, 147
Cixi, Empress Dowager Vol 2: 10, 14, 141 Vol 3: 127
Clark Kerr, Archibald Vol 3: 154-5, 162, 199-200
Colbert, John Vol 3: 99-103
Colonial Office Vol 1: 178, 189, 192-3 Vol 2: 25-26, 96, 101
Commission, Claims (Britain-China) Vol 1: 263, 269-72 Vol 2: 33-5, 66-8 Vol 3: 74
Commission, Extraterritoriality see: Extraterritoriality Commission
Commission, International (Shanghai, 1925) Vol 2: 321-3
Commissioner of Foreign Affairs (Shanghai) Vol 2: 260, 261 Vol 3: 26-7, 28
Commissioner (Chinese Customs) Vol 1: 105, 245-8
Commissioner (US Court) Vol 2: 184-7, 235-7, 280 Vol 3: 168

Commissioner (Weihaiwei) Vol 2: 24-6
Common law of the United States Vol 2: 75, 83, 85
Companies, regulation of
  American Vol 2: 211-2 Vol 3: 87-9, 138-41
  British Vol 2: 106, 108, 113, 114, 211-2, 320 Vol 3: 69
Communists (China) Vol 3: 13-4, 57, 145, 146, 196, 197-8, 200
Communists (Soviet Union) Vol 2: 211, 255-7, Vol 3: 13-4
Consular Courts
  Belgian Vol 1: 135 Vol 2: 335
  Danish Vol 1: 78
  Decisions of non-British, recognition of in British Courts Vol 2: 32
  General Vol 1: 12, 183, 286, 426
  German Vol 1: 292-5
  Italian Vol 1: 13i
  Japanese Vol 2: 312-3, 315
  Prussian Vol 1: 78
  Russian Vol 1: 198
Consular Courts (British) - Pre Establishment of SCCJ
  Hearings in Vol 1: 70
  Jurisdiction of and appeals from Vol 1: 45-7
  Problems with Vol 1: 15, 39-40, 43-44, 44i
Consular Courts (British) - Post Establishment of SCCJ
  Appeals from Vol 1: 61, 135-8, 207, 274
  Hearings in Vol 1: 140-1, 161, 223, 273 Vol 2: 124 Vol 3: 121, 125, 126
  Hornby's role in building system Vol 1: 99-102, 104-5, 109, 129, 136-8, 179-180
  Kanagawa Consular Court, premises Vol 1: 213
  Kanagawa Consular Court, abolition of Vol 1: 210i, 211
  Jurisdiction of Vol 1: 61, 196, 198, 224, 227, 278, 323, 339 Vol 3: 128
  Renaming as Provincial Courts Vol 1: 61
  Shanghai Consular Court, abolition of Vol 1: 61
  Transfer of cases to SCCJ Vol 1: 234
  Witnesses, swearing of Vol 1: 321
  Visits by SCCJ judges Vol 1: 132, 136-8, 205-6

Consular Courts (United States) - Pre-establishment of US Court for China
Appeals from Vol 1: 45
Cases in Vol 1: 44-5, 78-9, 140-1, 150i, 150-1 219-222
Jurisdiction Vol 1: 39n, 44-5, 78-9, 196, 219-8
Problems with Vol 1: 15, 39-41 Vol 2: 74
Consular Courts (United States) - Post establishment of US Court for China
Appeals from Vol 2: 75-6
Cases in Vol 2: 86, 205, 208 Vol 3: 190
Concurrent jurisdiction (Shanghai) Vol 2: 184-7
Double jeopardy Vol 2: 86
Jurisdiction of Vol 2: 76, 86, 184-7, 237, 240-1, 254, 269, 360
Premises Vol 2: 185
Consular jails
Conditions in Vol 1: 40, 114n7, 388 Vol 2: 41, 129-30, 184
Construction of Vol 1: 113-4, 118
Escapes from Vol 1: 40, 45, 226
Executions at Vol 1: 97, 118-9 Vol 2: 41
Prisoners in Vol 1: 141, 215, 220, 247, 264, 360, 362, 396 Vol 2: 129-30, 240, 244, 356
Transfers to other prisons Vol 1: 141, 268, 362 Vol 2: 129-30
Consular Regulations (US), application of in US Court Vol 3: 81, 83-4
Convention of Kanagawa Vol 1: 34
Convention of Peking Vol 1: 32
Coolidge, Calvin Vol 2: 266, 323
Coolies (Chinese) Vol 1: 138, 148-157
Corea See: Korea
Court of Consuls Vol 1: 12 Vol 3: 67, 70, 160
Covey (barrister) Vol 3: 16
Creighton, G.W. Vol 3: 124, 127
Crosse, Charles Vol 1: 399 Vol 2: 125-9
Crown Advocate
Position and role: Vol 1 193-4, 325 Vol 2: 37, 41-2, 154, 314 Vol 3: 76,

145, 155-6, 203
Remuneration and benefits Vol 1: 194-5, 369-70 Vol 2: 58-9 Vol 3: 154
Cunningham, Edwin Vol 2: 192 Vol 3: 26, 28
Cushing, Caleb Vol 1: 21-23
Currie, Phillip Vol 1: 189-191, 303-306, 310, 380
Custodian of Enemy Property Vol 2: 200-1, 202, 332, 335 Vol 3: 203
Customs Service (China)
Authority of foreign courts, challenges to, by Vol 1: 105-7, 238-9, 240-2, 244-8
Enforcement against foreigners, by Vol 1: 305, 370
Foreign employees Vol 1: 14, 105, 270,
Offences by foreign Customs officers Vol 1: 159-65, 237-44, 263-9, 309-16, 316-7
Relatives of judges or parties Vol 1: 93 Vol 2: 498
Revenue, collection of Vol 1: 105 Vol 2: 203, 404
Structure Vol 1: 105
Customs service (Japanese) Vol 1: 143, 199-202

D

Deacon, Victor Vol 1: 270-1
Death Penalty (British and American courts)
Authority to try cases Vol 1: 45, 61, 132 (lack of), 178, 207
Commutations Vol 1: 81, 222, 361-2, 396 Vol 3: 118, 121-2, 162
Executions Vol 1: 45, 97, 118-9 Vol 2: 40-1 Vol 3: 12, 119-20 (failed)
Sentences of death Vol 1: 45, 80, 94-5, 118, 222, 360, 396 Vol 2: 40 Vol 3: 13, 33, 118, 162
Death Penalty (Japan) Vol 1: 37, 157, 395
Defence of the Realm Act (DORA), Vol 2: 197, 227
De Long, Charles Vol 1: 154
De Menil, Henry Vol 2: 88-92, 95, 137, 141, 143
Denby, Charles Vol 2: 116
Denby, Edwin Vol 2: 75-6, 116, 186
Disbarment of lawyers Vol 2: 82, 97, 229-30, 293-4, 302-4, 361
District Attorney, position and role Vol 2: 75, 81, 82

District of Columbia laws, application in US Courts Vol 2: 85, 184, 192, 252, 271 Vol 3: 81-2
Douglas, Archibald (Admiral) Vol 2: 64
Douglas, John
  Barrister Vol 2: 131, 133, 158-60, 188
  Case against former partner Vol 2: 152-156
  Death Vol 2: 196-7
  Registrar Vol 2: 27, 47, 50, 64, 145, 221
Drummond, W Vernon Vol 1: 325, 371-4, 378, 406n, 406, 407-8 Vol 2: 16, 47-8, 153
Dual Nationals See Nationals, Dual

E

Elliot, Charles Vol 1: 24-5
Ellis, Francis Vol 2: 28, 102, 103-4, 135-9, 226
Enemy Nationals Vol 1: 17 Vol 2: 200-203, 210-211 (See also Prize Cases)
Evans, R.T. Vol 3: 94-7, 94i
Extraterritoriality
  Description of Vol 1: 7-8, 12-4, 18
  Diplomatic statements on Vol 1: 21-3, 147-8, 171-2, 223-7, 312, 315 Vol 2: 20-1, 73 Vol 3: 43-47, 51-2, 114, 136-5, 147-8, 185-6
  Judges' personal views of Vol 1: 18, 59, 91, 105-6, 165, 321 Vol 2: 31, 118, 222, 336, 346-7 Vol 3: 138
  Judicial pronouncements on Vol 1: 76, 78-9, 106-7, 169-70, 323, 377 Vol 2: 129, 176, 268-9, 294, 334 Vol 3: 38
  Legacy Vol 3: 196-8
  Political statements on Vol 1: 327-8 Vol 3: 125, 136-7
  Public comments on Vol 1: 204, 320-1, 390-1 Vol 2: 74-5, 232-3, Vol 3: 106, 113-4, 125
  Treaty provision abrogating Vol 1: 329 396-7 Vol 2: 134 Vol 3: 189
  Treaty provisions establishing Vol 1: 22, 26, 29, 34-5, 277-8
Extraterritoriality Commission Vol 2: 249, 305, 323-5, 345

F

Far Eastern Bar Association 185, 238, 245, 263 Vol 3: 80
Faison, P. Vol 2: 353, 356
Feetham, Richard Vol 3: 50i, 50-1, 159
Feetham Report Vol 3: 50-1, 159
Fessenden, Stirling
Attorney Vol 2: 80i, 81, 82-3, 157, 166, 210, 232, 233i, 234, 235, 237, 238, 280-1
Biography Vol 3: 200
Lobingier, Charles, defence of Vol 2: 233, 241, 247
SMC Chairman/Director-General Vol 2: 263-4 Vol 3: 13, 61, 134-5, 135i
Speaker/toastmaster Vol 2: 192, 246, 263-4, 266
Fischer, Oscar Vol 2: 231-2, 231i, 276, 321 Vol 3: 16, 68, 68i
Fish, Hamilton Vol 1: 154
Fleming, William
Attack on Lobingier Vol 2: 230-47, 263
Attorney Vol 2: 88-89, 141-143, 157, 166, 211, 284, 315, 353-6
Francis, John J. Vol 1: 238-43, 267, 322
Franklin, Cornell
Attorney: Vol 2: 253-4, 258-264, 353-6, 359 Vol 3: 83-4, 94, 97, 200
SMC Chairman: Vol 3: 134-5
Fraser, John Vol 1: 66i, 67-8, 73-4, 83, 90
Fraser (Foreign Office) Vol 1: 288n7, 289, 392
Foreign Affairs, Ministry of (China) (See also: Tsungli Yamen) Vol 2: 92, 207-8, 321 Vol 3: 53
Foreign Office (British)
Amalgamation of Judicial and Consular positions, by Vol 1: 189-91, 304-6, 379-81
Chief Justice, change in title of, by Vol 2: 46, 48, 49-50
Colonial Office, Agreements with for sharing judges Vol 2: 27, 179, 343-5
Consular Officers, appointment of Vol 1: 42, 83-7, 387-8 Vol 3: 37-8
Courts, Supervision of Vol 1: 15, 104, 111-4, 189-92, 204, 206, 223, 268, 304n2, 353-4, 356 Vol 2: 40, 60 Vol 3: 121-2
Crown Advocate, Appointment and supervision of Vol 1: 193-4,

256-7, 346-7 Vol 2: 32-3, 41-2, 58-9 Vol 3: 153-5, 187-8
Foreign Office Judicial Service Vol 2: 55, 146, 189, 218, 338
Judges, Appointment and supervision of Vol 1: 47, 51, 58, 66, 178, 212, 256-7, 303, 368, 384, 387 Vol 2: 53-5, 145-6, 147, 189, 216, 218 Vol 3: 74, 181, 187
Orders in Council, drafting: Vol 1 59, 204, 278 Vol 2: 2, 343-4, 49-50
French, George
Biography Vol 1: 192-3
Chief Justice Vol 1: 192, 229, 230, 234-7, 237-244 Vol 2: 53
Sickness and Death Vol 1: 249-252, 252i, 255-6, 364, 412
Wilkinson, H.S., praise for Vol 1: 215, 218
Fry, Marjorie Vol 3: 151-3
Full Court (Hong Kong) Vol 2: 175, 179-181
Full Court (Shanghai) Vol 2: 59-60, 216, 338, 342-345 Vol 3: 21, 162, 169-72

G

Gambling (in Shanghai) Vol 2: 56, 84-5, 269-271, 270i Vol 3: 67-72
Gaol, Ward Road Vol 3: 12, 106, 119-20, 133-4, 167, 168, 180
Gaols See also Bilibid Prison and McNeil Island Prison
Gaols, Consular: See Consular Jails
Garfield, James Vol 1: 224
Gauss, Clarence Vol 3: 141, 141i
Godfrey, C.W. Vol 2: 102, 111-3, 136
Gollan, Henry Vol 2: 322i, 322-3, 343-5, 344i Vol 3: 22
Gompertz, Henry Vol 2: 187, 198n
Goodwin, Agnes Vol 1: 64, 67, 124-5, 143, 146, 260, 354
Goodwin, Charles W
Assistant Judge (Shanghai) Vol 1: 67-70, 73, 91, 96-7, 101, 106-7, 118, 129, 134, 138-9, 260
Assistant Judge (Japan) Vol 1: 130-133, 142-6, 158, 179, 206, 207-8 Vol 2: 218
Acting Chief Judge Vol 1: 118, 132, 181-2, 206
Biography Vol 1: 16, 61-67
Court Building (and consulate fire) Vol 1: 120, 121, 124-5

Death Vol 1: 177, 183-6, 189, 208, 412
Family members Vol 1: 64, 67, 124-5, 143, 146, 184, 260 Vol 2: 51
Judge for Japan, offer of appointment Vol 1: 183
Supreme Court and Consular Gazette Vol 1: 101
Grain, Peter
Biography Vol 2: 218-9
Assistant Judge Vol 2: 118, 276-7, 287-9, 290-3, 293-5, 337, 340, 344i
Full Court, Hong Kong Vol 2: p181n3
Full Court, Shanghai Vol 2: 343-5, 344i Vol 3: 22-3, 22i, 69-71
Jewish, purported to be Vol 2: 219
Judge Vol 2: 346 Vol 3: 12, 21-2, 22i, 61, 62-67, 70-2, 76
Magistrate Vol 2: 313
Kentwell, Lawrence, relationship with Vol 2: 291-2, 295-6, 300, 302-4
Retirement Vol 3: 73-4
Weihaiwei, Judge of Vol 2: 339 Vol 3: 32-3
Grant Jones, Penrhyn
Acting Judge, Weihaiwei Vol 3: 37
Acting Judge, Shanghai: Vol 3: 116-8, 121-2
Assessor, Mixed Court Vol 2: 394
Assistant Judge, Shanghai Vol 2: 181, 302-3 Vol 3: 67, 74, 85, 152-3, 165-6, 170, 173, 175, 187
Biography: Vol 3: 37-42, 200
Consular Officer: Vol 3: 37, 48-9
Full Court, Hong Kong: Vol 2: 181n3
Full Court, Shanghai Vol 3: 162, 171
Sikhs, view of: Vol 3: 40-2, 155
Gregson, R.E., Vol 2: 135-6
Gumpach, Baron von Vol 1: 106-7, 129

H

Habeas Corpus Vol 1: 151, 222, 227 Vol 2: 97, 361 Vol 3: 151-3, 182
Haines, Cyril
Acting Assistant Judge: Vol 3: 118n13
Biography Vol 3: 36, 200-1

Coroner Vol 3: 147-9
Registrar Vol 3: 85, 115, 120, 162, 180, 181, 187
Hall (nee Goodwin), Agnes, see Goodwin, Agnes
Hall, John Carey
Acting Assistant Judge Vol 1: 260-1
Consular Officer Vol 1: 140-1, 142n29, 146, 364
Coroner Vol 1: 345, 349-51, 354-5
Hannen, Nicholas
Biography Vol 1: 93, 134
Acting Asst Judge (Japan) Vol 1: 131-9, 142-4, 153-5, 206, 208, 212
Acting Chief Justice Vol 1: 138-9, 249-51, 257, 258
Arbitrator (Siam) Vol 1: 382-5
Barrister Vol 1: 92, 94-6, 106-7, 161-3, 167-8, 235
Crown Advocate Vol 1: 194, 208, 210, 235, 238
Chief Justice,
- administering courts Vol 1: 304n2, 367, 369, 370, 389
- other mentions Vol 1: 17, 296, 304i, 320, 321n4, 326, 397-8 Vol 2: 51, 164
- sitting as Vol 1: 310-4, 322-4, 374-6, 379 Vol 2: 164
Chief Justice and Consul General, amalgamated role Vol 1: 303-7, 310-1, 314, 330, 379-81
Consul General (Shanghai) Vol 1: 307, 321n4, 325, 330, 332-333, 371-4, 376-9, 379-80
Consul General (Shanghai), other mentions 17, 296
Death Vol 1: 401-11, 412 Vol 2: 31-2
Judge for Japan Vol 1: 255-7, 259, 261, 282, 284-6
Knighthood Vol 1: 326
Shanghai Municipal Council, advisor to Vol 1: 210, 216
Harbin Herald Vol 3: 59
Harding, Warren Vol 2: 242-3, 246
Hardoon, Liza Vol 3: 62-67, 174-5
Hardoon, Silas Vol 3: 63
Harris, M. Reader Vol 2: 313 Vol 3: 17i, 22, 69
Harris, Townsend Vol 1: 34
Hart, Robert Vol 1: 105-7, 129, 237-8, 240, 242, 244-248 Vol 2: 13i
Hayes, Rutherford Vol 1: 222

Hayllar, Francis Vol 1: 234-5, 238-41
Hays, J. Vol 2: 102, 105, 106i, 110, 226
Heath, Neil Vol 2: 352-362
Heen, M.L. Vol 2: 283-7
Helmick, Milton
Biography Vol 3: 79-82, 202
Extraterritoriality, views on Vol 1: 18
Judge, sitting as Vol 3: 80, 81-84, 95-99, 99-102, 134, 139-141, 163-5, 175
Judge, other mentions Vol 3: 87-90, 138, 179, 190
Hereira (Capt) Vol 1: 152, 155i, 155-6
Hetherington, J.H. Vol 1: 337-34
Hinckley, Frank Vol 2: 79, 104, 115, 205 Vol 3: 84
Hiogo See: Kobe
Holcomb, Chauncy Vol 2: 205-8, 237, 251, 264, 267, 268, 355 Vol 3: 78
Home, Noel Vol 2: 81, 131, 152i, 152-6, 188
Hong Kong
Cases involving Vol 1: 151, 169-70, 189, 264-5, 309, 317 Vol 2: 328-32
Cessation of and lease of by China Vol 1: 26, 32, 335 Vol 2: 25 Vol 3: 187
Companies Vol 1: 104, 106, 108, 113, 114, 212 Vol 3: 192
Executioners from: Vol 2: 41 Vol 3: 119-120
Imprisonment in Vol 1: 81, 101-2, 268, 282, 362 Vol 2: 28 Vol 3: 134
Rule of Law in, comment on Vol 1: 190
Supreme Court See: Supreme Court, Hong Kong
Hong Kong Chinese See: Nationals, dual
Hornby, Edmund G
Appointment as Chief Judge Vol 1: 47, 51, 58, 59-60, 66i, 67-71
Biography Vol 1: 51-8, 93
Chief Judge Vol 1: 7, 14, 16, 52i, , 56-7, 73, 75-81, 91, 94-7, 106-7, 120, 159-163, 191
Consular (provincial) courts, supervision of Vol 1: 43-44, 99, 100, 104-105, 129-30, 141-142
Court Buildings, construction of Vol 1: 111-114, 121-5, 212
Coolies, on Vol 1: 148-153
Hart, Robert, on Vol 1: 105-6
Japan, Reform of British Court system in Vol 1: 129-132, 137-8,

170-1, 177-8, 205-6
Judicial abilities, comments on Vol 1: 55-8, 108-110, 163-4, 179-80
Mixed courts, on Vol 1: 95, 169-172
Paranormal experience Vol 1: 102-4, 178
Shanghai Volunteer Corps Vol 1: 70, 83n1
Supreme Court and Consular Gazette Vol 1: 99-102
Retirement (including discussions of) Vol 1: 108-110, 177-181
Wives Vol 1: 54, 179, 181
Hough, Frank Vol 3: 92, 95-6
Hsu, Showin Wetzen Vol 3: 31, 31i
Hull, Cordell Vol 3: 88-9, 136, 185-6
Hulme, John Vol 1: 46
Husar, Leonard Vol 2: 251-3, 260-1, 266, 269-271, 350i, 351-62, Vol 3: 169

I

Idzumo HIJMS Vol 3: 131-2, 176
Ingenohl, Carl von Vol 2: 328-336
Ingenohl, Frederich von Vol 2: 330
Ito Hirobumi Vol 1: 36, 328, 331-1, 370 Vol 2: 121-3
Iwakura Mission Vol 1: 147-8, 157
Iwakura Tomomi Vol 1: 147

J

Jacob, Mary Vol 1: 351-6, 362-4
Jails, Chinese Vol 1: 40, 275
Jails, Consular See: Consular jails
Jails, Japanese Vol 1: 141, 395
Jamieson, George
Acting Asssistant Judge Vol 1: 260, 279
Acting Judge for Japan Vol 1: 260-1
Assistant Judge Vol 1: 304i, 310, 316-7, 320, 322-4, 326
Judge for Japan, application for position Vol 1: 368
Biography Vol 1: 84, 86-7
Consul (Shanghai) Vol 1: 304i, 320, 330, 380-1

Consul General (Shanghai) Vol 1: 380, 387
Consular Officer Vol 1: 90
Retirement Vol 1: 370, 381-2, 409
Student Interpreter Vol 1: 87
Jernigan, Thomas Vol 2: 81, 117-8, 166
Johnson, Bertrand Vol 3: 190-2, 210
Johnson, Finley Vol 2: 322i, 322-3
Johnson, Nelson Vol 3: 54, 88-9
Johnson Stokes & Master Vol 1: 322, 371
Jones, Loftus Vol 1: 406n5, Vol 2: 32, 195, 197n
Judd, William Vol 3: 105-116
Judges (British)
Remuneration Vol 1: 192, 194, 215, 249, 380, 384-5 Vol 2: 59
Qualifications required Vol 1: 61 Vol 2: 26, 180-1, 343-5
Judges (US)
Remuneration Vol 3: 78
Special Vol 2: 184 Vol 3: 168, 190-2
Jury trials (British courts)
Abolition, proposed Vol 1: 177-8
Coroner's jury Vol 1: 339, 345
Criticism of Vol 1: 163, 269, 139-41, 469-70
Hong Kong, in Vol 1: 45, 151 Vol 2: 174
Japan, in Vol 1: 138, 182, 196-7, 215
Jurors, number of Vol 1: 95-6, 364 Vol 2: 135
Jury duty Vol 2: 58
Trials, criminal Vol 1: 79-81, 94-5, 104, 118-9, 159-63, 239-43, 267-8, 281-2, 284-5, 316-7, 348-59, 375-6, 386 Vol 2: 16-8, 40-1, 102-14, 135-39, 197, 284-7, 313-5 Vol 3: 12, 105-12, 116-8, 161-2, 170
Trials, civil: Vol 1: 107, 129, 196-7, 197i Vol 2: 43-4, 131-4, 305-6 Vol 3: 71-2
Weihaiwei Vol 2: 28 Vol 3: 32-3
Jury trials (United States Courts)
Coroner's jury Vol 1: 220, 339
Expressions of desire for Vol 1: 16 Vol 2: 232-3, 264 Vol 3: 95, 100, 102
Trial without, legality of Vol 1: 16, 219, 221, 227-8 Vol 2: 3, 75-6, 78

Vol 3: 94-5, 98-9, 182

K

Kagoshima Vol 1: 8, 35-6, 361 Vol 3: 148
Kanagawa See: Yokohama
Kearny, Lawrence Vol 2: 251-262, 357, 358
Kellog, Frank Vol 2: 323
Kemp, Joseph Vol 2: 343n7 Vol 3: 70
Kentwell, Lawrence
  Biography Vol 2: 273-6, Vol 3: 201-2
  Civil Actions, personal involvement in Vol 2: 280-1, 277-81, 290-3
  Disbarment 293-5, 302-3
  Grain, Peter, relationship with Vol 2: 291-2, 295-6, 300, 302-4
  Legal Practice Vol 2: 276-7, 287-9, 301
  Imprisonment Vol 3: 201-2
  Nationality Vol 2: 275, 297-9, 300, 355 Vol 3: 201-2
  Opium smuggling, possible involvement Vol 2: 354-5
  Prosecution of Vol 2: 281-7, 296-300 Vol 3: 201-2
Killings, Inter-racial
  British and Americans, of, by Japanese Vol 1: 35-36, 37 Vol 3: 127 (speculation), 146-9
  British, of, by Chinese Vol 1: 31-2, 172-3
  Chinese, of, by British Vol 1:79-81, 91, 94-97, 104, 159-165, 165-168, 237-244, 263-269, 316-7, 374-6 Vol 2: 135-141, 321-323 Vol 3: 105-116, 165-6
  Chinese, of, by Americans Vol 1: 280-2 Vol 2: 88-95, 141-3
  Japanese, of, by British and Americans Vol 1: 283-6, 394-5 Vol 3: 123-5
  Korean, of, by British Vol 1: 386
King, Gilbert W
  Biography Vol 2: 35, 35i, 219-222
  Clerk of Court Vol 2: 35, 35i
  OBE, awarded Vol 2: 337-8
  Registrar Vol 2: 145, 195-6, 201, 220i, 278, 283, 297, 306-11
  Assistant Judge Vol 2: 346, 346i Vol 3: 22, 35-6

King, Harold Vol 2: 35, 221
King, Wunsz Vol 3: 26
Kirkwood, Montague Vol 1: 213, 322
Knatchbull-Hugessen, Hughe Vol 3: 118, 133
Kobe
  Cases in Vol 1: 215, 284
  French, George, death and burial in Vol 1: 249-52, 364
  Hiogo, established in place of Vol 1: 34
  Incidents involving: Vol 1: 37, 140-2, 283-4, 338, 399 Vol 2: 36
Kong Sing Vol 2: 135, 141-3
Korea
  Cases involving Vol 1: 386 Vol 2: 9, 123-34
  Extraterritoriality in Vol 1: 14, 15, 22, 277-8 Vol 2: 3, 76, 134
  Japanese claims to Vol 1: 10, 330, 332 Vol 2: 4, 60-1, 121, 126-7, 134
Kung (Prince) Vol 1: 60, 268-70
Kuomintang (see Nationalist Party)

L

Lampson, Miles Vol 3: 44-5, 47, 53-4, 53i, 118
Land Law Vol 1: 235-236 Vol 2: 29, 160-167, 276-7
Land Regulations (Shameen) Vol 2: 317, 320
Land Regulations (Shanghai) Vol 1: 76-78 Vol 2: 165, 268-9
Law Officers of the Crown Vol 1: 54, 171, 196, 205-6, 223, 268 Vol 2: 37n13
League of Nations Vol 2: 209-10 Vol 3: 57-8, 62
Legal System (Japan)
  Traditional Vol 1: 14
  Reform of Vol 1: 37, 71-2, 147-8, 157, 283, 286-7, 327
Legal System (China)
  Qing Dynasty Vol 1: 14, 171-2 Vol 2: 20-1
  Republican Vol 2: 324 Vol 3: 14-5, 30, 137, 140, 198
  Reform of Vol 1: 71-2 Vol 2: 20-3, 141, 208, 324 Vol 3: 30-1, 43-5, 48
Levinson, William Vol 2: 225-30 Vol 3: 75
Li (Shanghai Magistrate) Vol 2: 88, 92, 137, 139-40, 143
Li Hongzhang Vol 1: 173, 330-3 Vol 2: 11, 14

Lichtfield, Henry Vol 1: 214, 284-5, 339-42, 346i, 348, 356, 399-400
Lin Zexu, Vol 1: 24-5, 27i Vol 3: 224
Lindsell, Roger Vol 2: 343n7
Lipson Ward, H. Vol 2: 293n, 297-8 Vol 3: 75
Lobingier, Charles
  Allegations against Vol 2: 230, 232-3, 236-8, 241-2
  Biography Vol 2: 182-3
  Chinese Government Decoration Vol 2: 246
  Far Eastern Bar Association Vol 2: 238, 245, 264
  Investigation of Vol 2: 242-4
  Judge, sitting as Vol 2: 205-7, 210-2, 234, 244-5, 237-40, 246-7, 252-62, 268, 280-1
  Judge, other mentions Vol 2: 191-2, 241, 244, 245-6 Vol 3: 79
  Reform of US Court for China Vol 2: 4, 183-7
  Retirement: Vol 2: 263-5
Lowder, John Vol 1: 143, 200-1, 204n, 213, 214, 284, 322, 345-64, 399
Lurton, Nelson Vol 3: 168-9, 202
Lu Chiang Hsiang Vol 2: 207
Luna Park Vol 3: 67-72

M

MacDonald, Claude Vol 1: 368
MacGregor, Atholl Vol 2: 343n7 Vol 3: 162, 171-2, 171i, 199, 202-3, 204
MacKellar, Patrick Vol 3: 161n4, 169-72, 536
MacLeod, R.N. Vol 2: 43-5, 284, 313, 313i, 315, 333-6 Vol 3: 17i
MacMurray, John Vol 3: 27
Macnaghten, Ernest Vol 3: 69-71
Maitland, E.T Vol 2: 297, 298i, 301, 309-10, 321n18 Vol 3: 15-6, 16i
Manchuria/Manchukuo
  Extraterritoriality in Vol 3: 58-60, 127-9, 155
  Japanese occupation Vol 1: 330, 332 Vol 2: 5, 61-4, 200 Vol 3: 48-9, 52, 57-8, 88, 123, 127-9
  Russian occupation Vol 1: 334 Vol 2: 15, 23, 60-1
Mandate Abrogating System of Consular Jurisdiction (Chinese)

Vol 3: 45-8
Mansfield, Robert Vol 1: 270
Maria Luz Vol 1: 137-8, 148-57
Martin, A.J. Vol 2: 284 Vol 3: 36
Master, A.P. Vol 1: 322
Master, R.F.C. Vol 2: 313
Mau Te-piau Vol 3: 106-13
McCord, United States v (McCord case) Vol 2: 82-6, 104, 107, 109, 111-2, 114
McDonald, Ranald Vol 2: 280 Vol 3: 22, 40-1, 108-15
McNeil Island Prison Vol 2: 350-1, 359-60, 361 Vol 3: 98-9, 165, 167, 169, 182
McNeill, Duncan Vol 1: 406n, Vol 2: 33, 42-6, 43i, 48, 148, 333, 339-40 Vol 3: 157
McNeill, John
  Barrister Vol 2: 340 Vol 3: 106, 109, 115, 148
  Biography Vol 3: 156-7, 203
  Crown Advocate Vol 2: 33 Vol 3: 156, 159, 160n2, 161, 170, 187-8
Mei, Hua-chuen Vol 2: 205-7, 280-1, 321n18 Vol 3: 80
Meiji Restoration Vol 1: 36
Miller, Robert Vol 1: 394-5, 395i
Missionaries Vol 1: 4, 14, 28, 42, 86, 89, 229-236, 309 Vol 2: 33, 204, 359
Mixed court (ad hoc) Vol 1: 166, 169-171
Mixed Court (French) Vol 2: 327
Mixed Court (International)
  Assessors Vol 1: 174, 371, 378, 382, 389 Vol 2: 65i, 67i, 247n Vol 3: 199
  Cases in Vol 1: 382, 389 Vol 2: 38n15, 65-6, 67i, 166-7, 231, 250, 276, 278-9, 284-6, 312-6, 321, 327 Vol 3: 37-9
  Constitution Vol 1: 173-5 Vol 2: 177, 322-3
  Disputes with foreign powers Vol 2: 64-68, 322-3
  Magistrates Vol 1: 97, 154-5, 155i, 378 Vol 2: 66, 67i
  Mock up of Vol 3: 223
  Municipal Council (Shanghai), and Vol 2: 65-6, 177, 322-3
  Rendition Vol 2: 299, 300, 323 Vol 3: 14i, 15-6, 27, 30

Morris, Idwal Vol 3: 36, 187
Mossop, Allan
Barrister Vol 2: 188, 196-7
Biography Vol 2: 188, 341-2 Vol 3: 203-4
Crown Advocate (China) Vol 2: 293, 303, 341-2, 343 Vol 3: 12, 76
Crown Advocate (China), acting Vol 2: 214-6, 225, 280
Crown Advocate (Weihaiwei) Vol 2: 188 Vol 3: 32
Custodian of Enemy Property Vol 2: 201
Executor of HP Wilkinson's will Vol 3: 85
Full Court, Hong Kong Vol 2: 181n3
Full Court, Shanghai Vol 3: 70, 162, 171
Judge, sitting as Vol 3: 81, 84-5, 105-114, 144, 152, 161-2, 173-4
Judge, other mentions Vol 3: 35, 74-6, 121n19, 126-7, 129, 159, 173, 181, 187
Legal Counselor to British Embassy Vol 3: 203-4, 205
Priestwood, Victor, relationship with Vol 3: 32, 75, 154
Report on Japanese take over of court Vol 3: 177, 180
Retirement: Vol 3: 203-4
Mowat, Robert
Acting Assistant Judge (Japan), not considered suitable Vol 1: 131
Acting Chief Justice Vol 1: 249, 257, 260, 307
Acting Consul General (Shanghai) Vol 1: 307-10, 314
Assistant Judge (Shanghai) Vol 1: 138, 193, 193i, 215, 258, 274-5
Biography Vol 1: 83-4, 86, 87-8, 357-8
Bourne, Frederick, views on appointment as Chief Justice Vol 2: 53
Deputy Chief Judge Vol 1: 181
Japan, strict enforcement of treaties against Vol 1: 320-1
Judge for Japan Vol 1: 208, 255, 303, 319-321, 321-3, 325, 345-62
Law Secretary Vol 1: 90-91, 92, 94, 97, 118, 124-5, 161, 183
Police Magistrate Vol 1: 166-8, 246-8, 295
Retirement and death Vol 1: 367-70, Vol 2: 343
Student Interpreter Vol 1: 87-8
Myburgh (Alexander or Philip) Vol 1: 217
Myburgh, Philip, Vol 1: 73, 80

N

Nagasaki

Dutch Factory Vol 1: 32-3

Incidents involving Vol 1: 70-1, 325, 367-8, 396

Nanking (Nanjing) Vol 1: 25-7 Vol 2: 171 Vol 3: 10, 47, 54, 57n1, 74, 133, 136

Nationalist Party (Kuomingtang)

Republican Revolution Vol 2: 171-3, 276

Canton, governments in Vol 2: 5, 173, 249, 296, 316, 318

Divisions Vol 3: 52-3, 149

Government, National Vol 2: 5 Vol 3: 14, 24, 43, 49, 51, 57, 60-1, 136, 140, 145, 151, 176n17

Northern Expedition Vol 2: 358 Vol 3: 9-11, 13, 61, 74

Recognition in British and American courts Vol 3: 17-21, 21-24

Nationals, Dual

- British Vol 3: 29-30, 84-5
- American Vol 3: 24-29, 84-5

Nationals, Enemy see Enemy Nationals

Nationality of corporations Vol 2: 318-20

Nelson, E. Vol 1: 371

Nelson, H.G. Vol 3: 164-5

Newman, K.E. Vol 2: 285 Vol 3: 162

Ninth Circuit, United States Court of Appeals See Appeals, US Court for China, from

Niigata Vol 1: 182, 204, 211, 218

Normanton case Vol 1: 283-6

O

O'Malley, Edward Vol 1: 238

O'Shea, Henry Vol 2: 12-13, 15-20, 98-99, 101-114, 106i, 135, 139, 145

Obama, Barack Vol 2: 274

Oe Taku Vol 1: 154-6

Okuma (Count) Vol 1: 287, 334

Oppe, Henry Vol 2: 153, 197n4

Order in Council, 1865 Vol 1: 60-1, 95, 106, 132, 136

Order in Council, 1878 Vol 1: 193, 207
Order in Council, 1884 Vol 1: 277-9
Order in Council, 1904 Vol 2: 46, 59-60, 135, 155, 159-60, 174, 215
Order in Council, 1907 (Bethell Clause) Vol 2: 123-4, 128
Order in Council, 1919 (Management of British Companies) Vol 2: 212 Vol 3: 138
Order in Council, 1920 (Publication of seditious materials) Vol 2: 305
Order in Council, 1925 Vol 2: 342-3

P

Page, Edward Vol 1: 237-244
Page, William Vol 1: 245-7
Parkes, Harry
  British Minister in China Vol 1: 259, 266, 269
  British Minister in Japan Vol 1: 37, 89-90, 142, 143, 147, 158, 178, 203i, 205i, 215, 291
  Consular officer Vol 1: 28, 31-2, 42
Pauncefote, Julian
  Attorney-General of Hong Kong Vol 1: 151, 178
  Foreign Office Vol 1: 189-194, 190i, 204-6, 268, 303-4, 307
Peking (Beijing)
  Attacks on Vol 1: 8, 25, 30-2 Vol 2: 9-14, 33 Vol 3: 123
  British Ministers quarters: Vol 2: 42
  Cases in Vol 3: 123-7
Peking Post Vol 2: 203-8
Penfold, Frederick Vol 2: 39-41
Penniston, John Vol 3: 77-8
Perjury, by British in foreign courts Vol 2: 157-160
Perry, Matthew Vol 1: 8, 33i, 33-4
Peterel H.M.S. Vol 3: 176
Peters, Ernest Vol 3: 105-26
Phillips, Herbert Vol 3: 153-5
Piggott, Francis Vol 2: 179, 181
Piper, Kenneth Vol 3: 141-4

Platt, W.C. Vol 1: 406n, Vol 2: 33-4, 47-8, 59, 182
Potter, Eldon Vol 2: 318-320, 320i Vol 3: 65
Pottinger, Henry Vol 1: 8, 25, 27i, 42
Practitioners, Legal (British)(See also: Barristers, Solicitors)
Attendance at ceremonies Vol 1: 143, 399, 406n5 Vol 2: 50, 196
War Memorial to Vol 2: 197
Priestwood, Gwen Vol 3: 75, 156, 199, 204
Priestwood, John Vol 2: 226 Vol 3: 75
Priestwood, Victor
Barrister Vol 2: 318 Vol 3: 32, 85
Biography Vol 3: 75, 204
Crown Advocate Vol 3: 85, 106, 109-11, 115, 116, 124, 145
Termination Vol 3: 153-6
Prison, Bilibid Vol 2: 185, 245
Prison, McNeil Island Vol 2: 350-1, 359-60, 361 Vol 3: 98-9, 165, 167, 169, 182
Prisons See: Jails, Consular and Gaol, Ward Road
Privy Council
Appeals to, civil (from China) Vol 1: 74, 107, 274-5, 322-4 Vol 2: 295, 335-6 Vol 3: 23
Appeals to, criminal (from China) Vol 1: 237, 247-8 Vol 2: 156
Appeals to, criminal (from Hong Kong) Vol 1: 151n Vol 2: 174-5
Appeals to, civil (from Japan) Vol 1: 204-7
Appeals to, criminal (from Japan) Vol 1: 364
Decisions of, relied upon Vol 2: 164-5, 293-4 Vol 3: 66
Jurisdiction Vol 1: 135-7, 191, Vol 2: 26, 59-60, 179, 322-4
Prize cases, WWI Vol 2: 198-200
Protests, formal
Chinese, by Vol 1: 268, 312 Vol 2: 92-3, 141, 143 Vol 3: 113 (lack of), 151
Japanese, by Vol 1: 204
British, by Vol 1: 377-9, 408 Vol 3: 17 (lack of), 29 (not made), 59, 128
Provincial Courts (see Consular Courts, British)
Provisional Court (Shanghai) Vol 3: 15-17, 16i, 25-6, 28, 30-1, 68

Pu, Keng-lung Vol 2: 88-91
Purdy, Milton
  Biography Vol 2: 265-6
  Cases, criminal Vol 2: 268-70, 349-51, 352-62
  Cases, civil Vol 2: 211, 268 Vol 3: 19, 20, 77-8, 82-3
  Judge Vol 2: 265-71, 350i Vol 3: 24, 76-7, 78-9
  Lobingier, Charles, on Vol 2: 265
Plunkett, Francis Vol 1: 286

Q

Qingdao - See Tsingtao

R

Raven, Frank Vol 2: 211-2 Vol 3: 90-99, 105, 113
Rees-Davies, William Vol 2: 175, 181, 198n, 199, 331-2, 335-6 Vol 3: 210
Reeks, Hugh Vol 3: 108-112, 115, 116-20, 151, 170
Reid, Gilbert Vol 2: 203-208, 280
Reinsch, Paul Vol 2: 191, 204-7
Rennie, Richard
  Biography Vol 1: 92-3, 208-9
  Barrister Vol 1: 92, 94-6, 106, 167-8, 183
  Chief Justice Vol 1: 255, 256i, 257, 258-60, 266-8, 274-5, 279-82, 291-2 Vol 2: 51, 215
  Judge for Japan Vol 1: 208, 210-5, 225i,
  Retirement and death Vol 1: 296-299
  Shanghai Municipal Council, advisor to Vol 1: 208-210, 218
Republican Revolution (China) Vol 2: 171-7, 260 Vol 3: 197
Rights of Audience, lawyers
  In non-national court Vol 1: 399-400 Vol 2: 80, 302, 313 Vol 3: 16, 17i
  Solicitors, in British courts Vol 1: 73-4 Vol 2: 154-5
Riots, anti-foreign
  Canton Vol 1: 46, 263-9, 265i Vol 2: 318
  Chungking Vol 1: 230
  Foochow Vol 1: 230, 233,
  Missionary, anti Vol 1: 230, 233, 307-8, 313

Shanghai Vol 2: 64-8, 321-3 Vol 3: 15
Yangtse Valley Vol 1: 307-8, 313
Robertson, Russell Vol 1: 89, 142, 143, 212, 215, 257, 257i, 258-9
Robinson, Alfred Vol 2: 284-5, 285i
Robinson, F. Alan Vol 2: 586
Robinson, Gower Vol 1: 337-44
Rockhill, W.W. Vol 2: 92-5, 94i
Rodger, Hewitt Douglas (H.D.) Vol 2: 234-9, 247 Vol 3: 18-20, 24-5, 88-9
Roosevelt, Franklin D Vol 3: 77, 103, 168, 528, 191
Roosevelt, Theodore Vol 2: 63, 73, 76, 97, 114-6, 117, 192, 275
Ross, John Vol 1: 45, 219-228
Ross, United States v and Ross v McIntyre (Ross Case) Vol 1: 219-228, 279 Vol 2: 3, 254, 360 Vol 3: 94, 98, 182
Russo-Japanese War Vol 2: 60-4, 61i

S

Samuel, H.B. Vol 3: 64i, 65
Sassoon, David, & Co Vol 1: 273-5 Vol 3: 63
Satow, Ernest
Student interpreter Vol 1: 89
Consular Officer in Japan Vol 1: 37, 43, 142
British Minister in Japan Vol 1: 334, 346-7, 353, 356-7, 359, 361-2, 367-9, 396-8
British Minister in China Vol 1: 409 Vol 2: 14, 37i, 41, 59, 64n15, 68-70
Japanese common law wife Vol 1: 90n16
Retirement Vol 1: 370 Vol 2: 51-2
Wilkinson, H.P., relationship with Vol 2: 32-3, 37-8, 53, 338
Wilkinson, H.S., relationship with Vol 1: 346-7, 353, 356-7, 368-9, 397-8 Vol 2: 32-3, 35-8, 42, 51-2, 53
Sausmarez, Havilland de
Biography Vol 2: 53-9, 54i, 191-3
Judge Vol 2: 56i, 58-60, 145, 148-52, 150i, 152-6, 174, 191, 196-8, 201-3, 220

Hong Kong Full Court Vol 2: 181
Retirement (actual and possible) Vol 2: 146-8, 213-5
Extraterritoriality, views on Vol 2: 222
Schuffenhauer, August Vol 1: 293-5
Schul, Ferno Vol 2: 235-7, 236i, 247, 280 Vol 3: 68, 68i
Scidmore, George Vol 2: 353-5, 399
Secretary of State (US) Vol 1: 22, 154, 224-7 Vol 2: 73-4, 86, 93, 97-8, 191, 323 Vol 3: 26-8, 88, 185-6
Secretary of State for Foreign Affairs (UK) Vol 1: 158, 224, 308n9, 367 Vol 2: 50, 60, 130 Vol 3: 49-54, 60, 62, 136-7, 177, 185-7
Sedition Vol 2: 5, 9, 123-9, 204-7, 305, 306-10 Vol 3: 11
Sellett, Thomas
Biography Vol 2: 352
Attorney: Vol 3 92-7
District Attorney: Vol 2: 353-359 Vol 3: 26, 28, 80, 81
Seward, George Vol 1: 44-5, 78-9, 171
Seymour, Horace Vol 3: 188
Shanghai International Settlement
Bye-laws, application outside Vol 3: 70, 107-8, 141-2
Constitution of Vol 1: 76-9
Laws, application within Vol 2: 215, 268-9, 308 Vol 3: 25-9, 29, 51
Military threats to
• Chinese Vol 1: 10-11, Vol 3: 9-11, 13, 61-2, 131-5, 132i
• Japanese Vol 1: 128 Vol 3: 61-2, 131-5, 132i, 135i, 160, 175-9
Shanghai Mercury Vol 2: 17, 32n3, 89-90, 107
Shanghai Municipal Council
Chairmen, statements by or actions of Vol 1: 183, 296-7, 380-1 Vol 2: 45-6, 263-4 Vol 3: 13, 134-5
Extraterritoriality, Feetham Report on Vol 3: 50-1
International Settlement, management of: Vol 1: 76-9, 108, 114n, 208-10, 215-7, 305, 308 Vol 2: 47 Vol 3: 134-5, 159-60
Mixed Court Vol 2: 65-6, 177, 322-3
Jury duty, obligations for members of Vol 2: 58
Legal actions, against Vol 1: 12 Vol 3: 67-72, 159-60
Legal actions, by Vol 1: 76-9, 76n7, 215-8 Vol 2: 298-300 Vol 3: 16-7

Special District Court, and Vol 3: 30-1
Supervision of Municipal Police Vol 1: 295 Vol 2: 65, 315 Vol 3: 30, 134
Shanghai Municipal Police
Arrests by Vol 2: 281, 297, 307 Vol 3: 25-6
Evidence in court by officers Vol 1: 217 Vol 2: 142, 285, 307, 355 Vol 3: 105-16, 117
Legal actions by Vol 1: 215-7, 292-5 Vol 3: 16-7, 134
Legal actions against officers Vol 1: 292, 295 Vol 3: 105-16, 116-22
Mixed Court Vol 2: 65-6
Police work Vol 1: 119, 216 Vol 3: 67-9, 133, 135-6
Riots, involvement in Vol 2: 65-66, 321-3
Sikh officers Vol 2: 148-152, 150i Vol 3: 11-3, 116-22
Shekury, Gabriel Vol 2: 157-60
Shields, Leighton Vol 3: 103, 133, 165, 168, 204
Shimonoseki Vol 1: 36, 331, 361
Siam, British Court for See: British Court for Siam
Sieh Taijen Vol 1: 312-6
Sikhs, issues with Vol 2: 148-152, 197, 306-11 Vol 3: 11-3
Simpson, Lenox Vol 3: 59-60
Singh, Atma Vol 3: 116-22, 134
Singh, Budda Vol 2: 305-6, 308 Vol 3: 11-3, 11i
Singh, Har Charan Vol 2: 305-6
Singh, Harbak Vol 2: 306-11
Singh, Harbant Vol 3: 11-2
Smale, John Vol 1: 151, 151i
Smith, Lindsey Vol 2: 145-6
Soejima, Taneomi Vol 1: 153, 154
Solicitors
Rights of audience: Vol 1: 73-4 Vol 2: 154-5
Soong, T.V. Vol 3: 21, 188, 189n9
Stark, George (Admiral) Vol 2: 252n, 255-62
State Department (US) Vol 1: 15, 151-2, 227, 384 Vol 2: 75, 77, 93, 114, 211, 233 Vol 3: 29, 76-7, 81, 88, 177, 185
Strawn, Silas Vol 2: 323

Student Interpreter Vol 1: 87-90, 140, 291, 387
Suga, Kitaro Vol 2: 322i, 322-3
Sun Yat-sen Vol 2: 171, 318, 365, 387
Supreme Court, Chinese Vol 3: 15, 30
Supreme Court, Hong Kong
Cases in Vol 1: 151, 370 Vol 2: 174-6, 199-200, 331-2
Judges or other staff of Vol 1: 42, 189, 267 Vol 2: 179, 181, 343n7, Vol 3: 118n13
Jurisdiction of Vol 1: 45-7 Vol 2: 26-7, 174
Full Court (Hong Kong) Vol 2: 179-81
Full Court (Shanghai) Vol 2: 343-5
Supreme Court, United States
Appeals to Vol 1: 227-8 Vol 2: 244-5, 332 Vol 3: 84
Building Vol 1: 111
Cases mentioned: Vol 1: 150 Vol 2: 240, 254
Ross case, decision in Vol 1: 16, 222, 227-8, 279 Vol 2: 3, 254, 360 Vol 3: 94, 98, 182
Supreme Court and Consular Gazette (including as part of North China Herald) Vol 1: 99-102 Vol 3: 76

T

Taft, William Vol 2: 76, 86-7, 117, 143, 192, 246
Taotai (Canton) Vol 1: 267
Taotai (Foochow) Vol 1: 169
Taotai (Shanghai) Vol 1: 77, 165, 311, 313, 314 Vol 2: 88, 92, 139, 141, 162-3, 166, 167
Terashima (Count) Vol 1: 147
Thayer, Rufus
Biography Vol 2: 117
Judge Vol 1: 128 Vol 2: 117-8, 141-3, 157-8, 165-7, 176, 192
Resignation 181-2
Thriftcor Bank Vol 3: 87-90
Tilotson, W.D. Vol 1: 339-434
Ting Jih Chang Vol 1: 234
Tinkler, R. Maurice Vol 2: 250, 281-2, 285, 307, 354-5, 355i Vol 3:

146-9
Tison, Alexander Vol 1: 339-342
Titlebaum, Sam Vol 3: 167-9
Treaty of Amity and Commerce (US-Japan) Vol 1: 8, 34-5, 225-6
Treaty of Amity and Commerce (Britain-Japan) Vol 1: 8, 9, 34-5, 147, 199-206
Treaty of Annexation (Japan-Korea) Vol 2: 134
Treaty of Bogue Vol 1: 26
Treaty of Commerce (US-China, 1929) Vol 3: 19
Treaty of Commerce (US-Korea) Vol 1: 277
Treaty of Commerce and Navigation (Britain-Japan) Vol 1: 328-9, 369, 396-7
Treaty of Commerce and Navigation (US-Japan) Vol 1: 329, 394
Treaty of Commercial Relations and Judicial Procedure (US-China) Vol 1: 174-5
Treaty of Friendship and Commerce (Britain-Korea) Vol 1: 277
Treaty of Nanking Vol 1: 10, 25-7 Vol 2: 222
Treaty of Shimonoseki, Vol 1: 327, 330-333 Vol 2: 60
Treaty of Tientsin (Britain/US-China) Vol 1: 29-34, 169-70, 239 Vol 2: 252, 323
Treaty of Versailles Vol 2: 208-10, 249, 303
Treaty of Wanghsia Vol 1: 21-23, 26, 29 Vol 2: 252
Treaty for the Relinquishment of Extra-Territorial Rights (Britain/US-China) Vol 3: 53-4 (drafts), 185-90
Treaty, Commercial (Britain-China) Vol 2: 21
Treaty, Peace (Russia-Japan) Vol 2: 63-4
Tri-Partite Intervention Vol 2: 333-4
Troup, James Vol 1: 182, 339, 345, 352, 354
Tsai Chun Vol 1: 371-9
Tsingtao (Qingdao) Vol 1: 334 Vol 2: 198-200 Vol 3: 144
Tsungli Yamen (Zongli Yamen) Vol 1: 28, 106, 172, 233, 244, 247, 268, 333
Turner, Skinner
  Biography Vol 2: 189-91
  Assistant Judge Vol 2: 189, 338-9

Extraterritoriality, views on: Vol 2: 346-7
Extraterritoriality Commission: Vol 2: 323, 345
Hong Kong Full Court Vol 2: 181
Judge
- Civil cases Vol 2: 279-80, 287-9, 306, 318-20, 327-36
- Criminal cases Vol 2: 284-7, 313-5
- Other mentions Vol 2: 276, 293, 311, 337-8, 339
- Special hearings Vol 2: 216-8, 225-6, 229

Shanghai Full Court: Vol 2: 343-5 Vol 3: 70
Retirement: Vol 2: 345-7
Twyman, B Vol 2: 65i, 65-6
Tyler, John Vol 1: 22

U

Ueno Kagenori Vol 1: 204
United States Court for China
Act establishing Vol 2: 75-6, 93-5 Vol 3: 192
Appeals from See: Appeals
Closing Vol 2: Vol 3: 177-9, 188-92
Establishment Vol 2: 4, 73-6, 77-8
Jurisdiction
- Companies, over Vol 2: 108, 185-7 Vol 3: 88-9, 140-1
- Consular courts, compared to Vol 2: 86, 240
- Difficulties in exercise of Vol 2: 118, 237
- Foreign nationals, right to bring action: Vol 2: 210-1 Vol 3: 140-1
- Geographic Vol 2: 121 Vol 3: 33
- Individuals, over Vol 2: 166-7, 360 Vol 3: 24-9, 169
- Treaties, enforcement of Vol 2: 253-5

Premises Vol 2: 116, 185, 436

V

Vincent, Arthur Vol 1: 117i Vol 2: 145-6

W

Wade, Thomas

British Minister Vol 1: 159, 163-4, 166, 172-4, 234, 237-8

Chinese Linguist Vol 1: 42, 87-8

Wainewright, R.E. Vol 1: 169, 248, 259, 274

Wake, U.S.S. Vol 3: 176

Wallis, Frank Vol 2: 317-20

Walsham, John Vol 1: 306

Wang, C.T. Vol 3: 43-4, 44i, 46-7, 53-4

Wang, Ch'ung-hui, Vol 2: 32

Wang Ching-wei Vol 3: 52, 149

Ward, John Vol 1: 30-1

Ward Road Gaol Vol 3: 12, 105, 119-20 133-4, 167, 168, 180

Warren, Pelham Vol 2: 17-8, 116, 136n, 141, 147

Washington Conference Vol 2: 249

Watson, Felthan Vol 3: 81, 92-7, 99-101, 103

Wei, Tao-ming Vol 3: 188

Weihaiwei Vol 1: 332, 335; Vol 2: 23-5, 24i, 64, 198-9 Vol 3: 31-3

Weihaiwei, High Court of, Vol 2: 23-9, 145, 187-8, 199, 216, 338, 339, 346 Vol 3: 32-4, 37

Werner, Pamela Vol 3: 126-7

Wheeler, Edwin Vol 1: 196, 339, 345, 350i, 354, 359, 364

Wilfley, Lebbeus

Allegations against: Vol 2: 97, 98-9

Biography: Vol 2: 77, 79i, 116

Defamation action against Henry O'Shea Vol 2: 101-114, 102i, 106i, 135

Examination for attorneys Vol 2: 79-82, 80i

Judge, sitting as Vol 2: 78-86, 88-92, 115

Judge, other mentions Vol 2: 76-8, 115-6, 192 (lack of)

Illustrations of Vol 2: 79i, 80i, 87i, 101i, 102i

Investigation of Vol 2: 99-101, 101i

Washington, support from Vol 2: 86-88, 97-8, 114-5 (lack of)

Wilkinson, Hiram P (Harrie)

Acting Chief Justice Vol 1: 385-6

Acting Assistant Judge (Shanghai) Vol 1: 386
Acting Assistant Judge (Siam) Vol 1 37-8, 49, 189
Barrister Vol 1: 292-5, 316-7, 322, 347, 371-2, 374-6, 389n32 Vol 2: 59-60, 195, 318-9 Vol 3: 64i, 64-7
Biography Vol 1: 89-90, 291-2, 295-6
Bravery award Vol 1: 325-6
Chief Judge, desire for promotion to Vol 2: 53, 146-7, 213, 215-6 Vol 3: 74
Claims Commissioner Vol 2: 33-5, 66-8
Crown Advocate (China)
- Advising as Vol 2: 154, 200-1, 220
- Appearance in court as (general applications) Vol 1: 406-7 Vol 2: 196-7, 213, 288-9
- Appointment as Vol 1: 325 (acting), 369-70 Vol 2: 33
- Organisation of practice Vol 2: 188, 431
- Prosecuting as Vol 2: 58-9, 102-114, 106i, 125-8, 135-9, 158-60, 273, 281-7, 313-5
Crown Advocate (Weihaiwei) Vol 1: 27-8
Judge, Weihaiwei Vol 1: 187 (acting), 188
King's Counsel Vol 2: 220
Marriages Vol 1: 296, 406 Vol 2: 147, 195
Pidgin English, mastery of Vol 2: 138
Retirement and death Vol 2: 338-9 Vol 3: 85-6
Wilkinson, Hiram S, relationship with Vol 1: 295-6, 319-20, 385, 399 Vol 2: 32-3, 37-8, 41-2, 51, 53, 105, 146-7, 314
Wilkinson, Hiram S
Acting Law Secretary Vol 1: 182, 195-207, 201i, 203i, 205i, 208, 210, 211i
Acting Assistant Judge (Japan) Vol 1: 212, 214
Acting Assistant Judge (China) Vol 1: 215-8
Barrister Vol 1: 258-9, 274-5, 292-3, 322
Biography Vol 1: 83-6
Claims Commissioner (Canton) Vol 1: 269-72
Crown Advocate Vol 1: 256-7, 263, 266-7, 278, 279-82, 310-5, 332-3, 346-61

Chief Justice Vol 1: 406 Vol 2: 4, 31-52
Consular Officer Vol 1: 90, 140-2, 143, 157-8, 178, 182, 211
Judge for Japan Vol 1: 324-6 (acting), 369, 385, 397-400
Judicial appointments, desire for Vol 1: 208, 255-6, 259, 319-20, 368
Knighthood Vol 2: 136
Parkes, Harry, relationship with Vol 1: 157-8, 178, 259
Retirement and death Vol 2: 41-2, 46-9, 51, 339, 343-4
Satow, Ernest, relationship with Vol 1: 347, 353-4, 357, 368-9, 398 Vol 2: 35-7, 42, 52
Student Interpreter Vol 1: 88-90
Wilkinson, Hiram P, relationship with Vol 1: 295-6, 385 Vol 2: 32-3, 37-8, 41-2, 51, 53, 105, 146-7, 314
Wilkinson, W.H. Vol 1: 87, 317
Wilson, Woodrow Vol 2: 204-6, 209
Wing, Tyco Vol 2: 288, 293-5
Wolfe, John Vol 1: 231-5
Wood, John Vol 2: 343n7 Vol 3: 118n13
Woodward, Tracy Vol 2: 351-360
Woosong Railway case Vol 1: 166-8
Wright, G.H. Vol 2: 85, 148, 421
Wushishan Case Vol 1: 231-237

Y

Yang Ki-Tak Vol 2: 127-8, 132
Yokohama
Cases in Vol 1: 142, 145, 148-57, 219-22, 337-44, 344-60, 394-5
Courts, location of principal British Vol 1: 129-33, 137-8, 143-4, 181, 205-6, 207 Vol 2: 32
Kanagawa, established in place of Vol 1: 34
Incidents involving: Vol 1: 35-6, 283 Vol 2: 241, 244
Mowat, Robert, life in Vol 1: 319-21
Young, John Russell Vol 1: 268-9
Yuan Shikai Vol 2: 11, 18, 68-70, 69i, 171-3, 172i, 200, 276

Z

Ziar, Y.S. Vol 2: 313 Vol 3: 15-7, 15i
Zongli Yamen See: Tsungli Yamen
Zung Zu-fung Vol 2: 135-141

Table of Cases

The following is a table of cases mentioned in this book. Civil cases have been indexed by the names of both the Plaintiff and Defendant unless they share the same surname. Criminal cases in the British and American courts are indexed under either "R v" or "United States v". Case citations are giving for those cases that can be found in law reports.

Abdoolaly Ebrahim & Co v MS Mehta	Vol 2 276
Ah Choy v John Grigor	Vol 1 198
Alexandre Pavlow v TCR Ward	Vol 2 59
Alger, Dallas v	Vol 2 161
American Food Mfg. Co., Ld., Yao Sudong v (Re Fitch's Estate)	Vol 2 186
Amistad case	Vol 1 150
Anderson, McDonald v	Vol 1 388
	Vol 2 164, 167
Archer v Heath, 30 F.2d 932 (1929)	Vol 2 361
Attorney-General of Hong Kong v Kwok A Sing (1873) Lr 5 PC 179, 42 LJ, PC 64	Vol 1 152
Bank of East Asia v Jamieson & Anor	Vol 2 317
Banque de l'Indochine, Trustee of Dent & Co v	Vol 2 329
Barchet's Estate, In re	Vol 2 166
Barkley Co., Inc. v. William E Maloney	Vol 2 186
Barnes, International Banking Corporation v	Vol 3 82
Bennertz v The Kiangnan Defence and Pay Department	Vol 1 372
Benson, E.S. v Jaffray, A.	Vol 1 145
Bethell, Ernest v North China Daily News and Herald Ltd	Vol 2 131
Blockley, Bridget, Kusumoto Masataka, Chiji of the Tokio-fu v	Vol 1 198

Boulon, Gaston, Williams and Wigmore v	Vol 2 234
Brooks, F.M., Gabriel Sherkury v	Vol 2 157
Browne, Fujiyama v	Vol 2 287
Cairney, Yu Chung Shing v	Vol 2 32
Caldbeck, MaGregor & Co, Mosley & Co v	Vol 2 145
Carmichael, Myers v	Vol 1 182
Casement v. Squier Warden, 46 F. Supp. 296 and 138 F.2d 909 (9th Cir. 1943)	Vol 3 182
Cathay Laundry Ltd, J Kobeneff v	Vol 3 175
Cathay Trust, In re Count Praschma	Vol 2 202
Chalaire, Walter v Cornell S. Franklin 81 F. 2d 105	Vol 2 440
Char, Nick, Jui Hsoh-hsien v	Vol 3 24
China Merchants Steam Navigation Company v William Hunt	Vol 3 140
China Merchants Steam Navigation Company, McElroy v	Vol 1 389
China Press Inc, Lawrence Kentwell v	Vol 2 278
China Realty v Kew & Anderson	Vol 2 343
Chow Chang Kung, Lin King Chun, Loo King Fah, Sat Keok Min, Directors of the Taou Shan Kwan Temple at Wu Shih Shan, Foochow, v Rev John R Wolfe, of the Church of England Missionary Society (Wushishan case)	Vol 1 231 Vol 2 164
Chow Kwei Ching v Lawrence Kentwell	Vol 2, 290, 297
Chun Nich Realty Investment v Clark	Vol 2 343
Clark, Chun Nich Realty Investement v	Vol 2 343
Clough, H.B. v G.R. Grove	Vol 2 278
Colomb, Captain P.H, Iwasaki Yataro v	Vol 1 197
Condon, T.C. v S.N. Condon	Vol 3 175
Consolidated Steel Corporation, Poo Shing Hing et al v	Vol 2 210
Cowen, T.C., Henry O'Shea v	Vol 2 16
Dallas v Alger	Vol 2 161
Dobree v Napier seven Bingham's N.C. 781	Vol 1 239
Dolan v Dolan	Vol 2 268
Douglas, John v Noel Home	Vol 2 153
Douglas, John v North China Daily News and Herald Ltd	Vol 2 131

Duncan, Andrew v Nestor Nicolay Nordenstedt (Judgment Debtor) and Charles John Strome (Garnishee)	Vol 1 198
Ellies, master of the British ship Zingra, H. Ahrens & Co v	Vol 1 213
Enslie Will case	Vol 1 399
Fang Chiao-Ho, Hu Tsing-Pang, Fang Ven-Tuck, and Tse Zay-Tsing v Shanghai Municipal Council	Vol 3 160
Fermus, R, Siberian Agricultural Corporation Ltd v	Vol 2 345
Finance Banking Corp Ltd v Luebbert's Pharmacy, Fed Inc USA,	Vol 3 82
Findlay Richardson & Co v Pitman & Co	Vol 1 135
First Trust Co v Indar Singh	Vol 3 41
Fitch, Alberta C.K., in re the estate of, Yao Sudong, v. American Food Mfg. Co., Ld.	Vol 2 186
Fleming v United States	Vol 2 242
Franklin, Cornell, Walter Chalaire, v	Vol 3 84
French v French, reports of Cases De- cided in the High Court of Chancery by shadwell VC, 1840-1841 p257	Vol 1 192
Fuhlee	Vol 1 291
Fujiyama v Browne	Vol 2 287
Gaston, Williams and Wigmore v Boulon	Vol 2 234
Gensburger, In Re	Vol 2 202
Gilfillan v Glover & Co.	Vol 1, 70
Glover & Co., Gilfillan v	Vol 1 70
Granada Estates v Kenneth Piper	Vol 3 142
Great American Fire Assurance Corporation, Republic of China v	Vol 3 18
Green, Langfeldt & Mayer v	Vol 1 138, 258
Greenfield v Rabbetts	Vol 3 84
Greyhound Racing Association (China) Ltd v Macnaghten & Martin	Vol 3 67
Grigor, John, Ah Choy v	Vol 1 198
Gromov v International Banking Corporation	Vol 2 211
Grove, G.R., H.B. Clough v	Vol 2 278
H. Ahrens & Co v Ellies, master of the British ship Zingra	Vol 1 213
Hanametal [1915] HKLR 3	Vol 2 198
Hanson v Watson	Vol 2 164

Hardoon, Ezra v Liza Hardoon Vol 3 62
Hardoon, K.B. Ezra v Liza Hardoon Vol 3 67
Hardoon, Liza, Probate Proceedings in the matter of the will of Vol 3 175
Hart v Gumpach, L.R. 4 P.C. 439; [1873] UKPC 9. Vol 1 107, 129
Hart v Herhausen Vol 1 210
Hereira, Capt, case against Vol 1 154
Herhausen, Hart v Vol 1 210
Home, Noel v North China Daily News and Herald Ltd Vol 2 131
Home, Noel, John Douglas v Vol 2 153
Hughes and Anor v O.C. Thomas Vol 1 206
Hunt, William, China Merchants Steam Navigation Company v Vol 3 140
Imperial Japanese Government v Peninsular and Oriental steam Navigation Company (Chishima case) [1895] A.C. 644. Vol 1 322
In Re SP Barchet's Estate, Vol 2 166
In the matter of a suit heard in HBM's Consulate at Foochow before a Mixed Court composed of HM's Consul Charles A Sinclair Esq, in conjunction with Pan Tautai Vol 1 169
Ingenohl v Olsen & Co, 273, US 541, (1927). Vol 2 332
Ingenohl v Olsen 1922 HKLR 4 Vol 2 332
Ingenohl v Wing On (1927) 44 RPC 343 Vol 2 333
International Banking Corporation v Barnes Vol 3 82
International Banking Corporation, Gromov v Vol 2 211
Iwasaki Yataro v Captain P.H. Colomb Vol 1 197
Jamieson & Anor, Bank of East Asia v Vol 2 317
Jui Hsoh-hsien v Nick Char Vol 3 24
Kentwell v The China Press Inc, Vol 2 278
Kentwell, Chow Kwei Ching v Vol 2 290, 297
Kentwell, Lawrence v Po Sa-tien & Ord Vol 2 284
Kentwell, Lawrence, In Re (application to disbar) Vol 2 293
Kentwell, Lawrence, Shanghai Municipal Council v, Vol 2 297
Keswick W, J Hose, T Hanbury, JC Coutts, G Nye and W Probst v the estate of G Wills and S Wills Vol 1 76
Kew & Anderson v China Realty Vol 2 343

Khoo, N. Moalle & Co v Vol 2 32
Kiangnan Defence and Pay Department, Bennertz v Vol 1 372
Kijima, Tsune & Ors, Peninsular and Oriental Steam Shipping Company Ltd v, [1895] A.C. 661. Vol 1 324
Kobeneff, J v Cathay Laundry Ltd Vol 3 175
Kusumoto Masataka, Chiji of the Tokio-fu v Bridget Blockley Vol 1 198
Kwok A Sing, Attorney-General of Hong Kong v (1873) Lr 5 PC 179, 42 LJ, PC 64 Vol 1 152
Langfeldt & Mayer v Green Vol 1 138, 258
Levinson, William, In re (application to disbar) Vol 2 228
Linke, In re Vol 2 203
Low Long-Yan, Sin Hong Chan v Vol 2 216
Luebbert's Pharmacy, Fed Inc USA, Finance Banking Corp Ltd v Vol 3 82
Mackenzie & Co Ltd, Shanghai Import & Export Lumber Co v Vol 2 345
Macnaghten & Martin, Greyhound Racing Association (China) Ltd Vol 3 67
Malcolm, Wilcox & Co, Yokuzawa Zensuke v Vol 1 198
Maloney, William E, The Barkley Co. v Vol 2 186
Maria Luz case Vol 1 154
McDonald v Anderson Vol 1 388, Vol 2 164, 167
McElroy v The China Merchants Steam Navigation Company Vol 1 389
McRae, Frank Raven v Vol 2 211
Mehta, MS, Abdoolaly Ebrahim & Co v Vol 2 276
Merchants Fire Assurance Corporation of New York, Republic of China v 30 F.2d 278 (1929) Vol 3 18
Mitchell, Nakajima v Vol 1 182
Moller v Wheelock Vol 2 43
Mosley & Co v Caldbeck, MaGregor & Co Vol 2 145
Myers v Carmichael Vol 1 182
N. Moalle & Co v Khoo Vol 2 32
Nakajima v Mitchell Vol 1 182
Norddeutscher Steamship Company v Ocean Steamship Co, Vol 2 32

Nordenstedt, Nestor Nicolay (Judgment Debtor), Andrew Duncan v, (Charles John Strome (Garnishee)	Vol 1 198
North China Daily News and Herald Ltd, Ernest Bethell v	Vol 2 131
North China Daily News and Herald Ltd, John Douglas v	Vol 2 131
North China Daily News and Herald Ltd, Noel Home v	Vol 2 131
O'Shea, Henry v T.C. Cowen	Vol 2 16
Ocean Steamship Co, Norddeutscher Steamship Company v	Vol 2 32
Ossim, H, Singh, Pakai v	Vol 2 277
Paklat [1915] HKLR 19	Vol 2 198
Peninsular and Oriental steam Navigation Company, Imperial Japanese Government v (Chishima case) [1895] A.C. 644.	Vol 1 322
Peninsular and Oriental Steam Shipping Company Ltd v Tsune Kijima & Ors [1895] A.C. 661.	Vol 1 324
Penniston, John, Mitsuko Shiga v	Vol 3 79
Pickwood & Co v Shanghai Mercury	Vol 2 32
Piper, Kenneth, Granada Estates v	Vol 3 142
Pitman & Co, Findlay Richardson & Co v	Vol 1 135
Pitman, John, Walsh, Hall & Co v	Vol 1 145
Poo Shing Hing et al v Consolidated Steel Corporation	Vol 2 210
Praschma (Count), In re Cathay Trust	Vol 2 202
R (Charles Penfold) v Martin, George	Vol 1 216
R (on the Prosecution of the Imperial Customs) v Hartley, John	Vol 1 199
R v Abbas, S.H., and O Abbas	Vol 2 197
R v Ali	Vol 1 75
R v Archer, Charles	Vol 3 175
R v Banks, Edward	Vol 1 166
R v Bellamy, John	Vol 1 399
R v Bethell, Ernest (No. 1)	Vol 2 123
R v Bethell, Ernest (No. 2)	Vol 2 124
R v Bigg, J	Vol 1 75
R v Bingham, Robert and Ducker, Thomas	Vol 1 142
R v Carew, Edith	Vol 1 344
R v Chang Yung-fu	Vol 3 32

R v Chi Hsing–Nan and Others Vol 2 29
R v Chia Yu-Wang and Others Vol 2 28
R v Chiang Lian-shi Vol 3 32
R v Compton Vol 1 46
R v Cooke, Herbert Vol 3 124
R v Drake, John Vol 1 285
R v Eckford, David Vol 3 160
R v Fawcett, Thomas Vol 1 160
R v Frerar, John Vol 1 75
R v Gabbutt, J.H. Vol 2 311
R v George, Robert Vol 1 91
R v Hunt, Ralph Vol 3 124
R v Ibrahim Vol 2 173, 422
R v Jackson, Robert Vol 1 316
R v Judd, William Vol 3 105
R v Kentwell, Lawrence Vol 2 281
R v Lee, George Vol 1 273
R v Lesley 29 L.H. M.C. 97 Vol 1 239
R v Line, Alfred Edwin Vol 1 142
R v Liscom, John Vol 1 282
R v Liu Chang-te Vol 3 32
R v Liu Huan-Chu Vol 2 188
R v Logan, James Vol 1 266
R v Ma Shuang-Hsi Vol 2 28
R v MacKellar, Patrick Vol 3 169
R v Main, David Vol 1 261
R v Mason, Charles Vol 1 310
R v Mohamed Vol 1 79
R v O'Neil Vol 1 386
R v O'Shea, Henry Vol 2 82, 102
R v Page, Edward Vol 1 239
R v Page, William Vol 1 246
R v Parrish, T.D. Vol 3 124

R v Penfold, Frederick Vol 2 39
R v Perry and Adler Vol 1 293
R v Peters, Ernest Vol 3 105
R v Prevot, Peter Vol 3 145
R v Procter, John Vol 1 75
R v Pyne Vol 1 282
R v Reeves, James, William Box and James Keell Vol 1 75
R v Reynolds & Holt Vol 1 76
R v Robinson, Daniel (Ice Cream Bob) Vol 1 215
R v Ross & Reed Vol 1 295
R v Ryan, Richard Vol 1 374
R v Sali Vol 1 75
R v Scarfield, Elizabeth Vol 1 195
R v Sherkury, Gabriel Vol 2 159
R v Sidney Vol 2 58
R v Singh, Amar & Dalup Vol 3 11
R v Singh, Atma Vol 3 116
R v Singh, Harbak Vol 2 306
R v Singh, Harbant Vol 3 11
R v Singh, Harnam et al Vol 3 11
R v Singh, Husara Vol 2 345
R v Singh, Sangat Vol 2 11
R v Stevenson, Thomas Vol 2 135
R v Turner, E.C. Vol 3 166
R v Wang Cheng & Chi Chiu Vol 2 28
R v Williams, William Vol 1 118
R v Wilson (Lieut.) Vol 3 126
R v Wilson, J.G. Vol 1 75
Rabbetts, Greenfield v Vol 3 84
Rakusen, Shanghai Municipal Police v Vol 3 70
Raven, Frank v McRae Vol 2 211
Republic of China v Great American Fire Assurance Corporation Vol 3 18

Republic of China v Merchants Fire Assurance Corporation of New York, 30 F.2d 278 (1929) Vol 3 18
Rey v Lecouturier Vol 2 331
Ross v McIntyre 140 US 453 Vol 1 227,
Vol 2 3, 254, 360
Vol 3 94, 98, 182
Roy, David, Inquest on Vol 3 162
Sassoon v Wong Vol 1 273
Sassoon, Wu v Vol 1 273
Scott v Brown, Dering , McNab & Co [1892] 2 QB 724. Vol 2 43
Secretary of State for Foreign Affairs v Charlesworth Piling & Co [1901] AC 373. Vol 2 165
Shanghai Import & Export Lumber Co v Mackenzie & Co Ltd Vol 2 345
Shanghai Mercury, Pickwood & Co v Vol 2 32
Shanghai Municipal Council v Kentwell Vol 2 297
Shanghai Municipal Council v Leontieff Vol 3 16
Shanghai Municipal Council v Maitland Vol 3 17
Shanghai Municipal Council, Fang Chiao-Ho, Hu Tsing-Pang, Fang Ven-Tuck, and Tse Zay-Tsing v Vol 3 160
Shanghai Municipal Police v Rakusen Vol 3 70
Shanghai Municipal Police v Stanoyevich Vol 2 250
Sherkury, Gabriel v F.M. Brooks Vol 2 157
Shiga, Mitsuko v John Penniston Vol 3 78
Siberian Agricultural Corporation Ltd v R Fermus Vol 2 345
Sin Hong Chan v Low Long-Yan Vol 2 216
Singh, Basant, Kagar Singh, v Vol 3 175
Singh, Bashant v Singh, Bihan Vol 3 42
Singh, Budda, Har Charan Singh v Vol 2 306
Singh, Har Charan v Budda Singh Vol 2 306
Singh, Indar v First Trust Co Vol 3 41
Singh, Kagar v Basant Singh Vol 3 175
Singh, Pakai, v Ossim, H Vol 2 277

Smoleff v Smoleff Vol 3 175
Thomas, O.C., Hughes & Anor v Vol 1 206
Tinkler, R. Maurice, inquest into death of Vol 3 145
Trustee of Dent & Co v Banque de l'Indochine, Vol 2 329
United States v Beardsley, E.J. Vol 2 269
United States v Biddle, Charles Vol 2 84, 184, 192 Vol 3 83
United States v Carney, Boatner Vol 3 190
United States v Casement, Gerald Vol 3 163
United States v Chapman, William Vol 2 349
United States v Colbert, John Vol 3 99
United States v De Menil, Henry Vol 2 88
United States v Fleming, William Vol 2 238
United States v Fuller Vol 2 268
United States v Heath, Neil Vol 2 352
United States v Hetherington, J.H. Vol 1 338
United States v Husar, Leonard 26 F.2d 847 (1928) Vol 2 352, 360
United States v Jones, Thomas Vol 2 141
United States v Jordan, J.F Vol 2 177
United States v Kearney, Lawrence Vol 2 252
United States v Kyau, Stephen Vol 3 134
United States v McCord, R.J Vol 2 82
United States v Price, S.R. Vol 2 86
United States v Raven, Frank & Brown, Warner Vol 3 92
United States v Reid, Gilbert Vol 2 205
United States v Riley, Jack Vol 3 167
United States v Ross, John Vol 1 219
United States v Slevin Vol 2 251
United States v Titlebaum, Sam Vol 3 167
von Gumpach v Hart Vol 1 107
Walsh, Hall & Co v John Pitman Vol 1 145
Ward, TCR, Alexandre Pavlow v Vol 2 59
Watson, Hanson v Vol 2 164

Werner, Pamela, inquest into the death of Vol 3 125
Wheelock, Moller v Vol 2 43
Wilholt, Mrs S.M. v H. Wilholt Vol 3 175
Wills, estate of, W Keswick, J Hose, T Hanbury, JC Coutts, G Nye and W Probst Vol 1 76
Wing On, Ingenohl v, (1927) 44 RPC 343 Vol 2 333
Wolfe, Rev John R, Chow Chang Kung, Lin King Chun, Loo King Fah, Sat Keok Min, Directors of the Taou Shan Kwan Temple at Wu Shih Shan, Foochow, v Vol 1 231, Vol 2 164
Wong, Sassoon v Vol 1 273
Wu v Sassoon Vol 1 273
Yao Sudong, v. American Food Mfg. Co., Ld. (Re Fitch's Estate) Vol 2 186
Yokuzawa Zensuke v Malcolm, Wilcox & Co Vol 1 198
Yu Chun Shing v Cairney Vol 2 32

Table of Jury Members

British Courts

Volume 1

K.D. Adams, R v Logan	Vol 1, 267
C.A. de Britto, R v Page	Vol 1, 239
William Christy, R v John Liscom	Vol 1, 282
W.J. Clarke, R v Fawcett	Vol 1, 161
H. Consterdine, R v Fawcett	Vol 1, 161
W.A. Cornabe, R v Fawcett	Vol 1, 161
J. Davieson, R v Carew	Vol 1, 348
Emberly, R v O'Nei	Vol 1, 386
J.M. Farmer R v Fawcett	Vol 1, 161
G.D. Fearon, R v Page	Vol 1, 239
R v Logan	Vol 1, 267
W.R. Fuller, R v Fawcett	Vol 1, 161
John Graham, R v John Liscom	Vol 1, 282
J.C. Grant, R v Ryan	Vol 1, 375
George Greenhill, R v John Liscom	Vol 1, 282
Hay, R v O'Neil	Vol 1, 386
Hodge, R v O'Neil	Vol 1, 386
R. Howie, R v Logan	Vol 1, 267
R.C.K. Johnson, R v Carew	Vol 1, 348
Kenmure, R v O'Neil	Vol 1, 386
N. Komberg, R v Logan	Vol 1, 267
C.J. La Fre, R v Logan	Vol 1, 267
A. McKelvie, R v Ryan	Vol 1, 375
D. Maclaren, R v Carew	Vol 1, 348

G.V.T. Marshal, R v Ryan Vol 1, 375
W.E. Mitchell, R v Page Vol 1, 239
J. Moosa, R v Ryan Vol 1, 375
J.D. Munro, R v Page Vol 1, 239
Murdock, R v O'Neil Vol 1, 386
David R. Orr, R v John Liscom Vol 1, 282
J. Patterson, R v Carew Vol 1, 348
W.T. Phipps, R v Ryan Vol 1, 375
George U. Price, R v John Liscom Vol 1, 282
R. Roberts, R v Page Vol 1, 239
A.H.C Watson, R v Carew Vol 1, 348

Volume 2

W.N.C. Allen, R v Stevenson Vol 2, 136
J. Bottenheim, R v Stevenson Vol 2, 136
W.J.C. Budd, R v Stevenson Vol 2, 136
H.E. Campbell, R v O'Shea Vol 2, 102
Ernest Clark, R v Wang Cheng and Chi Chiu (Weihaiwei) Vol 2, 28
T. Cock, O'Shea v Cowen Vol 2, 16
H.W. Daldy, Bethell v North China Daily News Vol 2, 131
G.F.C. Dobson, R v Stevenson Vol 2, 136
H.P. Dudley, R v Stevenson Vol 2, 136
F.E. Glanville, R v O'Shea Vol 2, 102
H.F. Gray, R v Stevenson Vol 2, 136
F. Griffin, R v Stevenson Vol 2, 136
H.C. Gulland, R v Stevenson Vol 2, 136
J.A. Hayes, R v Stevenson Vol 2, 136
C. Holdsworth, Har Charan Singh v Budda Singh Vol 2, 306
J.E. Judah, O'Shea v Cowen Vol 2, 16
W.H. Jackson, Bethell v North China Daily News Vol 2, 131
M. Joyce, Bethell v North China Daily News Vol 2, 131
F. Large, O'Shea v Cowen Vol 2, 16
S.E. Lucas, R v Stevenson Vol 2, 136
I.A. Levis, Har Charan Singh v Budda Singh Vol 2, 306

W.A. Lewis, R v Wang Cheng and Chi Chiu (Weihaiwei) Vol 2, 28
F.C. Mallett, R v MacKellar Vol 2, 52
P.W. Massey, Bethell v North China Daily News Vol 2, 131
A. Merrilees, R v Wang Cheng and Chi Chiu (Weihaiwei) Vol 2, 28
H.E. Middleton, Har Charan Singh v Budda Singh Vol 2, 306
F. Milner Har Charan Singh v Budda Singh Vol 2, 306
E.R. Morriss, R v O'Shea Vol 2, 102
E.C. Ockenden, R v Wang Cheng and Chi Chiu (Weihaiwei) Vol 2, 28
T.C. Ramsey, R v Wang Cheng and Chi Chiu (Weihaiwei) Vol 2, 28
A. Samson, R v Stevenson Vol 2, 136
A.J. Stokes, Har Charan Singh v Budda Singh Vol 2, 306
K.D. Stewart, R v O'Shea Vol 2, 102
R. Viccajee, O'Shea v Cowen Vol 2, 16
J. Valentine, O'Shea v Cowen Vol 2, 16
H. Veicht, R v O'Shea Vol 2, 102
R.M.C. Wallace, Bethell v North China Daily News Vol 2, 131
C.C.A Warn, R v Stevenson Vol 2, 136

Volume 3

J. Acheson, R v Harbant Singh Vol 3, 12
G.H. Ackerman, R v Harbant Singh Vol 3, 12
G.L. Atchison, R v Atma Singh Vol 3, 117
R. Bachrach, R v Harbant Singh Vol 3, 12
F.L. Barker, R v Harbant Singh Vol 3, 12
N. Boniface, R v Eckford Vol 3, 161
V.H. Bourne, R v Atma Singh Vol 3, 117
R.H. Box, R v Eckford Vol 3, 161
T. Brennen, R v MacKellar Vol 3, 161
W. Canning, R v Atma Singh Vol 3, 117
W.T. Cromby, R v MacKellar Vol 3, 161
A.G. Davies, R v Eckford Vol 3, 161
E.A. Dearn, R v Peters & Judd Vol 3, 106
W.J. Dexter, R v Harbant Singh, Vol 3, 12; Greyhound Racing Association (China) Ltd v Macnaghten & Martin Vol 3, 71

W.H. Ferris, R v Harbant Singh Vol 3, 12
J.S. Flood, Greyhound Racing Association (China) Ltd v Macnaghten & Martin Vol 3, 71
G.T. Gambling, R v Eckford Vol 3, 161
C.S. Gilson, Greyhound Racing Association (China) Ltd v Macnaghten & Martin Vol 3, 71
E.S. Hine, R v Peters & Judd Vol 3, 106
R. Hobday, Greyhound Racing Association (China) Ltd v Macnaghten & Martin Vol 3, 71
J. Huxley, R v Harbant Singh Vol 3, 12
S.A. Judah, R v MacKellar Vol 3, 161
C.S. Kemp, R v Peters & Judd Vol 3, 106
D.W. Leach, R v Harbant Singh Vol 3, 12
J. Macbeth, Greyhound Racing Association (China) Ltd v Macnaghten & Martin Vol 3, 71
P.J. MacKellar, R v Eckford Vol 3, 161
K. McKelvie, R v Peters & Judd Vol 3, 106
F.C. Mallett, R v MacKellar Vol 3, 170
J.R. Milligan, R v Harbant Singh Vol 3, 12
R.B. Moller, R v Eckford Vol 3, 161
J.R. Moody, R v Harbant Singh Vol 3, 12
G.A. Morris, R v Eckford Vol 3, 161
E. Noakes, R v MacKellar Vol 3, 161
P.T. O'Neill, R v Atma Singh Vol 3, 117
S.R. Owen, R v Atma Singh Vol 3, 117
A.J.G Parkhill, R v Atma Singh Vol 3, 117
G. Pickering, R v Atma Singh Vol 3, 117
K.R. Plowright, R v Peters & Judd Vol 3, 106
J. Prentice, R v Atma Singh Vol 3, 117
R.L. Reade, R v Atma Singh Vol 3, 117
C. Reeves, R v Harbant Singh Vol 3, 12
E.A. Richardson, R v Atma Singh Vol 3, 117
G.D. Smart, R v Peters & Judd Vol 3, 106
N.L. Sparke, R v Peters & Judd Vol 3, 106
H. Standring, R v Peters & Judd Vol 3, 106
H.K. Strachan, R v Peters & Judd Vol 3, 106

H. Stephenson, R v Eckford	Vol 3, 161
F.F. Sullivan, R v Eckford	Vol 3, 161
H.W. Sun, R v Chiang Liang-shi (Weihaiwei)	Vol 3, 32
R.V. Thomas, R v Eckford	Vol 3, 161
C. Trickett, R v Peters & Judd	Vol 3, 106
P.R.M. Wallis, R v Eckford	Vol 3, 161
H. Walton, R v Peters & Judd	Vol 3, 106
F.S. Ward, R v Harbant Singh	Vol 3, 12
J. Watson, R v Eckford	Vol 3, 161
A.A. Williams, R v Atma Singh	Vol 3, 117
R.V. Yarrow, R v Peters & Judd	Vol 3, 106

Table of Illustrations

Volume 1

Foreign Office Map of Main Treaty Ports
Scene from an Italian Consular Court 13
Caleb Cushing 22
Chinese blockade the Canton factories 24
Henry Pottinger forcing opium on Lin Zexu 27
British and French forces prepare to attack Tientsin and Peking 30
Commodore Perry arrives in Japan 33
Bombardment of Kagoshima 36
Chaos of a Consular Court 44
Sir Edmund Hornby 52
Charles Goodwin 62
Announcement of appointments of Hornby, Goodwin and Fraser 66
Shanghai in the 1860s 69
Richard Rennie 92
Supreme Court and Consular Gazette frontispiece 100
Original Courthouse of the SCCJ 115
View of SCCJ courtroom 117
Cacophony of Shanghai streets 126
Nicholas Hannen arrives in Japan (1871) 133
Kobe assault case: Hornby and Watson 142
Charles Goodwin returns to Japan 144
Embarking Coolies in Macau 149
US Consular General Court advertisement for the sale of the Cayalti 150
John Smale, Chief Justice of Hong Kong 151
Julian Pauncefote, Attorney General of Hong Kong 151

Magistrate Chen chases Capt. Hereira	155
Opening of Woosong Railway	166
View of Chefoo from Consulate Hill	172
H.S. Wilkinson name card	182
Julian Pauncefote, Foreign Office	190
Robert Mowat, promoted to Assistant Judge	193
Chiri Maru case	197
H.S. Wilkinson delivers judgment in the Hartley case	201
Harry Parkes forces opium on the Japanese	203
Wilkinson as a puppet of Harry Parkes	205
Opening of British Court for Japan (advertisement)	210
Richard Rennie arrives in Japan	211
A trial before Richard Rennie in Japan	214
US Consul General Thomas van Buren in front of the US Consulate in Yokohama	221
Ross case: Richard Rennie holds the scales of Justice while British and American officials look on	225
View of the Wushishan	232
Robert Hart	237
Edward O'Malley	238
George French's grave stone	252
Appointment of Rennie as CJ and Hannen as Judge for Japan	256
H.S. Wilkinson name card as Crown Advocate	256
Russell Robertson steps down as Acting Judge for Japan	257
Nicholas Hannen arrives in Japan (1883)	258
Rioting in Canton	265
The docks in Shameen	266
A Compradore	272
Capt. Drake demands money from drowning Japanese	284
Alfred Robinson, Drake's defence attorney	285
Japan Punch's view on the end of extraterritoriality and press freedom	287
Lyceum Theatre, Shanghai	294
Nicholas Hannen and George Jamieson	304

Vernon Drummond, Acting Crown Advocate 325
Foreigners fear being subject to Japanese Law 327
W.D. Tilotson, US Consul General, Yokohama 340
Walter and Edith Carew 344
Henry Lichtfield, Crown Prosecutor 346
Carew case: Sketches made during the hearing 350
H.P. Wilkinson, new Crown Advocate 369
F.S.A. Bourne, new Assistant Judge 387
Foreigner's worst fear of the end of extraterritoriality 393
Robert Miller and his victims 395
St Mary's Churchyard, Wargrave 410

Volume 2

Foreign Office map of Main Treaty Ports in Asia
Map showing foreign legations in Peking surrounded by Chinese troops 10
Daily Express, July 16, 1900, front page 13
Weihaiwei featured on the cover of the Eastern Sketch 24
Weihaiwei Walled City 27
H.S. Wilkinson C.J. 31
WC Platt, Acting Crown Advocate 34
Clerk of the Court 35
Ernest Satow 36
The Bund, Shanghai 39
Duncan McNeill, challenged H.S. Wilkinson 43
H.S. Wilkinson offers a toast 51
Havilland de Sausmarez 54
Havilland de Sausmarez as a chess knight 56
Battlefields of the Russo-Japanese war 61
B. Twyman, British Assessor in the Mixed Court 65
Eastern Sketch's view of the Mixed Court riots 67
Foreign observers watch Yuan Shikai and his new army 69
Lebbeus Wilfley and Arthur Bassett 79

The New Broom - Wilfley forces lawyers to take an examination 80
Thomas Jernigan 81
Wilfley presiding in the U.S. Court for China 87
John Clark, editor of the Shanghai Mercury 89
W.W. Rockhill, U.S. Minister to China 94
Wilfley returns from Washington, vindicated 101
Wilfley reading the China Gazette. What is a squid? 102
Sketches from the O'Shea trial 106
Korean Daily News 122
Hirobumi Ito feigns surprise at the Korean emperor's decision to abdicate 123
Main characters from Bethell v NCH 132
A richshaw coolie drives into the night 136
A sampan man 142
Sikh policeman, de Sausmarez, Capt. Barrett 150
Noel Home 152
The National Review welcomes the rise of Yuan Shikai 172
A soldier of a Baluchi regiment 174
Hong Kong Supreme Court 180
Charles Lobingier 182
Gilbert Reid: prosecuted for sedition 204
Gilbert King: admitted to the bar 220
Sapajou's view of the growth of Shanghai 226
Dr Oscar Fischer 231
Stirling Fessenden 233
Ferno Schul, US Commissioner 236
Judge Cornell Franklin 253
The Saddles, a popular recreation area and site of a Russian arms transfer 257
Illegal gambling in Shanghai 270
E.T. Maitland, Municipal Prosecutor 298
R.N. Macleod 313
Major Hilton-Johnson 314

Eldon Potter KC arguing on behalf of the Bank of East Asia 320
Kitaro Suga, Finley Johnson, Henry Gollan, International Commissioners 322
Poster advertising Ingenohl's cigars 328
Box cover of Ingenohl's cigars: "Removed to Hong Kong" 330
Warning notice published by Ingenohl 332
Duncan McNeil in the Mixed Court 340
Shanghai Volunteer Fire Brigade 342
First Appeal Court in Shanghai 344
Gilbert King promoted to Assistant Judge 346
U.S. v Husar: The Chief Personalities 350
Detective Inspector Maurice Tinkler 355

Volume 3

Foreign Office map of Main Treaty Ports in Asia
Sapajou does a round of the boundaries 10
Our Punjabi visitors 10
Sirdar Sahib Budda Singh, Assassinated 11
Sapajou on the rendition of the Mixed Court 14
Judge Ziar of the Provisional Court 15
A trial in the Provisional Court before Judge Chiu 16
Sapajou on Judge Ziar's ruling that barristers appear in Chinese robes 17
The Full Court in Session (1928) 22
Showin Wetzen Hsu, Judge of the Kiangsu Higher Court 31
C.T. Wang, Chinese Foreign Minister 44
Sapajou questions whether China will ever reach a final agreement with the foreign powers 47
Justice Richard Feetham of South Africa 50
Miles Lampson, British Minister to China 53
Access to Manchuria barred by Japan 58
Scenes from the Hardoon case 64
Bryan knocks out Schul and Fischer in the Wheel case 68

Luna Park: Advertisement 69
John Benjamin Penniston: My Philosophy 77
Frank Raven, fraudster 90
Sapajou on the collapse of AOCB 91
Thomas Sellett 93
R.T. Evans, Warner Brown's defence attorney 94
A now worthless AOCB banknote 97
Leighton Shields, new US District Attorney for China 103
Kenneth Bourne 106
Sir John Brenan, British Consul-General 121
Shanghai Doomed City 132
Stirling Fessenden defends against Japanese attacks 135
Clarence Gauss, U.S. Consul-General 141
Damage to houses on Hungjao Road 143
Japanese troops blockade the British concession in Tientsin 150
British Prime Minister Chamberlain in a Japanese headlock 151
Badge of United States Marshall for China 167
Atholl McGregor, Chief Justice of Hong Kong 171
A Golden Autumn in Shanghai 173
US-Japan tensions mount in November 1941 174
The Cathay Hotel – One of Shanghai's luxury hotels 178
Sapajou on Sino-Japanese tensions in 1937 198

Photographs

With the exceptions noted below, the majority of the photos reproduced in this book have been sourced from various contemporary newspapers, magazines and open sources. They are, to the best of the author's knowledge and belief, in the public domain. The individuals or organisations provided the photos listed below and have consented to their use. I thank them all. These photos should not be reproduced with obtaining prior permission.

Volume 1

Original Courthouse of the SCCJ	TNA
Shanghai Consular Compound	TNA
Sir Richard Rennie	University of Liverpool
Sir Nicholas Hannen	Pippa Pettifer
George Jamieson	China Association
Hiram Shaw Wilkinson	Hugo Read
Hiram Parkes Wilkinson	China Association
John Carey Hall	China Association
Seal of the SCCJ	TNA
Seal of the Yedo court	TNA
Victor Deacon	Deacons
Agnes Hall	Hugo Read
Jessie Hannen	Pippa Pettifer
Hannen's funeral cortege	Pippa Pettifer
Bourne and marines	Pippa Pettifer
Mourners at Trinity Cathedral	Pippa Pettifer
George French's grave	Douglas Clark
John James Enslie's grave	Ryohei Taniguchi
Walter Carew's grave	Douglas Clark
John Carey and Agnes Hall's grave	Douglas Clark

Volume 2

British Minister's residence	TNA
The British Supreme Court in 1913	TNA
The new second court	TNA
Hiram Shaw Wilkinson	PRONI
Sir Skinner Turner	Dr Michael Turner
Victor Priestwood	Richard Wheeler
Sir Joseph Kemp	Charles Kemp
A.B. Johnson and A.P. Stokes	China Association
Henry De Menil	Chatillon-DeMenil Foundation
Carl von Ingenohl	Edward Schneider
Lawrence Kentwell	Ann Curtis

Volume 3

Former American Club	Tomoko Yasuno
Ranald McDonald	Richard Wheeler
Kenneth and Jane Piper	John Piper
HMS Peterel	Richard Wheeler

TNA = The National Archives (UK)
PRONI = Public Records office of the Northern Ireland